Voyage
Beyond Doubt

Books by

Bruce Moen

Voyages into the Unknown,
Volume 1:
Exploring the Afterlife Series

EXPLORING THE AFTERLIFE
SERIES

VOL. 2

Voyage
Beyond Doubt

Bruce Moen

HAMPTON ROADS
PUBLISHING COMPANY, INC.
for the evolving human spirit

Cover design by Marjoram Productions
Cover Painting by Francine Barbet

For information write:
Hampton Roads Publishing Company, Inc.
134 Burgess Lane
Charlottesville, VA 22902

Or call: 804-296-2772
FAX: 804-296-5096
e-mail: hrpc@hrpub.com
Web site: http://www.hrpub.com

If you are unable to order this book from your local
bookseller, you may order directly from the publisher.
Quantity discounts for organizations are available.

Call 1-800-766-8009, toll-free.

Library of Congress Catalog Number: 98-71583
ISBN 1-57174-101-1
10 9 8 7 6 5 4 3 2 1

Printed on acid-free recycled paper in Canada

Dedicated to

The Mysterious Teacher, who wishes to remain anonymous (called Rebecca), without whose love, understanding, and support none of this would have been possible;

Robert A. Monroe, whose courage and technology provided the path and the tools;

The staff of The Monroe Institute, whose guidance and teaching taught me to explore the Afterlife;

My family, whose love and patience have been with me from the beginning;

My wife, Pharon, whose love and courage helped bring this into being;

My friends, physical and nonphysical, who have helped me learn to explore.

Contents

Voyaging Beyond Doubt

Epilogue

Prologue

Curiosity about our human existence beyond the physical world launched the ship I sail to explore There. Curiosity billows the sails that power my voyages. Like the Vikings and Columbus, through my voyages I've discovered our physical existence is not a flat earth whose edge we sail off into an unknown abyss at death. Beyond the edge of our physical world lies the Afterlife, a New World we all enter when we die. *Voyages Into the Unknown*, the first book in my *Exploring the Afterlife* series, recounts early experiences on my journey of exploration and discovery in the Afterlife. *Voyage Beyond Doubt* continues that story.

Some authors have been driven to write about this subject by a near-death experience. I've never had one. Neither psychic gift nor supernatural happening allows me to explore beyond death any better than you can. With nothing more than curiosity, any ordinary human being can be led to extraordinary Afterlife experience. If there is any difference between you and me, it is only that my curiosity has already taught me how to explore There. I want you to know it's something any of us ordinary human beings can do.

Voyages Into the Unknown left my story after I removed a pair of ghosts, the Dancers, from the home of a young woman. That experience marked a turning point in resolving my doubt about the reality of our Afterlife existence. Information I gathered during that experience was undeniably verified, yet still my doubt about the Afterlife's existence persisted.

Beliefs I'd taken on during my lifetime ran counter to my experiences and caused me to stubbornly resist accepting those experiences as real. After *Voyages Into the Unknown*, evidence continued mounting with each new voyage I took. Time after time I returned with verified information that pointed to the reality of human existence beyond death. My voyages brought back information about the circumstances of people's death, dates, and times, their physical appearance, their habits and mannerisms. Sometimes I returned with names and descriptions of their long-dead relatives, which I had no way of knowing. I repeatedly found verified information in my Afterlife voyages that should have convinced any reasonable person of its existence. Still my doubt persisted. Doubt, I discovered, is a strong force holding out against acceptance. It caused me to continually rationalize evidence away. In the confrontation between my beliefs and my experiences, doubt always stymied full acceptance of our Afterlife's existence.

Yet, my curiosity's hunger for solid, unequivocal evidence drove me to continue sailing beyond the edge of the physical world to gather more information. I returned from each voyage with more treasure. Using techniques I'd learned at The Monroe Institute, I continued using the vehicle of retrievals to explore the Afterlife. Retrieving people who had become stuck in Focus 23 after their deaths had opened my perception to the nonphysical world. Retrievals were, at first, my only port of entry into that realm. As my ability to perceive improved, I gradually developed more ways to enter and explore. There are, I discovered, experiences in our physical world that point toward verification of our Afterlife existence, like a verifiable ability to perceive the thoughts and feelings of other physically alive people. Communication with physically alive people across vast distance and time via the nonphysical world became routine. An ability to sense the timing of physical world events became commonplace. A feeling of connection to all things at a level where communication passes freely between us became the norm. Relationships with nonphysical friends developed to the point that I was able to verify their information. I came to value their input as I made decisions in my day-to-day life. I received information about things as simple as finding a parking space close to the grocery store entrance and as complex as an electromagnetic theory of gravity. Exploring some of the alternate realities I discovered was just downright fun!

Much of the evidence I gathered for the existence of an Afterlife over the course of three years was compelling, but still my doubt persisted. Gradually, I began to see an internal consistency to the information and comprehend how beliefs and actions in Thislife affect experience exploring the Afterlife. With each new voyage I continued building trust in the validity of my experience. That led to a growing trust in the support of the entire universe for assistance as I follow my path and purpose in Thislife.

In this book I want to pass along to you more of what I've discovered. Through my accounts of retrievals, I hope to illustrate how our beliefs and actions in Thislife affect our Afterlife existence. Through accounts of other experience, I hope to show some of the other possibilities. Remember, as you read, these are only my experiences. For me, they've led the way beyond doubt of the Afterlife as a reality we all enter at death. But I don't encourage or expect anyone to accept my word on the subject. On the contrary, I believe nothing a person reads or hears can or should have that effect. The three and one-half years of exploring it's taken for me to finally accept the Afterlife's reality have taught me that only direct experience can truly convert a belief to a known. It has also reaffirmed my conviction that such experience is possible for any ordinary human being who is curious enough to try.

By the time *Voyages Into the Unknown* entered my publisher's editing process, the sense of urgency I'd been feeling to get it into bookstores was becoming an uncomfortable, constant companion. I felt a building sense of pressure to do whatever I could to accelerate that process. It had been more than a year since Bob Monroe, founder of The Monroe Institute, had entered the Afterlife. Some of the pressure I felt to push my publisher harder was coming from him. While house-sitting in Virginia during July of 1996, things came to a head. I was in communication with Bob on a pretty regular basis, and it felt like he had already forgotten that in the physical world a guy can't just sit down and write books as his only activity. He seemed to have forgotten that in the physical world a guy still has to spend some of his time earning a living. One day while walking the quarter mile to the mailbox, I felt Bob's presence again. I wasn't feeling like being pushed any harder, and in our conversation I blew up at him.

"Well, Bruce, you seem a little frustrated at the pace of getting your book to the market," I felt Bob say.

"Bob, I'm pushing these guys as hard as I dare without making them angry."

"Yes, I see that. Still, it seems like things are dragging a little, doesn't it?"

"Look, damn it!" I mentally shouted, "I'm doing everything I know how to do. If you guys want it done faster you're going to have to take some of the responsibility."

"My, you are feeling a little frustrated aren't you!"

"Yes I am! Look, if you want the book on the market faster why don't you drop five thousand dollars out of the air into my hands right now! I'll use it to pay someone to edit it for me, get three thousand copies printed and sell them out of the trunk of my car!" I held my hands together out in front of me, palms up, waiting for the money to fall from the sky. "Come on Bob, five thousand dollars, in my hands right now, and I'll self-publish it and sell it out of the trunk of my car! You want it done faster, go ahead, drop it right here in my hands."

"I didn't come to pressure you about that, Bruce. You're right, you're doing everything that can be done."

"Thank you!"

"We'll take over from here getting the first one to market. If we need your assistance, it will be only small things. We'll let you know. Besides, we've already been putting things in line so you can get started writing the second book."

"I hope so. The way it looks now I'll have to go back to work as an engineer for a few months to save enough money so I can spend full time writing it. I can't do it two or three hours a day after work. I tried that with the first one and the result lacked coherence. I need to do it full time for it all to fit together in an understandable pattern."

"Don't worry, Bruce, that's already in the mill."

"Really, where's the money coming from? Gonna fall out of the sky?"

"You'll see."

After getting the mail I walked back to the house to continue working on changes my publisher had suggested to the first book's manuscript. As my butt hit the chair in front of my laptop computer, the phone rang. It was my publisher. His office is located thirty miles away in Charlottesville, which was part of the reason I took the house-sitting job. He asked me to come to his office in two days to meet with his partner to discuss publishing *Voyages Into the Unknown*. I left that meeting with a signed contract and an advance against royalties, something rarely done for first-time authors. That advance funded my writing *Voyage Beyond Doubt*.

"Now the way's clear for you to get started on the second book," I felt Bob say as I left my publisher's office. "Not out of the sky exactly, and not the figure you named, but it will get you started, won't it?"

"Yes, Bob. Thank you," I replied back to him with my thoughts, "Thanks."

I returned to Denver a week and a half later and started writing *Voyage Beyond Doubt*. As before, it's a true account of my continuing journey, with some of the names and places changed to protect the privacy of those who desire it.

As I mentioned at the end of *Voyages Into the Unknown*, I have too much information for publication in a single book. Since *Voyage Beyond Doubt* is the second in the series, you may bump into unfamiliar language. To assist readers' understanding of such terms, I've condensed some likely candidates in a glossary in Appendix D. You will understand more fully by treating the book you're holding as the second part of a continuing story.

Voyaging with The Mysterious Teacher

The art of sailing is best learned under the tutelage of one who knows the sea. Rebecca, The Mysterious Teacher, had been exploring the Afterlife for many years, and I was lucky enough to learn the art of sailing from her. Like we've all heard before, when the student is ready, the teacher appears.

CHAPTER 1

Dichotomyland, Exploring an Alternate Reality

Rebecca and I continued to meet nonphysically for the purpose of exploring the Afterlife together. As you may remember from *Voyages Into the Unknown*, much of the evidence piling up to support the reality of the Afterlife came through these nonphysical trips together. While living 1,500 miles apart, we'd meet in the nonphysical world to carry out retrievals and other activities. Afterwards, I'd write down everything I could remember about those events in my journal. Comparing notes the next day on the phone became a routine way of checking the validity of my experience. Our records always matched. Sometimes one of us would have more details than the other, but our basic information was always the same.

On one of these trips, I had just arrived at our nonphysical meeting place, expecting to "see" Rebecca when I heard her giggle.

"Ha, ha, hee, you can't find me," I heard her say between giggles. "It's hide and seek time. Hide your eyes and count to ten."

I felt her fly off with a loud whooshing sound and closed my perception to her movement, sort of the nonphysical equivalent of hiding my eyes. I floated there in darkness, feeling very silly all the while, and counted out loud in my mind to ten.

"Ready or not, here I come!"

Floating at our meeting spot location, I did a quick turning scan to locate her. I locked on to her signal and took off like a radar-guided missile in Rebecca's direction. Finding her was no challenge at all.

"That was awfully easy. You didn't hide very well!"

"I knew you could get in here if you didn't think about it too much," she giggled. "Last time I tried to bring you here you weren't able to get in."

"The last time you tried to get me into where?"

"Take a look around and tell me what this place feels like to you," she said, still giggling.

I opened up awareness to my surroundings to get an impression of where I was. As I focused in, stretching outward, I began to feel that, wherever I was, the place was huge. It felt two-dimensional and yet, impossibly, seemed to go on forever in all directions. I felt my Interpreter beginning to form a memory-linking conceptualization of where I was.

"This place is huge. It feels like the biggest place I've ever been in," I remarked to Rebecca. "If I could fly forever in any direction many times faster than the speed of light I'd never reach the end of it."

Just as I said that, the entire place began shrinking in giant steps until it was somehow the size of a two-dimensional sugar cube floating in space in front of me. I heard Rebecca behind me, chuckling. When I started to tell her what had just happened, whatever it was shrunk from sugar cube size to a tiny point of light and then disappeared! I was just about to tell Rebecca that wherever we were had somehow just gotten so small I couldn't see it. With a silent boom, puff puff, it was instantly back to its original, limitless, huge size. I could still hear Rebecca giggling behind me.

As other characteristics of this place presented themselves, I discovered it was a very strange place indeed. As soon as a concept formed in my mind to describe it, my perception of it would suddenly snap to that concept's opposite. It's fat, snap; no, it's skinny. Feels really tall, snap; no, it's very short. Any concept formed to describe it caused it to change its appearance into that concept's opposite. I decided the best name for this place was "Dichotomyland," the land of opposites. Dichotomyland is in some ways like the Flying Fuzzy Zone, described in *Voyages Into the Unknown*. It appears to be a level of consciousness with its own existence apart from my awareness of it. It's a very odd, alternate reality.

Floating in Dichotomyland, trying to form a stable concept of what it was, I remembered that Rebecca had tried to bring me here the last time we'd met. I realized why it had seemed like a boundary then, with an opening I couldn't get through. Every time I had thought to move closer to the opening, it moved unreachably far away. Then, when I'd thought it was too far away, the opening would suddenly be right in front of me again. Every time I thought it was open wide enough to enter, it closed so tight an electron couldn't pass through it. As soon as I thought, "the opening just closed and I can't get in," it would open again. After several cycles of trying to get through this mysterious, nonsensical opening I had given up. Rebecca had actually succeeded getting me here last time, but I got so caught up interacting with it I had no idea that it was a particular place. That's what Rebecca meant when she said she knew I could get in here if I didn't think about it too much, hence the little trickery of a game of hide and seek.

Not being one to easily accept the defeat of rational conceptualization, I decided to pull Dichotomyland's chain. I decided to see if I could outsmart it, trick it into being a stable concept. I began rummaging through my memory, searching for something that didn't have an opposite, until . . .

"This place is a football," I thought out loud into Dichotomyland, and then I waited to see its reaction.

The whole place started buzzing and shaking like a mad little kid in a tantrum. It was like I had overloaded its circuits with something it couldn't handle. I held on tightly to my visualization of a football. Unfortunately my Interpreter just couldn't keep quiet. Using its association hooks to other memories, my Interpreter jumped from the football to a football game. I could see the players on the field executing a running play. Then an association hook from my Interpreter caused the scene to jump from a mere football game to encompass the entire football stadium. Then I saw the enormous crowd of football fans cheering in the stands. As soon as I saw the enormous crowd, Dichotomyland had something to work with. My concept jumped to the opposite of an enormous crowd, no crowd. Then I watched as Dichotomyland switched my visualization/concept back and forth between an enormous crowd and no crowd. First there were full stands then, snap; an image of empty stands, snap; they were full again.

I lost that test of smarts, but had to try again. After all, rational conceptualization should be able to handle any challenge. Not to be outdone by Dichotomyland, I mentally shouted, "This place is a baseball," and waited to see what would happen. Dichotomyland demonstrated intelligence. The place has the ability to learn! It changed my visualization/concept from a baseball to the cycle of empty stands/full stands in quick, clean flashes. I heard Rebecca burst out laughing with glee at my antics.

Dichotomyland was not going to get the best of me! "What would happen if I give it nothing?" I wondered. "I'll be absolutely quiet." I floated there in silence without a thought in my mind. Dichotomyland began jumping around in all directions at once. The place was shaking and banging and vibrating like a screaming brat who wanted to do something really impressive, but couldn't settle down long enough to come up with a plan. It was very difficult to maintain an absolutely thoughtless state of mind! When the shaking, banging and rattling settled down I found myself immersed in the loud, blaring hiss of random noise. Dichotomyland got me again! Random noise is a mixture of everything, and that's the opposite of nothing.

Rebecca and I both left Dichotomyland laughing hysterically at my attempts at getting the better of it. While comparing notes with her on the phone the next day, I found that all the details of her little deception and my attempts to outwit Dichotomyland were confirmed. She repeatedly burst out laughing as she recounted what she'd seen me doing there.

Most of my voyages beyond the horizon of the physical world have had a more serious tone. This trip to Dichotomyland was more like a romp through a funhouse in the nonphysical world. I came away from playing there with the realization that it had its own lessons to teach regarding conceptualization. It was associations the Interpreter uses to store and recall events in memory that Dichotomyland had utilized to mirror back opposite concepts. Holding that quiet, conceptless state of mind is great practice for learning to achieve the

balance between the Interpreter and Perceiver. Through repeated experience within this realm, one can practice the ability to withhold conceptualization, allowing clearer perception
of what is really There. This skill is very useful in getting past
personal bias, like doubt, during interaction and information
gathering in any level of the nonphysical New World. It also
occurs to me that in my trying to hold the mind focused on
Nothing, Dichotomyland opened access to Everything. Kinda
makes me want to meditate more often.

CHAPTER 2

Magic Carpet Rides

There are times in our lives when we're faced with difficult choices. The spring of 1993 was such a time for me. My wife and I amicably decided to separate, and I turned over almost all of my financial assets to her and my children. Dissatisfied with my engineering career, I quit my job and started my own, one-man, consulting firm. By early summer, the urge to go to Virginia to follow my obsession with exploring the Afterlife was very strong, some might say obsessive. For months I was an emotional wreck, torn between my children, who lived 1,500 miles from Virginia, and my quest to know. At such times, no matter how painful, you know it's something you've got to do.

In preparation for the near certainty of being separated from my kids, and wanting to maintain more than letter writing, videotape and telephone contact, I decided to use my developing ability for interaction in the nonphysical world to experiment with another form of contact. I decided to embark on a different kind of voyage. This one was not intended to sail beyond the physical world to explore the Afterlife. Instead, these were voyages my kids and I started taking while they were sleeping, to develop a new means of contact. I'd go to their rooms nonphysically and meet with them in their dreams. Then I'd invite them to come along and ride with Dad on a magic, flying carpet. That may sound rather strange to some, but, at that time, it was one of the few sources of fun and joy in my life.

The first night I tried to do this, I wasn't exactly certain how to proceed. After closing my eyes and relaxing, I pretended a beautiful, ornate carpet would appear. A few moments passed and then a six-by-four-foot carpet materialized before my mind's eye, hovering close by. There were bright-colored, intricate designs crisscrossing its entire surface. Long, golden fringe and tassels hung down all around its edges. When it had fully formed in my imagination, I pretended to hop on. Sitting in the middle of my magic, flying carpet I thought about my daughter, Shaela, and pictured her room. The carpet and I began to move. Moments later we passed through an outside wall of her mom's house and Shaela's room came into view. Hovering a few feet from her bed, I could clearly see my nine-year-old sleeping. When I called her name, she awakened nonphysically into my dream and sat up looking at me, hovering not six feet away. After she excitedly climbed up on the carpet and sat down beside me, we flew through the walls of the house to her brother's room. My son, Daniel, then four years old, also awakened into our dream at the calling of his name. In wide-eyed glee he climbed out of bed, up onto the carpet, and sat down on my other side. Then we flew through the closed window and out into the night sky.

On that first trip Shaela wanted to fly to see Grandma and Grandpa and was a little disappointed they couldn't see her. Daniel decided he wanted to go to the zoo and found that almost all the animals were sleeping. Some of the ones who were awake looked at us as if they saw us fly by.

Each night that we went out flying together on Dad's magic carpet, my kids took turns deciding where we'd go. After picking them up in their rooms we'd fly out through the window, over the neighborhood treetops, and then to wherever they wanted to go. On one trip, Shaela wanted to go around the world to China just to see if it was really daytime there. It was. At Dan's suggestion another night, we flew around the moon.

A problem surfaced more than once during those first trips. We'd be on our way to somewhere when I'd get a "call" to assist with a retrieval. I'd tell Shaela and Dan I had to leave for a few minutes and that I'd be right back. I have to admit that sometimes the retrieval took so long that by the time I got back, Shaela and Dan had returned home on their own. They didn't like being left alone. I only half believed any of this was really happening until my wife asked me about it. I hadn't mentioned our nighttime flights to anyone, not even my kids, so I was surprised by what my wife had to say.

"Are you doing something with the kids at night?" she asked.

"Yes, we've been going on magic carpet rides off and on for the past two weeks or so."

"Shaela told me that's what you were doing, and that sometimes you disappear for a while."

"Yes, sometimes I have to leave for a short time to answer a call before we can continue on to where we're going."

"Well I think it would be better if you brought them back home before you disappear like that. Shaela gets scared when you leave."

"You're right. In the future I'll see to it they get safely back to their rooms if I have to leave to answer a call."

"And in the future," she said sternly, "before you start doing anything like this, talk to me first, okay?"

"Sure," I replied.

I just know that most people would think such a conversation could only occur between two total wackos. I'm sure it was a strain on my wife having to deal with things like this. She and her family had great concern over my activities in the "Spirit World" as they called it. This was another episode in our clash of belief systems. After that conversation, I made a change in our magic carpet ride routine to alleviate any fear Shaela and Daniel might have. The next time I went to my daughter's room, I didn't arrive on my carpet. After getting her attention, I told her it was time she learned how to make a flying carpet of her own. Standing next to her bed, with her watching nonphysically, I brought my hands together with all my fingertips touching. Then I drew them apart slowly with the intent of creating a carpet. As my fingertips separated, a rolled-up magic carpet appeared. After unrolling it I left it hovering in the air nearby. Then I asked Shaela to think about what she wanted her magic carpet to look like. After a few seconds, she brought her fingertips together and pulled them apart. Her carpet materialized, much to her surprise, all rolled up as mine had. She grabbed the end and unrolled it with a snap. By the time she was finished changing its colors and texture and adding tassels all around the edges, it was a thing of beauty. Then we each climbed up on our own carpets and flew into her brother's room.

After Dan was shown how to make his carpet, he unrolled it and began adding his own touches. True to his boyhood, Dan's carpet needed pedals, two actually, one to make it stop and one to make it go. He also added a steering wheel, explaining that he needed it to turn his carpet in the air. After he was satisfied with it, Dan hopped on and out through the window we went.

I know this all must sound pretty crazy, but what can I say, we had a ball. We flew all over the world making more trips to China and back to the zoo. Side by side, we'd silently glide over the treetops, watching whatever there was to see. We practiced splitting up, flying to different places and then meeting back at home. Our practicing built up my kids' confidence in traveling on their own, and if necessary, returning home on their own. On one of our trips, they wanted Mom to come along. We flew into her bedroom and invited her along. She climbed up behind me and we flew out through the wall.

After Shaela and Dan learned to make and fly their own carpets with confidence, I didn't hear any more complaints when I had to leave to do a retrieval. They found it pretty boring, having to wait for their fun, and usually opted to fly around on their own until I got back. Sometimes they'd follow me to see where I went and see what I was doing. They even followed and assisted me on a retrieval, an experience re-counted in *Voyages Into the Unknown*. Hovering nearby, they watched as I worked at retrieving a little boy who'd been run over and killed by a tank. They made moving him to Focus 27 easy when he jumped at their invitation to climb aboard one of their carpets. It must be a fantasy for many little kids to fly on a magic carpet. To this day, sometimes as I'm dropping off to sleep, I remember those times we had together. Then off we go, joy riding again across the nighttime sky.

By early fall, 1993, I'd decided to move to Virginia to pursue my obsession with exploration of human existence beyond the physical world. That was the hardest, most emo-tionally wrenching decision of my life. I cried for miles while driving away in the U-Haul van, reliving the image of my young children waving good-bye to Daddy.

CHAPTER 3

Wahunka & Shared Alternate Realities

Soon after I arrived in Virginia, the subject of shared alternate realities came up in a conversation with Rebecca. She'd read an article by Charles Tart, a researcher in the field, and explained shared alternate realities by telling me about experiments he was doing. Our discussion led to an interesting landfall in my nonphysical world explorations on an island I call Wahunka.

Tart used two student volunteers in his experiment who were excellent hypnotic subjects; that is, they could be easily hypnotized to a deep trance state. To start, one of these subjects hypnotized the other, and then the second hypnotized the first. They alternated hypnotizing each other until they were both in a very profound trance. When sufficiently hypnotized, Tart would suggest a scene where they were both to go. They would enter that scene and interact with each other.

In one of his experiments Tart had suggested a sandy beach scene at the ocean. Taking his suggestion, both subjects reported going to a sandy beach. Not just imagining themselves to be there alone, but actually being present together at a vivid, completely realistic beach by the ocean. As I recall, they could see, hear and feel each other to the point that they could swim together in an ocean that felt completely real. They reported feeling the sand under their feet. They could have tossed a beach ball back and forth. To their perception, they were at a beach in an alternate reality, indistinguishable from the physical world. That's a shared, alternate reality.

This sounded like an incredibly fascinating, fun experience, and we immediately began talking about how we might attempt to experiment with this ourselves. I off-handedly suggested we could start by both trying to visualize something, which would exist in the nonphysical world. I reasoned that when we could both see it, it might serve as the seed for a complete, shared, alternate reality like the ones Tart's subjects described.

"What kind of object would you suggest?" Rebecca asked.

"How about a big orange ball? Something the size of a beach ball."

"A big orange ball? You engineers and your vivid imaginations!"

"Well, it's a place to start. If all we have to be able to do is both see the same thing, a big orange ball seems like an easy thing to visualize. It would be a small shared reality, grant you, but it's a start."

"Where should we see it?"

"Let's stand about three feet apart and visualize it in the air between us."

We stood facing each other and tried to visualize a big, orange ball in the air between us. I had the vague impression of a ball, but I certainly couldn't actually see anything. Nothing spectacular happened. We didn't enter into any shared alternate reality right then. In fact, we both started laughing at the silliness of the whole idea and I promptly forgot the whole thing.

A couple of weeks later, I was telling Rebecca about this odd sensation I had been able to switch on and off since the early 1970s. It's hard to describe. It's a strange feeling. When I intended to switch the feeling on, I experienced a mildly electric, fuzzy ball of something at the base of my skull, in back, right where the spine ends and the skull begins. I had no idea what it was or what use it might have, but I'd been curious since it first started happening, twenty years earlier. Since Rebecca was very skilled at sensing various states of consciousness, I thought she might be able to shed some light on it.

"Can you make yourself feel it right now?" she asked.

"Sure, I just have to close my eyes and feel for that spot at the base of my skull."

"Go ahead, switch it on and I'll see if I can sense anything about it."

Rebecca closed her eyes and let out a long breath to relax. I closed my eyes and searched for the mildly electric, fuzzy feeling. Once I found and focused my attention on it, the odd sensation intensified as usual.

"Hmm . . . I'm being catapulted into a tunnel!" Rebecca said.

I opened my eyes and switched off the strange feeling.

"Are you okay?" I asked, a little concerned.

"Seem to be, try it again."

I closed my eyes, felt for it, focused on it and let it intensify again.

"I'm back in a tunnel again, moving very fast," she said. "Keep it going a little longer."

Suddenly, I too could see the walls of a tunnel, perhaps six feet in diameter, rushing past me. They were a grainy, black and white blur rushing by so fast I couldn't see any detail.

"I'm in a tunnel too!"

"My tunnel just turned down and to the right," Rebecca remarked.

Mine had made the same turn just before she said it. I continued to focus on the strange sensation as I watched the tunnel walls whiz by. Then my tunnel veered upward in a steep, ninety-degree turn and I stayed in the center, moving automatically along its path.

"Did yours just make a sharp upward turn too?" I asked.

"Yes!" And after a few seconds, "The walls just changed to a kind of pattern, like they're made of bricks."

"Mine too!"

We continued moving through our tunnel until I lost my awareness of the strange feeling. As soon as I brought my attention back to the feeling, the visual image of rocketing through a tunnel returned. We played with this strangeness for about five minutes, and then I couldn't find the feeling anymore, so we stopped.

A couple of weeks later, we were sitting in a hot tub, close to midnight, looking up at the stars in the dark, country sky.

"Bruce," Rebecca suggested, "let's try that thing again, that funny feeling in the back of your neck thing."

"Okay," I replied. "You know I really ought to come up with a name for it. It's getting cumbersome to always refer to it as, 'that funny feeling at the base my skull.'"

"Have you got a name in mind?"

"How about, Wahunka?" popped into my mind and out my mouth.

"Wa what a?"

"Wahunka."

"Okay, let's try Wahunka again," she said laughing.

I closed my eyes, felt for Wahunka, focused on it, and let the feeling at the base of my skull grow and intensify. It went from something the size of a grape to something more the size of a tennis ball in fifteen or twenty seconds, and changed from a mild, fuzzy, electric feeling to the sensation of something gripping. Then I saw the strangest thing. From high above the hot tub, something falling toward me caught my nonphysical eye. A huge, orange ball plummeted from out of nowhere, hit the water in the hot tub without a splash, and continued on, out the bottom of the tub toward the center of the earth. When I snapped my physical eyes open I could see Rebecca's were already open very wide.

"Did you just see what I just saw?" I asked.

"If it was a great big orange ball, like an orange the size of a beach ball, yes, I saw it!" she replied.

"So did I!"

We both burst out laughing insanely as we realized the brief, forgotten exercise that we had tried weeks before had just now been successful. The orange ball had appeared, not exactly as I had imagined it weeks before, stationary and floating in the air between us, but dropping like a boulder out of the sky. When we both finally got control of ourselves enough to stop laughing I switched on Wahunka again.

"I'm back in a tunnel," Rebecca said.

"Me too!"

Every ten or twenty seconds one of us would describe what we were seeing in as few words as possible. The tunnel changed direction, texture, color and pattern. Then I exited the tunnel and found myself in a small room. It was a vivid, full-color, very realistic room about ten feet square with a ceiling so high I couldn't see it. A woman I didn't recognize stood near the opposite wall, facing it. I walked to the left, to a corner of the room, to get a better look at her.

"I'm in a room. I see a woman standing about three feet from the wall she's facing," I said.

"I'm in a room too. I'm close to a wall, looking up at a light shining down into the room," Rebecca replied.

"There's a beam of light shining on the woman's left shoulder," I said, describing what I was seeing. I saw the woman's head move as she appeared to look at her left shoulder and then back up at the source of the light.

"Yes, the light is shining on my left shoulder."

The woman turned her head back and forth, stopping when she was looking directly at me.

"Is that you standing in the corner?"

"Yes." Then waving my nonphysical hand at her, "It's me standing over here in the corner waving at you!"

Rebecca waved back at me. "It's me standing here waving back at you!"

"Is that a fireplace in front of you? Looks like a fireplace from where I'm standing."

The nonphysical Rebecca knelt down, looked at the fireplace, and then got down on her hands and knees and started crawling toward it.

"No, it's not a fireplace. It looks like another tunnel of some kind," she was saying, as she crawled into it and disappeared.

I walked over, got down on my hands and knees, and crawled in after her. When I came out the other side I was high in the air, looking down at a beautiful, round, deep blue pool. It was surrounded by complete blackness. From my position, about thirty feet above the pool, I could clearly see a metal ring about fifteen feet in diameter with perhaps twenty small, gold colored pipes sticking out of it, evenly spaced around its periphery, and just above the water level in the pool.

"How close are you to the pool?" I asked.

"I'm just a little above the water. I can see the whole pool and some sort of little pipes sticking out of it."

"I think I'm quite a ways above you. I can see the pool and quite a bit of the surrounding blackness."

Tiny flames, like candle flames, began coming out of each pipe simultaneously. The flames spread outward from the center of the ring and grew in size until they were perhaps five feet long. The flames were wide near the pipes and tapered in a graceful curve out to a point. They were wide enough that their edges near the little pipes were almost touching one another. They were colored like candle flames, vivid reds, yellows and oranges, spectacularly beautiful against the deep blue of the pool. The flames held their size just long enough for me to realize that what I was looking at resembled a beautiful, perfect lotus blossom.

"The flames on the pool look like a lotus blossom," I heard Rebecca say.

Then the flames flew upward explosively. A tubular column of beautiful flower petal-sized flames rose from the pool and shot up past me, forming a towering column of flames that extended as far as I could see above me.

"You see a column of flames rise up from the pool too?" I asked.

"Beautiful isn't, it?" Rebecca replied.

I floated there, watching the wall of little flames go by until I lost the Wahunka feeling and the scene faded out. When I opened my physical eyes Rebecca's were still closed, and I stayed silent until she opened them.

"Wow! What was that?" I exclaimed.

"I'd say we were just in a shared, alternate reality," was her reply.

We must have compared notes for at least half an hour, going over what each of us saw and felt. It was such an unusual, interesting experience, Rebecca and I continued to explore alternate, shared realities for quite some time. Exploring with Wahunka became a game. In honor of Charles Tart's research, and the hot tub where we first experienced a shared alternate reality, we named the game "Hot Tub Modified Charlie." I've played it with two to eight people at a time. The rules of Hot Tub Modified Charlie are simple. Everyone gets relaxed and closes their eyes. I switch on Wahunka and let its intensity build. Then everyone takes turns describing, in as few words as possible, any impression they have. Within five minutes of starting, everyone is in a shared, alternate reality. Sometimes they're fantastic, surrealistic scenes like the pool and column of flames. Sometimes an entire story unfolds like a scene from the distant past.

There were some side effects to experimenting with Wahunka, nothing serious, just side effects. One afternoon I was whipping up a big pot of my famous spaghetti sauce. It's one of the few things that really stands out in my culinary repertoire, which says volumes about my cooking. With all the ingredients in the pot just beginning to simmer, I began to wonder if the application of Wahunka would affect the sauce. Without giving it a second thought, I switched it on and let its intensity build. I felt silly to be focusing Wahunka energy into a pot of spaghetti sauce as I slowly stirred it with a big wooden spoon, but that's what experiments are for, to find out what happens. I'd been at it for about thirty seconds when the phone rang.

"Bruce, this is Rebecca, what are you doing?" I heard her voice say with a little irritation.

"Making my famous spaghetti sauce, why?"

"What else are you doing?" she asked, impatiently.

"Well, I know it sounds silly, but I'm trying to focus Wahunka into the sauce," I said a little sheepishly.

"I thought so!"

"Why, what happened?" I asked.

"I'm at the Institute doing a booth session with someone. I'm at the control panel switching in different Hemi-Sync sounds and monitoring the person in the booth. I'm supposed to be assisting her, providing guidance to her exploring."

"And?"

"And all of a sudden I'm being catapulted into a tunnel. The walls are rushing by so fast I can hardly maintain focus on my control room duties!"

"And I was just holding a very intense level of Wahunka, focusing on the spaghetti sauce!"

"Yeah, this session's going to take another forty–five minutes or so. Could you stop experimenting with your sauce until I'm done, and give me time to drive home before you start again?"

"Sure! Sorry, I didn't realize Wahunka would have any effect over a distance of eight miles."

"Well, now we know it does. I have to get back to the session so I'll talk to you later."

With that, Rebecca hung up, and I went back to stirring my sauce, sans Wahunka. From then on, I was more careful to experiment with it only when Rebecca was present or knew about it ahead of time. It was my first experience with having such an effect on another person at a distance. I learned there are responsibilities to consider in working with such energetic "toys."

The experimentation Rebecca and I did with Wahunka was like exercising a muscle. I discovered I could use that muscle as a tool for exploration of the Afterlife. Often, after relaxing to do a retrieval, or just to explore, I'll switch it on. When I do, it greatly facilitates my perception of nonphysical realities. Like the Shee-un spot, described in *Voyages into the Unknown*, it has become a tool for exploration. I'm not certain where I acquired this tool. My sense of it is that Wahunka is a natural, human ability we all have; I just got lucky and noticed it. Like a muscle that is seldom used, it has very little strength for most of us. I suspect that as I worked at developing the ability to perceive within the nonphysical world, I was unknowingly exercising this "muscle." At a certain level of strength, I began to notice its presence. It's possible that some of you who've been on this path of discovery have noticed something similar. Some of you might have noticed a mildly electric, fuzzy ball sensation of pressure at the base of the skull. I suspect that those of you who embark on a voyage of discovery past the edge of the physical world may someday notice an odd sensation such as I've described. If you do, I encourage you to experiment with it. Find another person you can work with, someone who won't think you're totally wacko, and try your hand at Hot Tub Modified Charlie. If your experimentation shows any sign of a shared, alternate reality, you've discovered the island of Wahunka, one far beyond the physical world's horizon, on the ocean of the Afterlife.

CHAPTER 4

Grandma and the Skunk

Our sense of smell is the most acute of our physical senses. It can detect odors from concentrations of things measured in parts per billion. In other words, one speck of something mixed in with a billion specks of air is detectable to our normal sense of smell. We have a nonphysical sense of smell too, as I discovered after hearing a story about Rebecca's grandmother.

Sometime after her grandmother died, Rebecca took a long road trip to visit the family farm. After a late start, and six solid hours behind the wheel, she was tired and still had two hours of night driving ahead of her. On a dark, two-lane, country road, she became aware of her grandma's presence in the back seat.

"Hi Grandma, I know you're sitting in the back seat," Rebecca said in her thoughts.

"Thought maybe you could use some company. It's after dark and I can tell you're getting tired," Grandma replied.

"Thanks, Grandma."

Now you have to understand that since she was a little child, Rebecca has always loved the smell of skunk. As a child on the farm, she couldn't understand why everyone else shunned a dog that'd had the misfortune to be sprayed by a skunk. It just made the dog all the more special to her. Not many people appreciate that odor, but for some reason, Rebecca has always loved it. Just after Grandma made her entrance in the back seat, the scent of a skunk began to fill the car.

"A poor little skunk, probably hit by a car," she thought to herself.

"No," Grandma said, "I know you like that smell, so I brought it with me, Dear. To help you stay awake for the rest of your trip, I'm going to bring that smell to you every so often until you get to where you're going."

According to Rebecca, every twenty minutes from then on the scent of skunk filled the car.

Since I'm the rational-minded type, I figured Grandma just arranged for a skunk to be hit by a car in Rebecca's path every twenty minutes. I realize that's no less irrational than Grandma magically bringing the scent of skunk into the car, but somehow it seemed like a more logical, reasonable explanation to me.

A week or so after I heard that story, long after sundown, I was sitting in a room with Rebecca in a house in the Virginia countryside. The air outside was the kind of warm, absolutely still air that doesn't rustle a single leaf or evaporate a single drop of sweat. Suddenly, the smell of a skunk filled the room. I don't mean I caught a whiff of the odor and then it gradually got stronger. I mean that from one instant to the next it went from nothing to full-blast, almost choking strength. That smell is not one of my favorites, and it was so overpowering that I felt my eyes would start watering.

"Whew! Smells like a skunk has gotten into the house and sprayed in here somewhere. Geez I hope it's not rabid," I remarked nervously, looking around the room for sharp, vicious teeth and a raised white tail.

"No, Grandma's here to visit."

"You have a pet skunk named Grandma?" I asked incredulously.

"No, silly," she replied, "It's my Grandmother, remember, I told you about my road trip?"

"But the smell is so incredibly strong."

"Yeah, isn't it a wonderful smell?" Rebecca said, beaming.

"It's got to be a real skunk, and it's somewhere in the house with us. Geez, sometimes skunks are rabid. Maybe we better try to find it and get it out of here before it comes after one of us!"

I was looking around the room, certain that a foaming-at-the-mouth skunk was going to jump out and attack at any moment. I had visions of getting those incredibly painful shots for rabies.

"There's no skunk, Bruce, calm down! It's just Grandma, she came to visit us."

"That's impossible!" I said, with college-educated certainty. "She couldn't do a thing like that!"

In the next millisecond, the smell of skunk disappeared. I don't mean it gradually dissipated and finally went away over a period of time. I mean it went away like the light from a bulb when you flip the switch! Zero! None! Absolutely gone! I couldn't believe my nose! I jumped up and started running through the house from room to room. I knew it was impossible for such a strong smell to instantly disappear from every room at once, but I couldn't detect the odor anywhere in the house. Rebecca was laughing at my antics.

"What are you doing?" she asked pointedly.

"That smell couldn't have disappeared that fast everywhere in the house at once. There has to be a least a faint odor of it somewhere!"

"I can still smell it here where I'm sitting."

I ran over to where she was sitting and sniffed at the air.

"It's not here, I can't smell it!" I told her.

"Well, I can! Grandma's still here, and I can still smell skunk," Rebecca insisted.

I made her get up and follow me around. We sniffed air in rooms all over the house. I couldn't smell a thing. She claimed to be able to smell skunk everywhere we went. To my nose it was completely, unexplainably, gone.

"Did you learn anything from Grandma's visit?" Rebecca asked later, after she claimed Grandma had left.

"Learn anything? Like what?"

"You were smelling the odor of a skunk so strongly you said it felt like your eyes would start watering. Something happened, and then you couldn't smell it any more. What do you supposed made it go away in an instant?"

Thinking back, I remembered that just before the smell went out like a light, I'd said, "That's impossible! She couldn't do a thing like that!" At that moment, my perception of the smell had instantly vanished without a trace. "I had just expressed my doubt about the possibility of a nonphysical person being capable of inducing the smell of a skunk in my nose."

"Would you say you were expressing your *belief* that such a thing was impossible?"

"Yes, you could put it that way. I don't believe it's possible."

"Yet, you claim the way it disappeared from the house is also impossible, didn't you?"

"Yes, based on my understanding of chemical concentrations and air movement through a house, that was also impossible. In the absence of air movement, on a still night like this, the smell would have to diffuse its way out. For a house this size, with no wind, it could easily take an hour or more before the last traces were gone. If the skunk sprayed in the house, it could take days."

"And yet, you experienced both things, didn't you?"

"Yes, and that's not possible either!"

"What possible explanation could there be for your experience?"

I pondered that question. I had just experienced two things that were not only physically impossible, but also mutually exclusive. I sat there dumbfounded for several moments. Then the answer flared inside me.

"It's not physically possible, but it might be nonphysically possible."

"Keep going," Rebecca said, grinning.

"I sensed the smell before I had any time to make a judgment about it based on my beliefs and doubts. I experienced a nonphysical sense of smell that detected the presence of your grandmother. As soon as my rational judgment and doubt kicked in, I expressed the impossibility of my experience, based on my beliefs. My experience conflicted with what I've come to accept as *true reality*, and so I denied the possibility of my own experience. As soon as I denied it was possible, the smell disappeared from my experience. How am I doing so far?"

"I think you might be on to something. Keep going."

"It was my denial of the possibility of my direct experience that prevented me from continuing to experience it. After I could no longer smell Grandma's skunk odor, you still could. The nonphysical reality of that smell can only be perceived if

I'm willing to accept that my own direct experience of it is real. If I deny its existence, I have no way to experience or detect it."

"Very good; now what might that imply about your awareness of other things?" Rebecca asked.

I pondered again, although the answer should have been obvious. Then I realized the huge impact beliefs have on my perception! Disbelief or doubt blocks and prevents the perception of whatever is believed impossible. I can be caught off guard and perceive something I believe is not possible, but as soon as my doubt has time to kick in, the perception will stop. Suddenly so many things made perfect sense.

"People can't see ghosts because they believe ghosts don't exist. If they do see one, it will disappear as soon as they decide a ghost is what they're seeing. Their doubt blocks their perception of the ghost. Miracles don't happen to some people, because they don't believe they're possible. If they believed they were possible, any miraculous event conceivable could happen to them. They could experience one of those totally unexplainable, spontaneous healings from a deadly disease no matter what their physical condition. Beliefs are incredibly powerful things. With a complete lack of doubt in the possibility, a person could probably fly through the air in full view of a crowd."

"Or walk on water?" Rebecca asked.

"That's how He did that! That Guy had complete trust in the possibility of anything! He had absolutely no doubt about the possibility of walking on the surface of a lake!" I realized out loud.

"And what does this imply about your ability to perceive while you're exploring the nonphysical world?"

"I'll bet my ability to perceive There is blocked by my continuing doubts about the reality of what I'm experiencing."

"Bingo!" Rebecca laughed.

"But it seems dangerous to allow myself to believe just anything I *think* is real, really is! Isn't that part of the definition of insanity? Don't they put people in the booby hatch who see and hear things that aren't really there?"

"Bingo!"

"Geez, that's a belief that's probably responsible for lots of my difficulties perceiving There. Probably why I never see or hear anything There. Probably why I had to trick myself into perceiving There at all by claiming I was only getting impressions. Not something real, just impressions. Imps I used to call them. Even a sane person can have impressions."

"Bingo!"

These insights into how perception operates, and how incompatible beliefs block it, were coming so fast I could barely keep up with what I was saying. My mind flew back to my first Lifeline program, when I was perceiving *absolutely nothing* in Focus 27. I couldn't understand then why other program participants were claiming contact with all sorts of nonphysical people and places, and I was experiencing a complete void. Now I understood why! My beliefs about the definition of insanity, and probably other things as well, were blocking my perception! It was exactly like what had just happened with the smell of the skunk. What I was attempting to perceive conflicted so deeply with my beliefs it was completely blocked!

My mind raced back to my understanding of the Interpreter. Every time my Perceiver began to bring something nonphysical, *not real*, into my awareness the little voice of my Interpreter had shut down awareness of it. The Interpreter accomplished this by connecting associated images in pre-existing memory to whatever my Perceiver brought into awareness. I'd caught myself thinking about *bananas in Brazil* and learned how to relax the Interpreter to allow perception of the nonphysical world to continue. Now I understood that when the Interpreter brought associated images to mind to build memory of the new information, it brought associated beliefs as well. Stored in my memory, along with images, sounds and smells, are associated beliefs connected to those things. When the Interpreter brought the images to mind, the associated beliefs came as well. If these beliefs conflicted with what the Perceiver was bringing to awareness, the beliefs shut down the perception.

"So, what do I do to prevent my disbelief from shutting down my perception in the nonphysical world?" seemed like the next logical question to ask Rebecca.

"You know you can perceive There. How have you been doing it?"

Just like Rebecca, instead of giving me an answer, she asks another question. I'd have to experience figuring out this one for myself.

I was quietly pondering again. When Grandma's skunk smell first entered my nonphysical awareness it was a real, nonphysical perception event. I experienced it, and then experienced its sudden, impossible disappearance. It happened so fast, I fell off the tightrope on the side of my Interpreter before I knew it was happening. I had beliefs, based on knowledge of chemistry and physics, which conflicted with my experience of the nonphysically perceived smell of the skunk. There was a narrow window of time between perception of the smell and its disappearance. I'd used that window to my advantage during that first Lifeline program, when I'd learned to relax the Interpreter. I'd forced the internal commentary to stop. Carlos Castaneda might call it *stopping the world*. As I'd learned to recognize and limit the activity of the Interpreter, the window of time in which I could perceive the nonphysical world had lengthened. Once I'd found the Balance point between the Interpreter and Perceiver, I was able to cruise for long periods of time both perceiving in the nonphysical world and storing the information in memory. The experience of Grandma's skunk smell was just another example of my loss of Balance.

I'd learned how to maintain my Balance by becoming aware of the process of losing it. Losing my Balance toward the Interpreter diverted my perception with a string of associated images leading to *bananas in Brazil*. Losing my Balance toward the Perceiver had prevented storage in memory of anything I perceived; I'd click out. I could remember none of my experience. By recognizing the impending loss of Balance at the slightest deviation from the perfect mixture of Interpreter and Perceiver, I had learned to Know. As I came to know more about the nonphysical world, I began building trust in the reality of my experience. That, in turn, placed new beliefs in memory that were associated with the new nonphysical world experience. Later, when I began to perceive nonphysically, those new, stored images and beliefs didn't conflict with the experience and perception. Granted, my perception was still limited by the remaining doubts I held, but my ability was definitely far greater than when I first started exploring. So, my continuing to explore promoted a gradual process of changing beliefs and removing doubt, thereby improving perceptual ability. The answer was obvious. I'd have to continue recognizing my doubting beliefs and limit their effects. By continuing to explore and build trust in my experience, my ability to perceive would continue to improve. My doubts would continue to dissolve.

"What I've done before is find the Balance between the keeper of my beliefs, my Interpreter, and my ability to perceive, my Perceiver. I've learned to suspend disbelief, at least temporarily, in order to allow continuing perception to occur. By remaining open to the possibility that there are real things beyond my present experience and beliefs, I've gradually built trust in my perception. Building trust changes or eliminates my conflicting beliefs and doubts. That's how I've been removing old, outdated beliefs, by building trust in my experience."

"Bingo again," Rebecca remarked, laughing. "Trust is always the first issue!"

"Yeah, the process of improving my perception to explore the Afterlife is the process of changing beliefs and removing doubt by building trust in my experience. I still wonder a little about where the borderline is between sanity and insanity. I know some of the doubts I hold are related to that. I guess that too is a matter of Balance."

"Bingo, Bruce, I think you've got it!"

As I first sighted and approached the island of Grandma and the scent of a skunk, it seemed pretty tiny and insignificant. If Rebecca hadn't pushed the point, I might have easily sailed right past it looking for a bigger, more dazzling landfall. It would have become just one of those strange, unexplainable, meaningless experiences that happen to all of us sometimes. *Gee, I thought I smelled a skunk and then realized I didn't*, would have been the entry in my journal. But, as I've said before, you just never know what buried treasure of information and insight you're likely to uncover on a voyage beyond the edge of the physical world. This treasure turned out to be one of my most important finds. For her part in embodying The Mysterious Teacher who's guided my voyages all along, Rebecca has my unending gratitude.

Some of you might recognize old, outdated beliefs that are impeding your desire to explore and learn. In Appendix B, you'll find a method to change or eliminate such beliefs. What I've written there is based on what Rebecca taught me. It works for me and, for those of you interested, I hope it helps.

CHAPTER 5

Earthquake in India

When great numbers of people die all at once as the result of a large-scale disaster, is there anything we, as living human beings, can do to assist them? When so many people make the transition to living in the Afterlife in such a short span of time, what happens to them?

Voyages into the Unknown readers may recall its first chapter was the account of my nonphysical experience with the Oklahoma City bombing in April 1995. In relating that experience, I mentioned a group of Helpers I'd met previously at an earthquake in India. What you are about to read describes my introduction to and first interaction with those Helpers.

Shortly after I'd settled into my new life in Virginia, I began participation in a Lifeline research group led by Dr. Rita Warren. This was part of an ongoing effort by The Monroe Institute to further explore and map areas of the Afterlife that humans inhabit. The group met once a month and was open to any Lifeline program graduates living in or visiting the area. Because I'd previously attended two Lifeline programs, I qualified, and eagerly joined in the research. Each group member had developed some level of the skills necessary for exploration, contact, and communication within the nonphysical world, and all were interested in and excited about the opportunity to do so as a group.

Each month Dr. Warren prepared for our gathering by selecting a research topic and preparing a detailed questionnaire. Questionnaires provided a means of collection and documentation of results used to build a database of information. We generally met on a Friday in the early afternoon and finished two to four hours later the same day. The Institute donated use of their facilities and Hemi-Sync tapes. Each group member used one of the same CHEC units (Controlled Holistic Environmental Center) used by program participants during our exploration sessions.

In a typical session, our group first met in the dining room for a briefing led by Dr. Warren. Afterwards, we followed the routine familiar to those who have attended six-day programs at the Institute. After we proceeded to our CHEC units, a control room operator played an appropriate Hemi-Sync tape that we each heard through stereo headphones. Sound patterns on these tapes facilitated our tuning into the Focus levels we intended to explore. With a little training, it's relatively easy to focus one's attention into the desired "location" in the Afterlife.

After each exploration session, group members filled out the survey questionnaire to document any information received while it was still fresh in memory. In this way, each member's experience was recorded in a systematic way for future reference. The method insured that no member's information was "cross-pollinated" by others in the group. After finishing our writing, the group reassembled in the lunchroom for debriefing and comparing notes. At times these discussions led to adjustment of the instructions for the next session, taking into account what we'd just discovered. This pattern of briefing on the topic, Hemi-Sync tape sessions, documentation, and debriefing was common to all the research group gatherings I attended. These were exciting times for me, and I always looked forward to our monthly gatherings to explore beyond the physical world as a member of a group with a common intent.

In the fall of 1993, a week or two before our group was to meet, an earthquake in India killed some 68,000 people. Dr. Warren chose as a research topic the question, "Is there any way a group such as ours could be of assistance in a large-scale, natural disaster?"

During past experience doing retrievals, I'd discovered people sometimes get "stuck" after they die. Often the circumstances of their death or their beliefs about an afterlife are responsible for their being "stuck." Doing retrievals, one person at a time, I'd learned the most common element of being stuck is a person's inability to perceive those who already inhabit the Afterlife and are trying to assist them. Deceased friends, relatives or volunteer Helpers sometimes have a difficult time with first contact. Through Lifeline training, I'd learned a method of getting a stuck person's attention and transferring their awareness of me to whoever was trying to assist them. That's essentially what the retrieval process is. Before joining the Lifeline research group, I'd become familiar with such assistance and providing it on a one-to-one basis. After hearing Dr. Warren describe our research topic, I began to wonder if it was possible to retrieve hundreds or thousands of people at a time. This month's session gave me the opportunity to explore that question. After our first pre-session briefing, I grabbed a blank questionnaire and headed for my CHEC unit. There were eight or ten others that Friday afternoon ready to explore what felt like an interesting and unusual topic.

I entered my CHEC unit, plumped up the pillow, and lay down under a light blanket to stay warm for the next forty-five minutes or so that the session would take. Then I flipped on the ready-light switch, indicating to the control room operator my readiness to begin the first session. After slipping on the stereo headphones, I got into a comfortable position and relaxed, waiting to begin.

Our sessions used a tape from the Lifeline program called "Free Flow 27." With few verbal instructions on this tape, it's ideal for long, open-ended exploration in the Focus 23 to Focus 27 areas of the Afterlife. In the fall of 1993, I still felt the need to rely on taped Hemi-Sync sounds to assist my exploration of states of consciousness I'd accessed during previous Monroe Institute programs. Since then, I've realized program trainers were truthful when they told us that once we'd learned to focus our attention There, we wouldn't need the tapes any more. Needing the tapes was just one more aspect of my continuing doubt about the validity of my experience. Continued exposure gradually replaced my belief in needing tapes with the knowledge that I could do it on my own.

Relaxing into the taped sounds, I expressed my intent to learn how I might assist as a member of a group in the aftermath of the India earthquake. Then, peering into the 3-D blackness before my closed eyes, I waited for something to happen. In a short time I was cruising with Rebecca through Focus 25, the Belief System Territories. I could see a large influx of people moving into the area. It seemed as though many of the earthquake victims were drawn to specific areas of Focus 25 which resonated with their particular afterlife beliefs. I "saw," in the impressions that came to me as I watched, how by using certain of their religious symbols and characters, one could attract their attention and assist in moving them to Focus 27.

I also noted that the sudden, unexpected and unexplained appearance of so many people in Focus 25 affected those already living in these areas. From previous experience, I understood that people "locked" in a Focus 25 belief system could be loosened when they felt a conflict within their beliefs. Though I didn't understand the exact details, something about huge numbers of people materializing out of thin air in their midst caused some to doubt something critical in their beliefs. In these moments of doubt, some seemed to move automatically to Focus 27. Looking back, I suspect there were Helpers I didn't see assisting these folks in the move.

When I reached Focus 27, I again expressed my intent to learn how I might assist. I shifted to Focus 23 and peered, intently, into the 3-D blackness before my nonphysical eyes. In that field of blackness, a small patch of bright, vivid green appeared and attracted my attention. I felt myself accelerating toward the green patch. Moving through it, I emerged from its other side, flying perhaps eighty yards above the ground. In full 3-D color, like a vivid, holographic movie, I was cruising along at a pretty good clip, over low, gently rolling, lush, green hills. It was a clear, bright, blue-sky sunny day. On the horizon, a little to my right, I could see two thin columns of white smoke rising, close together, into the clear blue sky. Not knowing what to expect, I turned slightly and headed straight for the columns of smoke, curious about where they were coming from.

The next thing I remember is standing at the edge of what looked like a small tent city or relief camp. There were many big, gray tents set up in rows on perhaps half a square city block of green countryside. From my time in the Boy Scouts, I'd say these were eight-man wall tents, pitched side by side using standard ropes and tent stakes. I noticed that the tent flap entrances to all the tents were closed, giving the impression they were occupied. Streets between the rows of tents were conspicuously absent, except for a single, narrow one leading through the center of the camp from my left to my right.

There were people in small groups or by themselves walking toward this tent city from the surrounding countryside. Off to my left, people were walking in from the countryside almost continuously, feeding a line that entered the camp. Apparently victims of the quake, the people looked exhausted and dazed as they entered the camp via the only narrow path I could see among the tents. There were other people, camp workers, greeting them as they moved through the line and entered the camp. On both sides of the path, tables were set up from which camp workers handed out blankets, cups, water and food. The distance between the tables was so narrow it forced everyone to walk single file. Each worker handing out supplies instructed the quake victims to follow closely behind the person in front of them.

Near where the workers were handing out food, I recognized the source of the thin columns of smoke I'd flown toward earlier. There were cooking fires in a couple of places in the camp where food was being prepared. The smoke columns were rising straight up from there, high into the windless sky.

I turned my head to the right and watched the line of people as they moved through the camp single file. At the edge of the camp, off to my right, I could see the line of people entering what appeared to be a tubular opening of some kind. It was dark and looked like the opening to a cave that was incongruously sitting there on the flat, open ground. The opening led into a tunnel, also dark on the outside, whose walls were semi-transparent. Looking closely through the tunnel walls, I could see that the line of people continued on. Each walked along, continuing to follow the person in front of her or him as instructed. Dazed and not very aware of their surroundings, most were still carrying their bowls of food, blankets and cups of water. Some, looking around and ahead inside the tunnel, appeared curious about the lights and colors they were seeing, but continued to walk, numbly following the person ahead of them. None of them seemed to be aware that just a short distance away from the opening, the tunnel lifted up off the ground and continued upwards. It looked like a long, dark, twisting tube extending far off into the distant sky. From where I was standing, I couldn't see where the tunnel went as the other end was too far away.

I was wondering where the tunnel went when I first became aware of someone standing behind me and a little to my right. I later realized he had been there, talking to me, from the moment I set foot in the camp. He was describing and pointing out various features of the camp and how it operated. I can't say I ever heard his voice, it was more like I felt it, and although I met him twice during these research sessions (and again several years later in Oklahoma City), to this day I've never seen him.

"It's a method we use to transport large numbers of people from here to what you call 'Focus 27,' 'The Park' or 'The Reception Center,' " I felt him say. On the other end of the tunnel there are more 'Helpers,' as you call them, who meet individually with each person as they arrive. Those Helpers make contact with each of the people and assist them in making their transition to life in their new environment. To some, it's explained that they died in the earthquake and they are now in a safe place. Others are allowed to come to this realization in their own time. Some of these Helpers are friends, relatives or loved ones who've come to meet and to help handle the influx of people from the quake. Others are volunteers who join in to help on their own."

As I continued looking around, he explained that the smoke from the cooking fires was one of the ways they attracted people to the camp. He told me that some of them had, no doubt, seen such camps or pictures of them while they were still living in the physical world, and this camp had been constructed by Afterlife inhabitants to look just like one of those. In that form, it fit in with what people expected to see. That way, he explained, people tended to remain calm and were much easier to assist since they felt themselves to be in familiar surroundings. He also explained the arrangement of the tents, with no walkways between them except the central, narrow path.

"It's an unobtrusive, subtle way of directing people to the line they must join to move to your Focus 27. As they approach the camp, the close spacing between the tents offers no easy way in except the path we intend for them to take. They automatically walk to where they see others gathering, and enter the line. It's an effective way of organizing and directing large numbers of people into a manageable means of retrieving them, as you would say."

Judging by the timing of events on the Hemi-Sync tape, it must have taken twenty minutes or so for him to show and explain the what and how of this camp's operation. Somewhere late in our conversation, I heard the verbal instructions on the tape saying it was time to return to my CHEC unit in Virginia. I explained to my host that I had to leave to go back and rejoin other members of my research group. I assured him that I'd return in a little while to learn more about how I could be of assistance. He seemed to understand what I was trying to communicate to him. Then I turned my attention back to the sounds of the tape and followed them to my familiar place in the physical world.

I stayed in my CHEC unit for a minute or so after the tape ended, giving myself a little time to remember all that had happened. Then I switched off the ready-light to let the person in the control room know I was back, and moved out of the CHEC unit. Sitting down at a desk in the room, I filled out the questionnaire. After finishing the form, I walked to the lunchroom, grabbed a cup of coffee, and sat down to wait for the remaining members of the group. When everyone was back, we started our debriefing session and listened as each in turn shared what he or she had just experienced.

For the most part, at first, it seemed as though each member of the group had been to a different place than I. It was almost as though we hadn't been together as a group at the same site. I recognized some similarities as people talked about their experiences, about the countryside they had seen, or the people they'd watched walking. A few had been in contact with people; some of these sounded like earthquake victims, others like various kinds of Helpers. As we all talked, I began to realize each had a story, at this point in our exploration, which indicated that most had arrived at different aspects of the earthquake site. None of us yet saw how our own individual experience fit together to form an overall picture. Each seemed to be involved in areas quite different from the others.

The following descriptions of activities during our first group session are taken directly from copies of the questionnaires. Dr. Warren graciously provided them to me in July 1995 as background information for an article I was writing.

One member of our group, BW, had met with some Guides in Focus 27. Their advice was that we should, "act as a group in sending Light" into the area. They explained that a large number of people were "stuck in the darkness of fear, frustration, and hopelessness." Sending "the energy of Light could lift these so they could go on."

Another participant, ND, described how, after placing her intent, "many people began to appear instantly. At first I was a little worried (that I might let them down) but almost immediately a tunnel opened up on my left. A kind of gang plank was put down." People, earthquake victims, "began filing up the plank" in large numbers. ND then went on to describe that people on the other side of the tunnel "were reaching out their hands to help them through the door of the tunnel. Large masses of people moved out steadily and calmly."

Rebecca described standing behind me in Focus 23, watching as a "known Indian leader" was "telling Bruce about the needs of his people. People seemed to be in hovels, attempting to care for themselves and each other. Bruce and I communicated with those in Focus 27 to receive instructions. All was in place for those in the 'camp' to go to areas of food distribution, and for us to float over the crowd and call to people to follow us. Many would go to Focus 25, and that would cause a disturbance there, and many from Focus 25 would also go to Focus 27 in the confusion."

Two other group members described being up in the air examining some sort of tube in the sky. Another received the message that our group should try to educate more people on Earth about death and dying. This would help because fewer people would become stuck in Focus 23 in the first place.

It was interesting to reread the questionnaire I'd filled out immediately after that first session. Doing so jogged my memory and added detail I'd forgotten in the two years since the experience. In response to the question, "What information did you receive?" I'd written:

"Relief 'tent city' as a means of gathering many together, use religious beliefs, to act as a 'floating figure' above the crowds."

Focus 25 retrievals could be done.

In such cases 'tent cities' have been formed with a focus on providing food and shelter. These can be a means of concentrating the newly dead. In their stunned, dazed state this is what they expect to see. Calling them to a nonphysical version of these (tent cities) is a starting point.

Focus 25 serves as a buffer. There's an opportunity to assist large numbers in NOT stopping in Focus 25 by portraying figures the people will see as Spirits. Floating or flying above crowds, calling to them to follow can induce many to do so."

Responding to the "other features of the experience" question, I'd written: "Located Rebecca and was in contact with her throughout most of the tape."

BW had, in her words, "been given a tour of an area of rubble" by a guide she met in Focus 27. Many people had been buried alive and were "stuck in fear, disorientation, and loss of energy." She reported that she and the Guide "sent light energy" into the piles of rubble as the guide explained this "would provide a 'spirit pathway' for those who had been buried alive."

Another member, RW, "saw moving streams of people both in Focus 23 and Focus 25." She "observed this while holding a golden light on the flow" of people.

As we each told the stories of our experience, a picture of our group interaction at the India earthquake began to emerge. We began to see how each of our experiences fit together to form an overall picture. We each had arrived at the site in different locations. Some were in different parts of the camp

I'd been in. Others were out in the countryside, with people who'd died in the quake. Still others had been up in the air assisting Helpers with the tunnel that exited the camp and went up to The Reception Center at Focus 27. Some members of our group had been aware of each other nearby, carrying out similar activities. Realizing we could gather together, we decided as a group that during our next tape session we would try to meet and set up our own mass retrieval station.

After completing our debriefing session we began preparation for exploring in the next phase of our research. In the second session we were to try to recontact any one we might have met during the first session and ask how we might be of assistance. After Dr. Warren made sure we all understood what we were to do, we each picked up another blank survey questionnaire form and headed back to our CHEC units.

After settling in with the headphones on, I switched on the ready-light, then relaxed, waiting for the tape to begin. I was excited at the prospect of going back to the earthquake site and again communicating with the guy I'd met previously. When the taped sounds started, I focused my intent on the camp and waited. In a few seconds, I found myself standing on the ground in the relief camp. I could feel the one I'd met last time, standing, still unseen, behind me and a little to the right. I opened my intended conversation with him by asking if he was there.

"Yes, I'm here," I felt him say.

"Well, I'm back to visit with you again."

"Yes, I knew you'd be coming, so I waited here for you."

"This time I'm here to ask if there's anything I can do to assist you and your team of Helpers? I'd like to assist in some way if I can. Is there any way I can be of help?" I thought out to him.

"As a matter of fact there is," he replied, "we can use you as bait."

"As bait?" I asked, a little puzzled at his use of the term.

"Yes, part of our problem is attracting people into the camp who are wandering around too far out in the countryside. We rely on our cooking fire smoke and there are some of us who fly over the area trying to get people's attention. Since you still live in a physical body, it will be much easier for them to see and hear you. We'd like to fly you around, beyond sight of our smoke, close to the ground. If you'd just get the attention of anyone you see and direct them toward the camp, it would be a great help."

"Okay, if being 'bait,' as you put it, would be a great help I'm willing to give it a try."

"These two will accompany you and provide an attention-getting function that will make your part easier to play."

As he said this, I was joined by two of the brightest, most brilliant, shining lights you can imagine. A feeling of peace and loving acceptance radiated from them. It took me a few seconds to realize these were humans in a form with which I was unfamiliar. Each of them was easily twice my six-foot, four-inch height and perhaps four times the diameter of my waist at the middle. They were long, slender oval shapes, gently tapering from their four-foot diameter middle to perhaps a foot and a half diameter dome at both the top and bottom. And their Light! Dazzling! They shone so brightly that I couldn't bring myself to stare directly into their light. I guess that's a trait I share with most other humans; concern about damaging our eyes by staring into very bright lights, a totally unnecessary concern I might add, since I was not looking at them with my physical eyes!

This brings up a point I'd like to cover in some detail. Avoiding staring into extremely bright lights is something I call a *human force of habit*. We physically alive humans are subtly influenced by many such habits, and that's part of the reason I could be used as bait. Without a second thought, we accept things such as gravity, the solidity of matter, and the privacy of our thoughts. As a result, we tend to act physically human even when we're in a nonphysical environment. We tend to project these human forces of habit out into nonphysical environments, and that, somehow, makes it easier for the newly deceased to see and hear us. They evidently pick up on our subconscious projections, making us more familiar and recognizable to them than Helpers who exist in the nonphysical world. So, the fact that I still reside in a physical body meant that I could best assist as bait.

The two bright-light people had positioned themselves on either side of me so that our "waists" were side by side, and they each extended about three feet above my head and below my feet. Thinking back on it later, we must have looked like a giant butterfly. In the center, I might have looked like the body of a butterfly with the two bright-light people on either side as wings. We could have also looked very much like some people's descriptions of an angel, a human body with a bright halo of wings. No doubt, the sight of us must have been similar to some Being in the religious beliefs of many victims of the quake. Shortly after joining me, the bright-light people and I gently lifted up off the ground, accelerated away from the camp, and flew toward the horizon.

At first, I was busily scanning ahead, looking for people on the ground below us. Sometime after the camp was out of sight, beyond the horizon behind me, I spotted the first people ahead of us, walking. As we approached, they looked up, and I could tell the bright-light people beside me had first attracted their attention. So, they were bait too. What we must have looked like to those first people I saw on the ground! Two brilliant lights up in the sky, outshining the sun, on either side of a man waving his arms and legs, pointing toward the horizon and yelling.

"There's a relief camp over that way, they've got food, water and blankets. Look for the smoke rising up from the cooking fires and follow it to the camp."

I'm sure the two light people got a good chuckle or two at my animated, amateur theatrics. I didn't realize, at any time during this experience, that the two bright-light people ever spoke to me. I remembered it much later, but, at the time, I wasn't consciously aware of it. After encountering the first few people walking below us, with the unspoken influence of the bright-light people, I toned down my act. No more waving arms, yelling, and pointing. We established a pattern of approaching from low in the sky, perhaps twenty-five feet off the ground. We maintained that altitude until the people on the ground noticed the bright lights. Then, moving toward them slowly, almost majestically, we'd gently descend. Hovering just above the ground, close to them, smiling, I'd talk in a more conversational tone. I'd explain about the relief camp, the smoke columns, food, water, and blankets. Then, extending my arm slowly, I'd turn, pointing in the direction of the camp. I was striving to appear like an angel to the people we encountered. I drew on every Sunday school angelic tidbit I could remember to give a really convincing performance.

After awhile, I caught on that I didn't need to look for anyone on the ground. The bright-light people did all that. These guys definitely knew what they were doing. All I had to do was play my part, smile, greet people, and point the way to the camp. The bright-light people handled all the locating. We had probably found 15 to 20 people when my role as bait was suddenly cut short. The sunlit, countryside scene with the image of those two brilliant lights by my side slowly faded into blackness. As it did, I thanked the bright-light people for their help in learning about being bait.

Next, I found myself standing on the ground, and Rebecca's smiling face came into view a short distance away. She was not looking directly at me, but rather had her smiling gaze turned toward my left, a far-off look in her eye. As I looked more closely at her, I could feel she was extending her Love outward, filling the countryside in all directions. The Love she was extending took the form of a bright beacon of light, shining outwards in front of her. Some of the light from this beacon was spread out over a wide area, illuminating a broad expanse of the nearby terrain. There was a central portion of this beacon that was more tightly focused, brighter and more intense. A little like a lighthouse beacon, the tightly focused part beamed a brilliant shaft of light deep into a black fog at the far edge of the countryside. I was a little surprised to see the black fog, as I hadn't noticed it in any of my previous activities. It seemed to form an edge of some kind between the area we could see and a dark unknown. Rebecca's Love/Light set up a field with an attractive force for anyone who came in contact with it. With her arms extended slightly downward and out to her sides, Rebecca's loving smile invited everyone.

I could also see what I would describe as an opening, forming behind her. This opening looked like the one I'd seen exiting the tent city relief camp. I moved closer to her, taking up a position on her left, joining in, intending to lend my energy to the beacon she was beaming outward. I noticed, as I joined with her, the intensity of the beacon increased not twofold, but more like four to six times its previous brightness. The dark, black fog area receded farther, the countryside extended farther away from us, now illuminated by our combined energy. The tightly focused part of the beam had expanded in diameter, penetrating a larger, deeper area into the dark fog.

As we stood there, I watched other members of the research group join us, one by one, lending energy, adding to the size and intensity of the beacon. Each one's joining increased the intensity of the beacon by orders of magnitude rather than by the simple addition I kept expecting, illuminating more of the countryside, extending it to the horizon before the last person joined our group effort. Members joined at all different levels, some above me, floating close by in the air, others beside or behind me. All of us were connected, as though we were holding hands, but not with our hands. It seemed as though our individual outer boundaries became thinner and thinner until we joined into one entity, projecting the Light of Love into the darkness of Focus 23. Looking out into the countryside, I could see quake victims turning toward the beacon we were projecting. I knew that they felt attracted to our beacon, and I could see them walking toward us. I watched as they moved closer and entered the opening that we had made.

Looking back, over my shoulder, I wanted to see where our opening led. It transformed into a tubular structure that lifted up off the ground and headed into the sky. It looked just like the one I had seen at the camp. I could clearly see the two research group members who had earlier been examining that tunnel. They were behind me, high up off the ground, and appeared to be directing their intent toward forming and maintaining our tunnel to Focus 27. I could see through the tunnel walls and saw the people who had entered. They were walking easily, unafraid, some wide-eyed and marveling at the view ahead as they moved forward. We continued as a group, providing the beacon, opening a tunnel to The Reception Center until the tape sounds indicated it was time to return. Our group then separated, reformed our boundaries as individuals, then moved apart and returned to Virginia. I don't know what happened to the opening we made. I left with a feeling of accomplishment and gratitude for the opportunity to learn through the experience.

At our debriefing session, all but one of our group had some recollection of the group activity we'd taken part in. As we talked, I found myself looking closely at each member. Some of them I'd met for the first time that day, and I was not entirely familiar with their physical appearances. I found myself comparing how they looked now with how they had looked as we had gathered together, forming a retrieval station in India. I decided the similarities were not so much in how they each looked, but rather in how their appearance made me feel. I left that day feeling much closer to those people and grateful for their participation in our research.

Looking back at the original intent of the research project we carried out, I find the results fascinating. Before this research session I'd met Helpers who'd assisted me in doing retrievals of individuals. We learned in this experience, however, that there are teams of Helpers who work together in large-scale disasters. These Helpers put together a scenario, based on what was known about the people they expected to find. In this case, the tent city relief camp was used because it fit in so well with what the people would expect to see. It was such a smooth, well-planned operation. Their system was designed to minimize any shock people might experience at learning that they had died. The subject didn't come up for any of them until they were already transported to The Reception Center in Focus 27. Most arriving There were allowed to become aware of their deaths in their own time, at their own pace. All were allowed to gradually move from the earthquake site to a place where they were greeted by and reunited with friends, relatives, or Helpers. I still marvel at the gentle, effective manner in which this team handles such situations. Using the smoke from cooking fires to attract people to the camp was so simple and so natural. It used victims' desire for food, water, and shelter to ease them into communication with those waiting to assist them. From understanding gained during my retrieval experiences of individuals, this is an important point. Without such contact shortly after dying, some people become stuck in Focus 23 situations of their own making. If they get stuck, it can be very difficult to reach them, not unlike trying to awaken them as a character in their own dream. The method this team used was to take roles in the *dream* most of the quake victims were already in. They worked together to fit into that dream of the aftermath of a devastating earthquake in a way that was completely acceptable to the newly deceased. There was no reason for them to doubt the reality of the relief camp or the people handing out supplies and words of encouragement. I still marvel at it.

The nice touches like giant, bright angels floating through the air to meet them were outstanding. These *angels* fit into the religious beliefs of people I encountered while being used as *bait*. I had watched some of those people walking away from where we lingered, the two bright-light people and I. Hovering just above the ground, I heard those people talking about us. They would look back at us, sometimes in disbelief, talking to other members of their little group excitedly, saying things such as, "Did you see that too?" They were completely unaware of the fact that they were dead. They were looking forward to telling others at the camp ahead that a Spirit Being had pointed the way. This team we'd met really had all the bases covered! I know they, or other teams like them, show up wherever they are needed to assist large numbers of victims in making their transition.

While taking part in Dr. Warren's research, I learned that a group of people still living in physical bodies can assist when large numbers of people die in a short span of time. We learned about being bait, about projecting Love and Light, and about making pathways to the Reception Center. We learned what it was like to work together nonphysically as a team, joining into one Being. Whenever I read in the newspaper or see a story on TV about some big disaster, I remember my experience with Dr. Rita Warren's research group in October of 1993.

I never suspected at the time of this exploration that I would ever meet the relief camp Helpers from the Indian earthquake again. I'm so grateful to have met them in India and learned a little about assisting in a large-scale disaster before the events in Oklahoma City on April 19, 1995. The experience in India was relatively calm, emotionally, compared to Oklahoma City. There, a terrorist bomb killed 168 people, many in the blink of an eye. The emotional energy at the site of that bombing was so powerful, I needed all the help I could get.

I'd like to take a moment here to express my love and gratitude to Dr. Rita Warren for this opportunity to learn.

CHAPTER 6

Scott's Murder

Scott was murdered in a restaurant in Oakland, California, in February of 1993. I didn't find out about it until I phoned his mother, a longtime friend, later that year in October. I'd been living in Virginia for a month or so when I felt the urge to call my friend Barb. She and her husband, Rob, had moved from Minnesota to South Carolina several years before when Rob took a position at the university in Columbia. I've known Barb since the early 1970s when we were neighbors living by a lake in suburban Minneapolis. We hadn't spoken in a long time, and I thought it would be nice to touch base and pass on my new address and phone number.

Early in our conversation I was saddened to hear Barb's news. "You know we lost Scott last February. He was murdered during a robbery in a restaurant in Oakland," she said.

Sadness, anger, and grief seeped through her voice as she told me what had happened. Three men entered the restaurant Scott managed, near closing time. After taking all the money they could find from customers and cash registers, they ordered Scott and two other employees to lie, face down, on the floor. For their cooperation, they were each shot once in the back of the head. Each had died instantly there on the restaurant floor.

As we continued to talk, Barb expressed concern for Bev, who had been Scott's wife for just a few months at the time of his death. Eight months after his murder, Bev was still having a very hard time accepting his death and moving on. She and Scott had both been struggling in their lives somewhat before they'd met and married. After their marriage, things just seemed to start coming together for both of them. They were happy and prosperous, and the joy of being together appeared to stretch out into a future full of promise. They had a house overlooking the ocean near San Francisco, and a sailboat tied up at a local marina. They were a happy newlywed couple. And then, in an instant of senseless brutality, Scott was dead. Bev had said, in conversation on the phone with Barb, that she could feel Scott around her now at times. Sometimes she could feel him standing just outside the glass doors that led to the patio with its spectacular view of the Pacific Ocean. Their dog, she said, sometimes acted as though he could see Scott in various places around the house. All of this continued to remind her of her loss and kept her grief close to the surface and unresolved.

Barb also mentioned that she, herself, was having great difficulty sleeping through the night for the last two to three weeks. She'd be awakened from a dream, often in the middle of the night, by the voice of a frightened little boy crying out for help. The voice's plaintive wail drove her to wake up to avoid the anguish she felt at hearing it. It was a source of torment for Barb, as these were just dreams to her, something she couldn't control. She questioned what they meant, but didn't know what to do about them. As she told me about her dreams, the impression that Scott was trying to contact his mother was firmly forming in my mind. It felt as though he was pleading for help from her like a frightened little boy calling out for his mommy.

I suggested to her that Scott might be connected with the voice in her dreams. Barb and I had spoken in the past about my Lifeline retrieval activities and I knew she was somewhat skeptical. When I offered to look for Scott and check in on how he was doing, she wanted to know what that meant. I explained that I would nonphysically go out and look for him. When I found him I would try to determine what sort of mental state he was in, and if he appeared to need assistance, I would offer it. I'm sure it felt odd for her when she said, "Yes, I'd appreciate it if you'd do that." I explained that it usually takes me several days to work up to it and that I'd call her back as soon as I'd made contact with Scott.

Still lacking full confidence, I enlisted Rebecca's help, since she, with her more extensive experience, was more adept at

Lifeline retrieval work than I. As it happened, the isolation booth in the lab at The Monroe Institute (TMI) was open one night that week, and we made arrangements to use the facility. The lab isolation booth is used during research into various states of human consciousness. It is a soundproof, temperature-controlled room, outfitted with a salt-water-filled waterbed and all kinds of electronic gear. It has an aura about it that I felt would give me added confidence. I was still in the stage of my learning that I felt using Hemi-Sync sounds was necessary to assist me in moving to Focus 27. Some of the electronic gear used in conjunction with the booth could supply those sounds. On the appointed evening, we went to the lab, and, using a Free Flow 27 set of Hemi-Sync sounds, went out together to look in on Scott.

Within a very short time we easily found Scott, who seemed to be in a somewhat confused state. He was very near Bev and this didn't seem to be helping either one of them. He was aware of Bev's almost overpowering grief and he wanted desperately to help and console her. Shortly after his death, Scott thought that by staying with her he could somehow help Bev move through that grief to a happier frame of mind. But as he tried to do so, he, himself, got caught up in her grief and felt it at least as strongly as she did. This greatly clouded his thinking, and, as a result, over the months since his murder Scott had become locked in a cycle of grief himself. He could no longer maintain any separation between himself and the grief he and Bev felt together. At the point we'd found them, this had become a sort of a mutually fed, perpetual cycle for both of them. If either of them began to heal, their emotional bond with the other would suck them back into grief, and the cycle would begin again. They had been at this for about eight months, and there was no end in sight for either of them. Scott was exhausted, dazed, and confused. He'd been at this so long that his power to think on his own, apart from their grief, had long since waned. He wanted to help Bev heal her grief, but instead he'd become so involved that he was now part of the problem. In his present, confused state of mind, there was no way for him to break free and move to a more objective perspective. With his thinking so clouded, he'd become locked in a cycle with Bev, stuck in Focus 23. He knew he was dead; that wasn't his problem. The power of the emotion was just more than he could handle. It was like being locked in a dream he'd have to awaken from to escape, but the power of those emotions kept the dream going.

Rebecca and I talked it over, nonphysically, and decided we'd split up. She would work with Scott; I would check in on Bev, and we'd compare notes later. I moved away from Scott to a place where the blackness before me was uniform and undisturbed. I placed my intent on connecting with Bev and peered into the blackness before me, waiting for something to happen. It didn't take long. A small, solid, black swirl drew my attention to one corner of my field of view. I focused my attention on the swirl, opening my awareness to whatever it represented. Moments later, a room materialized out of the blackness fully into view. It was a parlor in a mansion, my impressions placing it sometime during the American Civil War.

As I focused in on the black and white holographic image of the room, two women came into view. One was sitting on a chair that a present-day antique dealer would see as a fortune waiting to be realized. The other, the younger of the two, was standing with her back to a beautiful, dark, hardwood table. She was standing; facing a window, looking out toward the road that led up to the mansion. Looking into her eyes I could see the very life of her pouring out of her heart. It poured out through the window and down that road as she stood staring off into the distance. I knew the man she loved had left on that road. Out of his sense of duty, he'd gone off to the war to do his part, and the war had taken his life. She'd been told by a witness that there was no mistake about this. Her man was dead. Still she poured her life out that window and down that road every day. She wouldn't accept his death. It had to be a mistake. Some day, she knew deep inside, she'd see his smiling face coming back up that road and her life could start again. She'd waited until, while pouring out her life down that road in grief, she'd died. She never accepted that he wasn't coming back. She never healed the wound of grief she felt at his loss. She'd died at the end of that lifetime, locked into a grief from which she'd never recovered. This same woman from the American Civil War now lived in the Bay Area of California. Her name was Bev now and she was reliving that cycle of grief over her husband's loss. She was the young woman standing at the parlor window. In that lifetime, Scott was the one who'd never come back up that road from the war. All this information and more came to me in less time than it takes to tell it, as I looked at that young woman at the window. I backed away a short distance from her to take in all that the scene had to offer.

In a single ball of information, I knew more about Scott and Bev in their lifetimes during the Civil War. Scott and Bev had been man and wife then, too. They'd come into possession of a large plantation, and lived in a huge mansion on the property. It wasn't clear how they'd acquired it, but their lives were coming together nicely as a result. It had meant prosperity for them, a life of luxury. They were just beginning to reap the rewards of running the plantation together when the war broke out. Scott had felt a duty to join the war as a soldier, as many did. He had to fight for the way of life he felt was deserved by those on his side of the issues. There had been great sadness and hope at his leaving. She'd felt sadness that he would be in danger, away from her, and hope for winning the war and his safe return. He'd ridden away, down the road that led from the plantation. Bev had watched him leave, feeling the fear all wives feel when their husbands leave home for war.

Months later, his letters stopped coming. After what seemed like forever, someone who'd witnessed Scott's death came to the plantation and told Bev that Scott had been killed. She took it very hard. He'd been buried near the battlefield where he'd died. It was far away, and she never saw his body. Without seeing his body during that long ago lifetime, she had been able to deny it had happened. So, she spent all her days standing by the parlor window waiting for his return until her own death finally released her.

I turned my attention to the other woman seated on a chair not far from the young woman at the window. She was the older of the two, and, as I peered at her, I realized it was my friend Barb. There in the parlor, I watched as Barb talked to Bev, trying her best to console Bev and help her accept the death of her beloved. It wasn't completely clear what the relationship was between these two women during that life-time, but Barb seemed to be most like an aunt.

Barb was doing her best to close the wound to Bev's heart, which was pouring out the energy meant to sustain her very life. It wasn't working, and Barb could sense the futility of her efforts as Bev moved ever closer, day by day, to dying of a broken heart. The emotion of that scene began to get to me; it still does today when I remember it. There's a welling up of sadness that brings tears to my eyes as I remember the lost, forlorn look in Bev's heart, holding in her grief, staring out that window and down that road. It was clear to me that Scott's recent death was connected in some way to Bev's reaction to his death during the Civil War.

Feeling that I had enough information to understand Bev's situation, I moved away from the parlor, and the scene dis-solved into blackness. I focused my attention on finding Scott, and in a moment, he came into view. He and Rebecca were talking. He looked clearer now, alert, brighter in the face and eyes. His stupefying grief and sadness were gone, and he was clearly focused on his conversation with Rebecca. She was explaining to Scott the predicament he was in and offering to escort him to a place where he could gather himself together. Maybe later, she explained, when he was stronger, he could return to assist Bev. If he returned to be near her now, he'd most likely revert to his semiconscious state, locked in their cycle of grief .

Scott seemed to clearly understand what she was saying and the implications of his choices. He readily agreed to go with her to the place she described. I followed them both to Focus 27 where Scott was met by an older man he recognized immediately. The man felt like an uncle of sorts. We left Scott there with the man and returned to the isolation booth in the lab back at the Institute, opened our eyes and began to com-pare notes.

Rebecca filled me in on her interaction with Scott after I'd left to check in on Bev. She had done some energetic work with him which cleared away the effects of the emotional turmoil he'd been locked into for so long. With the clarity of mind she had facilitated, Scott had remembered how he'd become stuck. He'd wanted to help Bev work through her grief. By staying near her, trying to let her know he was all right, he'd felt her grief. He became so connected and focused into her emotional state that he'd lost the ability to think clearly. For the months since his death, he'd been only semi-conscious. He'd tried to contact his mother, hoping she could help him, but it had all been like a dream. In his state of mind, he hadn't realized that he could make choices on his own, much less act upon them. With Rebecca's assistance, Scott realized that if he went back to trying to help Bev as he'd been doing, he'd become lost in that dream of grief again. He understood that he had to put some distance between himself and Bev. He'd have to get stronger before any such effort could succeed. That understood, Scott had agreed to move to Focus 27 to be with people who could help him become stronger.

As we talked, it became clear that Scott's murder had been an attempt to heal the open wound of grief with which Bev had died long ago on a Civil War plantation. If she didn't succeed in healing that wound, their love for each other might draw them together in a future lifetime to try again. His death on the restaurant floor had been different from his death during the Civil War. It occurred in such a way that Bev was certain to see his body. He wouldn't be buried on a far-off battlefield in an unmarked grave, leaving the possibility open to her mind that he was still alive. This time she would have to face the reality of his death, and his fondest hope was that she would be able to accept it and heal. In a planned accident of the universe, he'd sacrificed his life to give Bev the opportunity to heal. Now it was all up to Bev. It was clear she had been holding the grief of both Scott's deaths deep inside her. To heal, she would have to get those feelings out into the openness of her awareness.

A few days later, after letting this all settle in, I called Barb to tell her what Rebecca and I'd found out. She confirmed that the tormenting dreams of the lost little boy calling out for her help had stopped the night we'd done the retrieval. As we talked, the similarities between the lives Scott and Bev shared in California and on the plantation long ago were striking. Up until they'd met, Scott was kind of aimlessly wandering, trying to find his place in this world. Bev was a very successful woman in business. When they married everything came together for both of them. Their prosperity provided the beautiful house overlooking the ocean and the sailboat they enjoyed together. They were in love, and everything in their lives seemed to be going their way. They had financial success, a wonderful home, and a life together that seemed to be just the beginning of a fabulous future for both of them. And then, in that instant on the floor in a restaurant in Oakland, it was suddenly, tragically, over.

Barb had been fulfilling the same role in *this* life she had tried to do in the earlier one with Bev and Scott. Several times a week she would call Bev on the phone and they'd talk. As best she could, Barb tried to help Bev work through the grief at her loss as she worked through her own. But it was apparent to Barb that Bev wasn't moving through her grief. At her best, she seemed to be stuck in it; at her worst, she was losing ground. Bev had been seeing a counselor off and on, but it didn't seem to be helping her deal with her problem.

I nonphysically checked on Bev again later in the week. It was clear from that visit that her trips to the counselor only aided in avoiding the pain, his therapy only serving to cover over the emotional pain so that she wasn't expressing it anywhere. What she needed was to face it and let it out. On this trip, Coach, a nonphysical guide I introduced in my first book, *Voyages Into The Unknown*, suggested Bev consider joining a support group made up of people who had suffered the same kind of loss. Her healing could be accelerated, he said, by interacting with other people whose loved ones had been taken from them by a sudden, unexpected, senseless act of violence.

Barb passed the advice on to Bev in one of their later phone conversations. It's my understanding that she took the advice, and, within a couple of months, started living her life again. She left that house full of memories overlooking the ocean and moved to southern California to start over. Last I heard, she was healing and doing much better, but that's not the end of this story.

About six months after I last saw Scott, as we left him with his "uncle" in Focus 27, I took my kids on vacation to Minnesota. We landed at the airport heading to a visit with Grandma and Grandpa at their home by the lake. Barb and Rob had moved from South Carolina back to the Minneapolis area, and offered the use of one of their cars. My mother came down to pick us up at the airport, and we all stopped to visit with Barb. As we sat outside on the patio chatting over a snack, I could feel Scott was there with us. Whenever I focused my attention on him, he was sort of happily bouncing around and I could feel his voice in my mind.

"Say purple and gold to my mother, Bruce, purple and gold," I kept hearing him say.

I had no idea what this meant; it made no sense to me. It seemed a little strange, and I didn't feel at all comfortable talking out loud about it in front of everyone there. So, I stayed behind for a few minutes after my mom and kids started off in the car for the two-hour drive to the house by the lake.

I was better able to focus in on Scott after they'd gone, and it was clear he wanted to get a message through to his mother. The flavor of it tasted like a graduation of sorts, like he had been in school since he moved to Focus 27. He wanted his mother to know he was about to graduate from that school. As a way of opening my conversation with Barb, I asked how she was doing now with Scott's passing. She said that she had worked through her anger and grief, but was troubled by dreams that had started again just recently. They were different in character from the ones before, but had the feel of Scott trying to contact her. Hearing that, I felt better about relaying Scott's new message.

"Scott is here right now with us, and he insists that I say 'purple and gold' to you. Do those colors mean anything to you?"

After a moment, the blank, questioning expression on her face suddenly changed as though a piece of a puzzle had just fallen into place.

"Purple and gold are the colors of the high school Scott went to. He wore them at his graduation."

At that point, it became clear to me what the message was that Scott wanted to get through to his mother.

"I'm graduating, Mom," he seemed to be saying. "I'm fine. I've been going to school here, and my graduation is coming soon."

I didn't know enough about what it meant to graduate from a school in Focus 27 to explain it to Barb. It had the feeling of celebration to it as he told me, but that's all I could get. Shortly thereafter I left in their car and drove the two hours northwest to rejoin my kids and my parents.

A week later, our vacation was over, and we returned to Barb's and Rob's house to return their car. The character of Barb's latest troubling dreams had changed, and she was sleeping better. She and Rob had arranged to gather some friends, including Scott's brothers and sister, for an evening house party. The night of visiting drew to a close, friends said their good-byes, and after a while only family and a few of their close friends were left. Sitting around the dining room table, Barb asked me to share what I'd told her, starting at the beginning and including my latest contact with Scott. After I'd gone over it in detail, Scott's younger sister excitedly shared information about Scott that she'd gotten recently. She'd been talking with a friend of hers, a psychic, two weeks ago, when the subject of Scott had come up. Her friend had also told Amy that he was about to graduate. I took this as a form of independent confirmation of what Scott had told me. A small bit of evidence, but evidence nevertheless, that I'd made contact with him and correctly passed along his message to the family. My confidence in the reality of the experience added to my growing trust and further reduced my doubt about the Afterlife's existence.

CHAPTER 7

Third Lifeline: Dr. Ed Wilson Returns

Dr. Ed Wilson was a medical doctor with an interest in subtle energy medicine. During my Gateway Voyage at The Monroe Institute (TMI) in the Fall of 1991, I was indirectly introduced to him through a rather peculiar experience. During a tape exercise, I saw a 3-D, nonphysical image of Skip Atwater's face in the fanning pages of a hardcover book. I met Skip physically for the first time later during a tour of the TMI lab. It was Skip Atwater, as *Voyage into the Unknown* readers may recall, who told me about work he and Dr. Wilson were doing to measure magnetic fields around the human body. During the same tape experience, I had also been shown a device identified to me as a magnetic anomaly sensor. The device seemed to be connected to the research Ed and Skip were doing.

Then, late in the summer of 1992, back in Colorado, I got a call from Rebecca. She was coming to visit with Ed, who lived in the mountains west of Boulder, Colorado. He was continuing to carry out experiments to detect magnetic fields around the human body. She wanted to introduce me to him on the chance my engineering background might be of help to his efforts. We met several days later and went to one of those great, hole-in-the-wall Mexican restaurants for which Colorado is famous.

Ed had been diagnosed with leukemia, and was in remission when I met with him and Rebecca. We talked about his interest in sensing the magnetic fields of human beings as a possible medical diagnostic tool. He also had other, more esoteric, ideas about using magnetic-field-sensing equipment around humans. We had an interesting lunch together and talked on at great length. I agreed to help Ed by designing and building a piece of equipment to wind large coils of very fine copper wire for his experiments. Over the next couple of months, I used the machine shop after hours where I worked to fabricate parts for the coil winder. In my spare time, I assembled it on my workbench in the basement, but not much came of my efforts to help Dr. Wilson with his research.

The next time I met him was during my third Lifeline program in November of 1993, while living in Virginia. The dishwashing machine at the training center had broken down again, the same one that broke down before my second Lifeline program. As it had then, my repair of the dishwasher this time secured a spot for me in my third program. This program was filled to capacity, and normally no additional participants would have been allowed in, but the dishwasher had to be fixed, so I made it in.

Two days later my third Lifeline program began. On the first full day of that program, Dr. Ed Wilson died at his mountain home, west of Boulder. After that Ed was a constant companion during every tape exercise for the entire six days of the program.

He was very intent on establishing communication with me after his death. He seemed to know the intensive focus on Afterlife exploration during a Lifeline program was like a ticking clock. He had six days to build a means of communication that would persist into the future. Ed was very persistent! As soon as a tape exercise began, his voice would be there trying to communicate with me. Sometimes this was really exasperating. There are brief instructions on these tapes, voiced by Bob Monroe. Ed's voice was so loud it was like listening to two different people talking at once. I couldn't understand what either of them was saying, and more than once had to ask Ed to be quiet until Bob's voice finished on the tape.

Ed practiced communicating verbally, visually, and through direct thought. He stood in odd postures his friends recognized from my description. He showed me where he had taken up residence. On the thick, green lawn next to a huge, stone building, Ed had pitched a pup tent. The building was some sort of library in Focus 27. It had a smooth stone exterior that looked like a single, solid slab of polished granite. He had pitched his little pup tent not ten feet from the building. He spent his time poring over papers he'd evidently gotten in the library. Cardboard boxes filled with papers were stacked near his tent. At times, I'd have to look for him and would find him sitting on a stool in front of a roaring campfire, reading through papers. It was a pretty incongruous scene! Imagine the same thing happening next to a big modern library in the physical world.

Less then a week before he died, Ed had called Rebecca on the phone and talked to her about coming to Colorado. He wanted her to move out of the TMI environment and develop her creative talents. She had been carrying out Hemi-Sync sound pattern research at TMI. She'd been responsible for some breakthrough research, and Ed felt that if she were free to pursue it on her own, great things could happen. Through Ed's friendly brow-beating, he convinced her to "come and play" with him in Colorado. As soon as he and I established communications after his death, one of the first things he adamantly stressed was that I make sure Rebecca lived up to her agreement to move to Colorado.

"You get her out of there!" he tersely repeated. "Don't you tell her I'm pushing you to make her leave until I've had a chance to talk to her about it. If she won't listen to me, then you get her out of there!"

It had been two months since I'd seen my son and daughter, and the prospect of moving back to Colorado to help "get her out of there" was a welcome thought. As it turned out, I didn't need to get pushy with Rebecca. In her After-life contact with Ed, he'd reminded her of her commitment, and she'd agreed to keep it.

Ed and Bob Monroe were friendly rivals while they were both alive in the physical world. During this Lifeline program, I asked Ed if he had a message for Bob. When I did, the scene changed. It felt like a formal garden with a slow moving stream winding its way under overhanging trees. In a dark scene, like images at dusk, the stream emerged from under the trees into the open, spilling quietly over a small, three-tiered, man-made waterfall.

Rebecca had also received a message for Bob from Ed. In a scene that looked like an ancient monastery, Bob and Ed were chuckling about the results of a project they had completed together. They had erected a structure from which hung a huge bell. They had positioned the bell near one of the buildings in such a way that when the wind blew just right, it caused a reverberation and sound from the bell. They were chuckling because this sound from the bell often occurred during the silent prayer and meditation of others in the monastery. Not everyone enjoyed the disruption of the sound. It seems Bob and Ed had shared a lifetime together in which they played with sound.

After the Lifeline program, I continued to be in contact with Dr. Wilson. Each time I checked in with him, the stack of boxes filled with papers from the library had grown. His campsite was becoming a bit of a blight on the neighborhood. No one seemed to mind too much. He was fond of digging up information in the nonphysical world and passing it along. Ed passed on all sorts of things he'd been curious about while he had been living in the physical world; among these was an electromagnetic theory of gravity.

I awoke one morning while still in a conversation with Ed and two other people. Ed had found these two in his wanderings, and wanted to assist them in passing along their theory. I knew as I awoke that our discussion had something to do with gravity, but that was all I remembered. During the remainder of the day, I jotted down details that came back to me from that dream conversation and listened to Ed's continued descriptions. It's a long, detailed theory. Those who are interested will find it in Appendix A.

A week after his death, Rebecca and I drove to Tennessee for Ed's memorial service. We told family members there about our contacts with him since his death. Though skeptical, they were accepting of what we had to say. After the service at the church, everyone went to the cemetery for a service to pay his or her respects. Everyone stood in a circle around Ed's grave marker and listened to brief stories about him by those gathered there. When the officiating minister asked everyone to bow their heads for a prayer, I got quite a surprise. After closing my eyes and bowing my head, I became aware of a whirling cyclone of energy. It was swirling like a silent tornado with a base the diameter of the circle of the people praying. As I focused my attention on the energetic whirling, I realized Ed was there with us. He was walking around the circle, stopping in front of each person to say a few words. When he got to me I could clearly see him, with my eyes closed. He stepped toward me.

"Bruce, I'm looking forward to working with you when you get to Colorado," I felt him say.

"Ed, I'm happily surprised to see you here and look forward to our work together too."

Then he stepped back and moved to the next person, Rebecca, standing to my right. I saw him step toward her and they exchanged a few words, which I couldn't hear. He then moved to the last person he visited with before he left. She was his mate during the final years of his life Here. He stepped toward her and they embraced in a dazzling shower of pink and golden light. As the minister's prayer ended, Ed stepped back away from her, rose skyward and disappeared.

Just before leaving Virginia to move back to Colorado, I was given another message for Bob Monroe. This time it wasn't from Ed Wilson, it was instead from Nancy Penn Monroe, Bob's wife, who'd died earlier that year. Bob had invited me up to his house on the mountain to watch a Sunday afternoon football game. After several cans of diet pop, my bladder was full and urged a trip to the bathroom. I'd just closed the door and lifted the lid when I felt Nancy's presence in the room.

"Bruce, I'd like you to pass along a message to Bob for me if you would," I felt her say.

"Of course," I said, almost absent-mindedly as I proceeded with what I'd come into the bathroom to do.

"Oh! Pardon me! I'll avert my eyes until you're finished."

"Thank you, but that's quite all right. I gave up on the illusion of privacy a long time ago," I responded, laughing.

When I'd finished, she returned to her request.

"Please tell Bob I'm still here and I still love him very much. Tell him I'll be waiting for him when the time comes for him to make his transition here."

"I'll be happy to, though I'm not sure he trusts my ability enough to believe I have actually been in contact with you."

"It's okay if that's the way he reacts. Will you do it?"

"Yes of course."

I felt Nancy thank me, and then she was gone. When I returned to watching the football game I told Bob what had happened in the bathroom and passed Nancy's message on to him. By his reaction, I could tell he didn't put much credence in what I said. He talked about his belief that no one spent more than six months where Nancy had gone before they moved on. Saying that brought a look of pain to his face, and I wished he could believe me. It might have brought him comfort to know that the love of his life was still waiting.

Within a month and a half I moved back to Colorado with Rebecca. I was so happy to be back, living close to my children again. My purpose in leaving them had been satisfied. I'd let them go and now they'd returned to my life.

CHAPTER 8

DEC'd by a Scepter

Remote healing is a technique taught during almost all Monroe Institute programs. At least one Hemi-Sync tape exercise is devoted to learning to use the remote healing tools of their Dolphin Energy Club (DEC). One of these tools is the visualization of a dolphin helper who assists with the healing process. Participants are encouraged to let the visualized dolphin carry out the energetic healing process that's taught. Group practice sessions are held a couple of evenings during the program in a large conference room during a week-long program. After moving all the chairs into a circle, participants close their eyes, relax, and follow the Hemi-Sync sounds and verbal instructions played over loud speakers in the room.

Prior to the DEC group practice sessions, trainers are given the name of someone who has requested a remote healing. None of the participants know anything about that person except his or her first name. After the name is given to the group, the tape is started and everyone practices together. During the first practice session of my third Lifeline program, everything went pretty well. I sent my dolphin, "Decky," I call him, out to observe the person named and sent healing energy through him at the appropriate time. After the session, the trainers discussed the person's reason for the healing request. As usual, I'd been very close in my "diagnosis," having accurately described the person's physical condition and the malady. I felt I was getting pretty proficient. In fact, I was feeling smug.

Two nights later, in another practice session, we were to do a group healing on each other instead of an individual at a distance. Everything went along just fine until the point in the taped instructions where I was to visualize Decky. Looking

down at my left side, with my eyes closed, of course, I expected to see my smiling little nonphysical dolphin looking up
at me. He always seemed so happy and eager to help! But this
time, he wasn't there. Instead, I could clearly see something
that looked like a scepter. Its two-foot long, ornate wooden
handle was topped with a spherical, milky white ball that
could have been glass or quartz. The ball looked to be about
five inches in diameter and had a dull appearance. This scepter
was just hovering in the air on my left side in the place where
before I'd always found my cute little dolphin.

When I heard the tape instruction to make sure my dolphin
was clean, clear, and bright, I began to feel some concern. The
ball on top of this scepter didn't look clear and bright at all.
On the contrary, it looked like a cold, lifeless piece of stone.
My rational mind took over and I began to worry that whatever this thing was, it didn't look right. I had no idea what to
do with it! This was a DEC exercise and Decky, my dolphin,
was supposed to appear, not some strange looking scepter! I'm
supposed to send Decky around the room to each person
sitting there. What if this thing is dangerous? Not knowing
what else to do, and completely forgetting trust is always the
first issue, I did what any good engineer would do. I decided
I'd better test this thing before I used it on everybody in the
group.

That decision made, I looked up (physical eyes closed the
whole time) and was surprised by the fact that I could see all
the participants sitting in their chairs in the circle. Turning my
nonphysical head, I looked over the entire group, all sitting
there with their eyes closed, no doubt working with the DEC
dolphins like they were supposed to. As I looked them all
over, I was trying to rationally decide on which of them I
should test this thing. Reasoning that there might be a different effect on men and women, I picked one of each. Since
both trainers were women, I had to pick a man from our group
as one subject. I stood up, nonphysically, holding the scepter by
the handle in front of me with both hands. It felt like I'd done
this before. It had the feel of a ritualistic ceremony, but I have
no connection with such things in this lifetime. The way I
walked and held the scepter felt oddly familiar. I nonphysically

walked across the room toward the man I'd chosen as my first test subject. When I stopped, I held the scepter in front of him, about three feet away from his body, and watched for a reaction. With a startled look on his face, his eyes suddenly snapped open and his body lurched forward in the chair. Then he closed his eyes and relaxed back into the chair. I couldn't tell much from his reaction so I walked back to my chair and sat down.

Figuring the trainers could probably better handle whatever this scepter might do, I chose one of them as my next test subject, rather than one of the participants. It came down to which one was sitting closest to me, and I chose that one. Standing up nonphysically, I carried the scepter in front of me, again feeling that sense of having done this before. Stopping a short distance away, I held the scepter about three feet in front of her, watching closely for any reaction. At first, I saw a smile form on her face as her body relaxed a little more deeply into the chair. Then, all of a sudden, her nonphysical eyes snapped open wide with a look of fright in them. Her head whipped from side to side once, like she was looking at everyone in the room. The fright spread from her eyes down her body in a wave and in the next instant I saw her frantically trying to claw her way backwards, up and over the back of her chair. As quickly as I could, I pulled the scepter back and covered the ball with one hand, trying to stop whatever it was doing, and not having the foggiest idea what that was or how to stop it. I scurried back to my chair and sat down. Putting the scepter back where I'd found it, I kept the ball covered with my hand and hoped I hadn't caused any injury. Worried and concerned, I sat there until the exercise was over, grateful I hadn't used the scepter on everyone in the group. At the close of the exercise, participants began to share their experience in a debriefing session. When my turn came, I described the scepter and what I had done with it. Asking the trainer what had happened when I saw her trying to climb out of her chair with fright, she said:

"I have only two words to describe it. Root chakra!"

At that, everyone in the room burst out laughing. I had to talk to her in private later to understand what she meant.

"At first, my body became warm and I experienced very pleasurable feelings. They had a strong, sensuous, sexual tone, and I relaxed into the chair. The feeling built up to such a high level that I could feel the insides of my thighs beginning to vibrate. It felt very good. Suddenly, it struck me that I had no idea where this energy was coming from, and that worried me! By that time the pulsating vibration was so strong I could almost feel my inner thighs slapping together. Not knowing from where or whom the energy was coming, I tried to break free of it. That's probably when you saw me frantically trying to climb backwards out of the chair."

"I hope I didn't do any harm!"

"If I'd known what was happening, I'd have relaxed into it and enjoyed it. It felt very, very good."

After checking quietly with the man on whom I had also tested the scepter, the trainers reported back that he'd not really been aware of anything out of the ordinary during the exercise. No harm done there either.

In the aftermath of the experience, I began to kick myself for not having trusted the appearance of the scepter. I realized it had appeared because it was supposed to be used during the group healing exercise. I'd let my rational mind, with its belief in fear of the unknown, take control. Later that evening, I did my own DEC healing exercise to try to rectify that mistake. Before I drifted off to sleep, I went to each of the participants nonphysically, one by one, and offered the scepter's energy to them. All of the women in the group relaxed and took it in with smiles growing on their faces. The men were evenly split between those who seemed to take it in and those who registered shock and pulled away.

Several times during the remainder of the program, I wondered about the origin of the scepter. I recalled walking with it, carrying it in a particular way that had felt so familiar, like a ceremonial ritual I'd done many times before. During a couple of the Lifeline tape exercises, I asked about it and got bits and pieces of information. The picture I put together shows an ancient school where I was a teacher in a previous lifetime. That school taught techniques of spiritual development through the building and utilization of sexual energy. The scepter was used in both ritual and ceremony to collect, focus, and supply that energy to students. It was used to boost students to ecstatic levels of sexual arousal that they then learned to utilize for their spiritual growth. I discovered one of my fellow teachers in that school is someone I know in my present lifetime. She remembered our being together as teachers in that school, and was able to give me details that matched what I already knew from the Lifeline tape sessions. It was comforting to have that confirming evidence. My acceptance of reincarnation had come years before this experience. Nevertheless, it's always great to have what you know to be the truth confirmed by an independent, second source.

In my continuing exploration of the Afterlife, once in a while I uncover tools such as the scepter I've used in previous lifetimes. In your journeys of exploration and self-discovery, you may come across similar tools. A strong, unexplainable attraction to some ancient artifact in a museum. The feeling of familiarity with the use of a tool you've never seen before. Oftentimes these are clues pointing toward a part of yourself buried deep in your subconscious awareness. If you come across such an item, from my experience, it's worth spending a little time wondering why you're attracted to it. Bringing the image of such a tool into your meditation and being aware of any impressions that result may begin another journey of self-discovery. That's what the strange-looking scepter did for me.

CHAPTER 9

The Banshee

Gwen's mother had been living in Boston when she died, leaving Marty, her sixty-six-year-old husband, a widower. Within a month of her death, Marty had a serious stroke. Doctors told Gwen that his prognosis wasn't good, and that he had a month, maybe two at the outside. Then Gwen's mother appeared to her in a dream saying Marty would be joining her soon. Gwen didn't want her dad to die alone, far away in a Boston area nursing home. So, at great expense, she'd had him flown to Colorado to live out his last few days in her family's home near Nederland. He'd arrived in November of 1993.

Rebecca and I were also now in Colorado, continuing to explore the Afterlife together. Gwen contacted us in March of 1994 through our association with a small metaphysical newspaper in Boulder. Since the day her father arrived, he'd been screaming in terror at the top of his lungs, from the moment he fell asleep until he woke up. Gwen and her husband hadn't had a full night's sleep since her father arrived. She called to see if there was anything we could do. In our effort to assist, I learned one of the *Laws of Nature* in the Afterlife. The law is that Love and Fear cannot coexist in the nonphysical world, and it's a law as solid as our physical world's law of gravity.

The first thing we did was to go together nonphysically to find Marty and determine the reason for his screaming. After peering into the 3-D blackness before my closed eyes, a small, black, swirling mass attracted my attention. I intended to move toward it, felt myself moving through blackness, and popped out on the other side. I was standing in a barren, desolate desert. Pale moonlight illuminated sparse vegetation scattered over the flat, empty terrain. Then I saw Marty., crouched down in a fetal position, his arms wrapped around himself, he was trembling. The blackness of fear surrounded him. I soon saw what Marty was afraid of. Moments after Rebecca and I arrived in the scene, a huge, stereotypical Banshee appeared. It looked like one I'd seen in an old Walt Disney movie, a green, vaporous apparition with a hideous face and the shape of flowing robes trailing behind it.

Marty looked up and saw the Banshee just as it began a swooping, downward lunge toward him from above, ten feet in the air. After just missing his head, the Banshee swooped back up into the sky and turned toward Marty again. With each swoop the Banshee made, Marty's fear built. Shivering in fear like a hunted quail, he squatted there, his fear and anxiety building up until he just couldn't take it any more. Then like a quail flushed from its hiding place, Marty jumped up screaming and started running as fast as he could. I could feel his intense hope of finding a hiding place in the barren desert. He ran until he was exhausted. Then he stopped and crouched down to hide again, quaking in fear. He'd stopped next to some sagebrush that was shorter then he was. It offered no real value as a hiding place, but he had hope. Besides, he had to stop running and rest. Hoping against hope to escape the Banshee, he huddled there waiting. It was no use. Shortly after he squatted there, the hideous apparition reappeared and began swooping down at him again, scaring him witless. He took it as long as he could, and then jumped up screaming and started running again.

Rebecca and I stood watching as this pattern repeated several times; then she moved in close to Marty and got his attention. As she spoke to him, I could see her gesturing with her hand. As the Banshee approached the next time, she moved her hand close to her heart and then extended it outward and upward, toward the green, vaporous terror. When she did, the Banshee faded and vanished like fog evaporating in the warmth of the sun. She spoke to Marty again. The Banshee reappeared, swooping toward both of them in a terror-inducing display. Rebecca touched her hand to her heart again and extended it toward the Banshee. Again it evaporated into the night sky and disappeared.

The next time the Banshee appeared, with Rebecca's encouragement, Marty mimicked the movement she'd shown him. The horrible apparition again disappeared. Marty was delighted! Several more times, as Rebecca stood nearby, Marty practiced the movement successfully. Each time he succeeded I could see more of the blackness of fear surrounding him leave. Unfortunately, on the Banshee's next approach a little twinge of fear caught Marty off guard. He forgot to extend his hand from his heart toward the beast, and his fear took over. He was terrified, off screaming and running again. That was all we could do, so we had to leave Marty running and hiding in fear.

We both then connected with other family members to get more about Marty's situation. We learned that he was afraid to face his wife again in the Afterlife because of things he had done during his lifetime. That, coupled with his strong fear of death, caused him to resist dying. When we compared notes later, Rebecca explained that the Banshee was fabricated from Marty's fear of death. His fear took the form of a Banshee and terrorized him whenever he slept and could see it. That was the source of his night-terror screaming. The gesturing I'd seen her making, and then Marty mimicking, was intended to teach him to use the *Love and Fear Law of Nature* in the Afterlife. By extending his love to the Banshee, rather than his manifested fear, it would cease to exist. When love is brought into any situation arising from fear, whatever is a product of that fear will disappear. While Marty had been able to extend his love toward the Banshee, it had worked. When he felt his fear again, the Banshee—his fear being mirrored back to him—would reappear to further terrorize him. Marty was actually locked in Focus 23 while he was still physically alive, delaying what would have been, considering his physical condition, a merciful death.

During the check-in on Marty, it was also apparent that there were issues between his daughter and him that were holding him in the physical world. In a meeting with Gwen some time later, we passed along all the information we had. Unfortunately, there was nothing else we could do for Marty.

As I think back about my experience with Gwen and Marty, I'm grateful for the opportunity to have learned more about the inner workings of human existence. The fact that Love and Fear cannot coexist in the Afterlife is a valuable lesson with application in any world, physical or nonphysical.

CHAPTER 10

Max's Hell

The church I grew up in described Hell as a place of eternal, punishing suffering. If I broke the rules during my one and only lifetime, they said, my soul would spend the rest of eternity being tortured in Hell. Within the beliefs of most all religions of the world, there are many variations on this theme, and none of them are pleasant. During one of my Afterlife voyages I met Max, a man who deserved to be in Hell if ever there was one. His Hell wasn't quite what I expected.

During his most recent lifetime in the physical world, Max was a psychotherapist. From descriptions by some who knew Max, he could also be called an emotional sadist. He enjoyed inflicting mental and emotional pain and anguish on people. His education and practice as a psychotherapist made him really good at it. He knew how to find people's vulnerabilities, knew how to probe someone's mind for their deepest, darkest secrets and fears. He knew how to use those secrets and fears to inflict exquisitely agonizing mental and emotional torture. I'm not saying that's all he used his education and training for. He might even have done some good for some people. But his friends, loved ones, and associates were often targets of his pull-the-wings-off-of-flies mentality. One of Max's favorite games was what I've heard called, "I want to watch you and him fight."

Over time, with subtle probing, Max would learn your darkest secrets and fears. He was a skilled psychotherapist and could gather all the information he needed in seemingly normal conversation. A little question here, a little question there, it didn't really matter how long it took him to gather what he needed, as long as he got it. Once he knew and understood the inner workings of your vulnerabilities, he'd select someone else he'd already probed who would attack your weakness out of theirs.

For example, suppose he discovered it was your greatest fear that someone might find out you were gay. Not just ordinary concern, you understand, but obsessive, anxiety-provoking, deep-seated, in-your-gut fear of being exposed. Maybe you worried constantly that your career in the government would be over if your constituents knew their councilman's secret. In your case, Max might arrange an encounter between you and a gay-hating newspaper reporter whose deepest fear was that gays in the government were destroying the world. He'd choreograph that meeting so he could be present and watch the fireworks. Before the two of you met, Max would drop hints to both of you to feed your anxiety. His hints weren't always that subtle; after all, he wanted to be sure the fight got started when you met so that he could watch.

One more example will suffice, I think, for you to get a good understanding of Max's emotionally sadistic nature. In his polite, party conversation, after introducing himself as a therapist, he might steer the conversation to your deepest, darkest fears. It's all right; he's a doctor. You might have seen him at several house parties in your circle of friends. You've begun to trust him enough that you think maybe he could help you deal with the fear only Valium keeps at bay. Your fiftieth birthday was a few months ago, and you obsessively, unreasonably fear growing old. The loss of your once youthful beauty spawns all sorts of thoughts that haunt you. Maybe one of your greatest fears is that some gorgeous young woman will make a play for your husband and he'll take the bait. In that case, Max might plan to invite someone special to a future house party. She might be a gorgeous young woman who gets her kicks from seducing husbands in front of their older, once beautiful wives and then hates herself for it. Max would, of course, set up your meeting in the most innocent of circumstances. But you can bet he'd have primed everyone involved with whatever hints would ensure a really good fight. And if Max had his way, this fight would be just the beginning of as many emotionally painful encounters as possible.

I realize I'm painting Max as a classic villain. What can I say, the guy was a mean-spirited, gifted, emotional sadist. To the best of my knowledge, Max died unrepentant. By the rules of the church I grew up in, he was a good candidate to be spending eternity in Hell.

Soon after Rebecca and I moved back to Colorado, we had reason to try to find Max in the Afterlife. Earlier in her life she had known him and been a target of some of his shenanigans. We were going to see if there was anything we could do to assist him. By this time, I was getting confident enough in my ability that I no longer felt I needed Hemi-Sync tapes to explore the nonphysical world. The truth was I hadn't needed them for quite a while, but sometimes it's hard to throw away your crutches and walk, even when you know you can. In my interest of gathering more evidence of the reality of my Afterlife activities, we went There nonphysically together and compared notes afterwards.

After briefly relaxing with my eyes closed, I entered the familiar 3-D blackness. Waiting there for something to happen, I moved toward the first dark swirl I saw. When I emerged from it on the other side, I saw Rebecca standing in front of me. She was being held by the throat at arms length by a man I soon discovered was Max. That's the only time I ever saw a look of fright on Rebecca's face. Her eyes were wide open, telling her feelings of terror. Max was squeezing her throat very firmly.

"Rebecca, I'm standing right behind you," I said, quietly but firmly, trying to get her attention. "Count to ten . . . relax. He can't really hurt you. Rebecca, count to ten."

The look on Max's face had a wickedness to it. He was trying to use something he knew about her to paralyze Rebecca to his will. He held her for fifteen seconds or so, then his grip relaxed and he let go.

Through impressions, I began to get a picture of the world in which Max lived. It had rocks and trees, houses and cars. It didn't look much different from the physical world he'd lived in before he died. But as the impressions kept coming in, I realized the world Max now lived in was different. It was a Hell made to order for him. Everyone living there with him, every man, woman, and child, had the same emotionally sadistic nature he did!

In one impression I saw him laying the groundwork for another of his schemes to inflict pain. He'd set up two of the other inhabitants of the place to meet at a restaurant so he could watch them fight. He'd told each of them something the other had supposedly said about him. The game he was running on them was intended to build anger and rage toward each other. He'd done a good job of setting them up. When their screaming insults and innuendoes erupted, everyone in the room stopped to watch. Max had positioned himself at a table nearby to watch as their anger and rage escalated. He was smiling, very pleased with himself, long before the two men jumped up out of their chairs. With outright glee he watched their punching, kicking, roll-on-the-floor violent display of rage.

But Max wasn't alone in this world. There were others living there who'd developed and honed their art to a level he couldn't begin to compete with. In the next scene of impressions, Max was sitting at a restaurant table with one of the previous combatants. This time someone I didn't recognize was sitting alone at a nearby table, smiling as Max's face flushed red and the veins stood out in his neck. This time Max was the one who'd been set up. It was so expertly done that he had no idea the emotional pain he was feeling had been choreographed. He was just the dancer on display to another's ruthless desire to inflict pain.

This is the Hell Max had lived in since he died, condemned to do in the Afterlife what gave him great pleasure throughout his previous physical lifetime. He was free to inflict the same anguish he'd sadistically enjoyed to the fullest of his capability to do so. Free to carry out his schemes and run his games as often as he could possibly arrange them. Now, however, the only targets for his schemes were others who shared his delight for inflicting such agony. When he was living here in the physical world, Max might have thought himself to be very good at what he was doing. He'd been a big fish in a little pond. Where Rebecca and I now found him living, I suspect Max is closer to the middle of the food chain. Think of history's most disgustingly evil characters, some sadistically cruel beyond normal human imagination. In the pond where we found Max swimming, he's in with some real pros!

Now that doesn't really sound much different from the version of Hell my Sunday school teachers described. There may be a little more detail, but it sure sounds like a fitting Hell for the likes of Max. Yet, as I continued to gather impressions, I discovered it's not a place of eternal punishment. In fact, it's not really punishment at all in the sense that some outside force put him in his Hell to suffer. Best I could determine, Max's Hell is in Focus 25, the Belief SystemTerritories. He was simply attracted to a place in the Afterlife in which everyone shares a common set of beliefs. It's my understanding that there's a place in Focus 25 representative of every set of beliefs held by human beings since way back in the distant past. It was his own beliefs that attracted Max there, and it's only his beliefs that hold him there. During this Afterlife voyage, I realized that the moment Max turns his back on the beliefs that are holding him There, he's free to leave. Somehow that struck me as perfect justice. Max's Hell is not externally enforced punishment. It's exercise of his free will to choose to live in an Afterlife environment that supports his choice for as long as he desires it. It's a nonphysical environment by our standards, but that doesn't mean anything to Max. For him, it's as real as the physical world he left. If he ever begins to question his choice of beliefs, it will be the beginning of leaving his Hell. If he decides he doesn't like living as an emotional sadist, changing his mind will reduce his attraction to it. With his commitment to stop being an emotional sadist, he'll fall out of the place and be free to leave. He can then pursue a life in accordance with his new set of beliefs.

The impressions of Max's Hell were still trickling in when I realized Rebecca was getting ready to leave. Her contact with Max had been difficult, and nothing she could say or do would have any effect on his situation. With a look of sadness on her face, she pulled away from Max's Hell and I followed her out.

When Rebecca and I returned from checking in on Max we compared notes. Fear and terror had indeed gripped her when he held her by the throat. She hadn't heard me telling her to relax and count to ten at first. Once she'd recovered from the initial shock of his move, she'd been able to release her fear and he'd let go. Rebecca's impressions of the world Max lived in matched mine with, as usual, more detail. It was another example of evidence gathered that was at least consistent with another witness's account. Not totally convincing of the reality of all my nonphysical experience enough to wipe out all my doubt, but more evidence piling on top of evidence.

Since my one and only visit to Max's Hell, I've thought a lot about his situation. When people who know about my Afterlife exploration ask me if I've ever found Hell There, I tell them Max's story. As I'm writing, I'm feeling the desire to editorialize a bit about it.

First, let me stress I'm not trying to change anyone's beliefs about Hell. It's not my intention to replace anyone's belief about anything with mine. As I've stated in my prologue, I believe a person's own direct experience is the only thing that can or should be responsible for such a change.

From the information I gathered while visiting Max's Hell, I know he's not been put There by someone else as punishment. No one had to single him out, judge his life, and sentence him to Hell. The system is more automatic than that. He is There because his energetic makeup, the sum total of his beliefs, attracted him to that area of Focus 25 like a magnet to iron. His free-will choices of beliefs led him to live his most recent lifetime in our physical world as an emotional sadist. When he entered the Afterlife, the energetic makeup of his beliefs pulled him into his own Hell with its matching energetic environment.

The information I gathered also says he's free to leave his Hell at any time. All that is necessary is that he change his beliefs. When his beliefs become different enough from the Emotional Sadist area of Focus 25, it will no longer exert an attractive force on him. When his beliefs oppose that area he'll be pushed out of his Hell by a repulsive force. Now that sounds good on paper, but it's not as easy as it sounds. Max is in pretty deep.

During his most recent lifetime on earth, other people around him displayed lives based on beliefs different from his. Not everyone in our physical world is an emotional sadist like him. He had the examples of other people's lives to observe and compare with his own. He could observe how their choices led to pain or pleasure. In those comparisons, he might have seen some positively reinforced reasons to change. When he died, he left that environment. Now he's in a place populated entirely by his *own kind*. Every man, woman and child There is an emotional sadist like himself. They all support emotional sadism as a way of life. Examples of positively reinforced reasons to change are nonexistent.

In Max's Hell, he is under constant attack by other emotional sadists. Although watching the two men fight as a result of his choreography gave him great delight, when he was a target, he suffered. His life now is filled with painful suffering in a place that supports and demands retaliation. He's locked in a vicious circle of sadism. Again, this isn't much different from the Sunday school version of Hell. Max probably spends quite a bit of his time *in anguish, wailing and gnashing his teeth*.

It would have been easier for Max to change while he was living Here in our physical world. By observing the lives of others, he might have easily picked up some clues. In Max's Hell it could be a very long time before a reason to change even occurs to him. No one There models a different set of beliefs. As I said before, he's in pretty deep. If he was aware at all of his situation, it could easily seem like eternal suffering in Hell.

Again, I'm not trying to replace anyone's beliefs with mine. Still, my visit to Max's Hell does suggest the wisdom of something else I remember from Sunday school. They called it the Golden Rule: "Do unto others what you would have them do unto you." Max's Hell sure seems to embody that rule. Makes me wonder about karma and reincarnation. Makes me wonder just how many different kinds of Hell there are. Makes me wonder just what it will take for Max to get out of his Hell and how long he'll want to stay There.

CHAPTER 11

Old Habits Die Hard

Several years before I moved to Virginia, the pastor of my church caught me coming in, between services, to pick up my daughter from Sunday school. I hadn't been to a service in quite a while because my personal beliefs were too much in conflict with the content of some of his sermons. It just didn't feel like I belonged there. So there I was, caught in the church just coming in to pick up my daughter. The pastor approached with a line I'd heard before.

"Well, hello, Bruce. Haven't seen you here in a while."

"You know, Pastor, I'd come more often, but it doesn't feel honest."

"How's that?" he asked, smiling.

"I'd come more often if we could come to some understanding about my past life," I replied.

"Well, I know we all have things in our past we're not proud of, it's part of being human," he said, still smiling.

"No, I mean past like a lifetime in the mid-eighteen hundreds as a farmer in southwestern France."

"I see," the pastor said, his expression turning pensive, ". . . maybe you'd like to come to our Saturday morning Bible study?"

I immediately gave him credit for not rejecting me and walking off to greet better Lutherans.

"What time does the group meet?"

"About 8:30 in the morning. Come any Saturday," the pastor said, smiling again.

It was the first time in my life anyone from the religion of my youth had been open enough to refrain from jumping at the chance to help someone who'd gone astray. The following Saturday morning began a period of several years in which I had the privilege of meeting once a week with a wonderful group of people. All were interested in gaining better understanding of the Bible and what it had to say about living their lives. I learned more about what the Bible's message means to me than at any other time of my life. No one was there to convert anyone. It was a small, closeknit group of friends who came to understand that I didn't necessarily share all their Lutheran beliefs. My favorite retort when I was feeling defensive, which wasn't often, was always the same:

"You know the man whose beliefs this church is founded on, Martin Luther, was a Catholic priest who couldn't swallow every belief his church tried to feed him. So he struck out on his own to find the truth for himself. My only basic disagreement with Lutheranism is that it encourages people to profess Martin Luther's beliefs, instead of encouraging them to do what he did."

Fortunately that crack was always met with good-natured laughter. Our discussions were often lively, fun, and interesting. Many had come to this church from a different belief system or denomination of Christianity. Not many agreed with the beliefs I held at the time, but they were willing to allow me to have and share them. What a gift that pastor and the rest of the group gave me. I continued meeting with them until a couple of weeks before I moved to Virginia. Within a few months of returning to Colorado, I was a regular again on Saturday mornings. Sadly, now I live so far away it's difficult to find the time to get there.

During one of our Bible studies in March of 1994, we were sharing our images of what comes after this life on Earth. When my turn came, I talked about some of the experiences I had had exploring the Afterlife and some of the things I'd found There. After our Bible study ended, a friend named Marla approached me. Her grandmother had died a little over a year ago, and she asked me if I would check on her. A little surprised she felt okay asking me to do such a thing, I told her I'd be happy to. After explaining all I would need was her grandmother's name, Marla wrote it down for me: Gwendilyn Eudora Winterlax.

That facet of doing retrievals still fascinates me. It always works, but I'm still amazed that just a person's name serves as an unerring address to find them. Marla's grandmother's name was certainly not common; some might even call it unusual. But it doesn't matter how common the person's name is. I know that if I were looking for John Jones I'd be led to the right one. It always works.

For as many times as I had done retrievals by then, you'd think I'd be supremely confident. Well, I wasn't. After Marla gave me her grandmother's name, I followed my usual pattern. I put it off and put it off, feeling anxious with *maybe I won't be able to do it this time* thoughts occasionally drifting in and out. The time it takes before I actually try to find someone is a measure of my doubt. So Friday night came; I'd be seeing Marla the next morning, and I still hadn't tried to find her grandmother. It was part of still having doubt about the validity of my experience that made me worry that I'd be unable to find her. I had no good, rational reason to feel that way, as successful, verified retrievals had become pretty routine by then. But there was still that nagging doubt saying that someday I'd discover, somehow, I was making it all up in my head. My old beliefs would have to be challenged much more before I could accept this afterlife stuff I was doing as real. Relaxing on my waterbed, I shifted to Focus 27 and checked in with Coach.

"Coach, I'd like to be sure that information comes to me that will let Marla know I found her grandmother and that she's all right."

"Okay, Bruce. I'll be glad to help with that," came his reply.

Then I brought Gwendilyn's name to mind, and, moments later, I was moving through the familiar 3-D, grainy blackness at a leisurely pace toward an old woman sitting in a chair.

The chair appeared to be one of those old wooden kitchen chairs. It was sitting near an equally old kitchen table. The woman was small and frail looking, sitting bent slightly forward at the waist. She seemed to be in her kitchen, sitting in the only place familiar enough to feel safe to her. She looked to be in a very confused, distracted state of mind. It was as if she were unaware of anything in her surroundings beyond her wooden chair. It felt as though she had almost no contact with any form of reality you or I would recognize as coherent or sequenced in any way. Whatever was in her awareness seemed fragmented, to the point that she had long ago given up trying to make any sense of things happening around her—like being locked in a continuous, fragmented dream where none of the disjointed bits and pieces related to each other.

Slowly, I moved closer to her, stopping about six or seven feet away. I had no particular plan in mind as to how best to help, so I just stood there, watching and waiting for Gwendilyn to notice me. I was waiting for something to happen or occur to me that would resonate with her situation, a way to approach and retrieve her that she'd be able to accept. By this time, I'd learned to refrain from jumping into the retrieval process and trying to figure the *right way* to do it. During my first retrieval with Rebecca, I'd almost lost contact with the little boy in the hospital because I was trying to figure out *the right way*. That bit of buried treasure taught me a lesson. At least now I sometimes remembered to wait for something to occur to me instead of trying to take control on my own.

As I stood there, Gwendilyn turned slightly in my direction and saw me. A puzzled expression swept over her face as she wondered who I was. In the next instant, I could feel Rebecca approaching from behind me and to my right. I hadn't told her anything about Gwendilyn or that I was planning to find and retrieve her. Still, I could feel her coming up behind me and she was moving very fast.

In a blur of speed, Rebecca passed between me and where Gwendilyn was sitting. She stopped, standing motionless, to my left and a little behind Gwendilyn's chair. Next, I felt the approach from behind and to my right of two other women. They were moving more slowly toward Gwendilyn. I watched as they moved, side by side, toward her. These two were dressed up in little-old-lady bodies and looked to be in their late seventies. The one nearest me I recognized as Rebecca's deceased grandmother, whom I'd met and worked with before. I didn't have a clue who the other woman was until Gwendilyn looked in her direction, and an expression of recognition filled her body and lit up her face.

"Maggie? Maggie?. . . What are you doing here?" Gwendilyn said.

The two old ladies walked to either side of the chair. Gwendilyn's open-mouthed gaze followed every move of the woman she'd called Maggie. It was like watching a scene in a nursing home with two older residents helping a frail old lady up out of her chair. One on each side of her, they slowly bent down, reaching for a hand and elbow. The two old ladies gently lifted Gwendilyn to a standing position. Her gaze was fixed on Maggie the entire time. After helping her take a few shuffling steps, the four of them began moving away. Slowly at first, they flew back in the direction from which they had come. Then, accelerating rapidly, they quickly disappeared into the blackness.

I had been waiting for something to occur to me as a way to assist Gwendilyn when the three women appeared. Instead of some clever idea coming along, it was all taken care of as I watched. It didn't occur to me there was anything else I needed to hang around for, so I opened my eyes and got up off the bed. After scrounging in the refrigerator for something to eat, I sat down at the table and wrote everything I could remember about the experience.

The next morning being Saturday, I went to Bible study as usual. After we'd finished, I took Marla aside and told her I was pretty sure I'd found her grandmother. We sat down in a quiet spot and I told her everything I could remember. I was feeling a little anxious about doing this, since it was an opportunity to gather evidence of the Afterlife from a *real world* source. Part of me was worried that none of what I told Marla about my experience would match with what she knew. Another part of me was just as worried that all of it would. But, in my compulsive habit to verify any information I could, I had to know.

Her grandmother had been very confused for the last six to eight months of her life. Although Marla didn't call it Alzheimer's, by her description it was that level of confusion. For the last few months of Gwendilyn's life, she spent much of her time in the only place she seemed comfortable. That was sitting, as I described, on a wooden chair near the table in her kitchen. Although Marla knew Gwendilyn's mother's name was Margaret, she thought it very strange that her own daughter would call her Maggie. Listening to Marla, I felt stunned.

It was obvious as we talked that Marla was very uncomfortable and concerned about some of what I'd told her. Her own beliefs held that when we die, we're set free from all physical afflictions, welcomed into Heaven and reunited with loved ones who'd passed on before. The idea that her grandmother had been stuck in that chair alone, confused, and lost for almost a year of our time greatly bothered her. I remember telling her that's one of the reasons I continued to do the retrieval work I'd learned. It bothered me too.

This retrieval brings up an example of how the circumstances prior to a person's death can affect their Afterlife experience. Gwendilyn's confusion near the end of her life Here had become a habit. When she entered the Afterlife, that habit persisted. She was no longer living in a physical body whose condition controlled her mental state, but the mental habits of confusion and disorientation she acquired in that body persisted. She had given up trying to make sense of her surroundings before she died, and, in the Afterlife, that decision retained its power. At her death, she had only been freed of the physical condition that caused her to make that decision. In the Afterlife she would have to change her mind to fully recover.

Comparing notes with Rebecca later, she confirmed every detail of what I'd seen just after she'd arrived with the two other women. Details as small as from which side she had approached me were all identical to my notes. I had some pretty strong evidence for my doubt to chew on.

The following week at Bible study, Marla told me she'd checked with her own mother, Gwendilyn's daughter. She confirmed everything, including Gwendilyn calling Margaret, Maggie.

When I got that piece of information from Marla, something inside me winced and squirmed. There was no rational explanation for my knowing Maggie's name. For a few brief moments, I felt the world around me quiver and shimmer like a mirage. I felt my Interpreter step to the fore to express the voice of my Doubt. I listened while it explained that bit of experience away in a string of associations.

"Rebecca, she was there. It must have been Rebecca's doing!" my Interpreter opened.

"I suppose it could have, somehow, been Rebecca," I reasoned to myself.

"Rebecca, oh yes, Rebecca. She's a mind reader; that's it, she just read Marla's mind!"

"Marla's mind?" I thought.

"Marla, oh yes, Marla. Marla knew Gwendilyn's mother's name was Margaret."

"I guess . . . "

"Guess, oh yes, guess. 'Maggie' was a pretty lucky guess on Rebecca's part."

"But how did I know?" I wondered.

"Know, oh yes, know. You know how to read minds, especially Rebecca's. You probably just read her mind; you really didn't get anything on your own—she did.

"This doesn't prove the existence of the Afterlife," my Interpreter exclaimed.

"Damn it! I don't believe it was Rebecca's lucky guess." I argued. "You're not getting out of this one that easily. If the Afterlife doesn't exist, there's no rational way Rebecca could know that 'Maggie' was the name. No other rational way!"

"Rational, oh yes, rational. There you go Bruce! You said it yourself, getting . . . that . . . name was irrational! Irrational . . . oh . . . yes . . . irrational. You know what happens to people who become too irrational, don't you!"

"Well, yes, go too far, and people might think I'm insane," I felt myself thinking.

"That's right! The guys in the white coats might come looking for you!"

"They might think I'm a real fruit!"

"Fruit, oh yes, fruit. Bruce, are bananas fruit?" my Interpreter questioned.

"Do they grow bananas in Brazil?" I found myself wondering.

The Interpreter, as the voice of my Doubt, is a deep baritone. It's not quite down there with James Earl Jones, but close to the same frequency range. That voice sounds very impressive. It doesn't rely on good logic to sway me from accepting my experience, as you can see from that internal conversation. Instead, it just keeps bringing associated thoughts and images into my awareness from pre-existing memory. Doubt just seems to pop up with those associations.

The undeniable fact that I'd correctly received Gwendilyn's mother's name, Maggie, should have been enough evidence to alleviate my doubt. It was enough to make my world shake and shimmer, but when that stopped, I still doubted the reality of the experience. I still wasn't absolutely certain it proved the existence of the Afterlife. All it proved is that beliefs and doubts can put up very strong resistance.

CHAPTER 12

First Afterlife Contact with Bob Monroe

The telephone pager clipped to my belt went off at work a little after 10:00 A.M. on a Friday. I recognized the phone number on the display as Rebecca's, and returned her call right away. It was Friday, March 19, 1995, the day Bob Monroe died, and Rebecca called just to give me that news. He succumbed to pneumonia in a Charlottesville, Virginia, hospital around 9:20 that morning.

After hanging up the phone, I sat there in my cubicle at work, reflecting briefly on what the man and his work had done for me. The Hemi-Sync technology he'd invented and developed had been a key to my learning to explore beyond the nonphysical world. The Institute he founded and all the people who work there are the reason I've been able to learn so quickly and so well. I took a moment to express my gratitude for the gifts I'd received.

Then I decided to see if I could find him. Maybe I could communicate with him and see how he was doing just a few short hours from his entry into the Afterlife. It's probably not good to admit that I was doing this on company time, but I closed my eyes and relaxed for a few minutes, to check on a friend who'd just died. As I opened up my awareness to him he was immediately present. To my surprise, so was Nancy, his wife, who'd died more than a year earlier. They arrived in my awareness together. Nancy was positively beaming as she hovered at Bob's left side.

"Well, hello, Bruce. Yeah it's me. And Nancy's here too!" Bob's voice carried excitement and joy.

"Yes, I can see her on your left and a little behind you," I replied. "She sure looks happy!"

"Boy, I can't tell you how wonderful it is to be back together with her again!" Bob said, smiling from ear to ear.

"So, you're doing all right?" I asked.

"All right?. . . All right? I'm doing better than all right. This is great!"

"I can tell there's another person there with you two, but I can't tell who it is."

"Over there?" he said, turning his head slightly and pointing with his chin in the direction of the person I was talking about.

"Yeah, who is that?" I asked.

"Ed Wilson; you remember the good doctor, don't you?"

"Yeah, I remember Ed, but I didn't recognize him. There's something different about him."

"Say, listen," Bob said with the excitement of a kid in his voice, "you'll never guess what I'm doing right now."

I just looked at him, waiting.

"Right now I'm in conversation with six other people besides you."

He sounded like a kid telling me about his newest toy.

"I'm actually with each of them, all at the same time. I can see myself with every one of them. I can hear every word I'm saying to each of them and what each is saying to me. I'm aware of everything about these six other conversations, and, at the same time, I'm here talking with you. What do you think of that?"

"Sounds like you're having a ball, like a kid playing with a fancy new toy."

"Well, I guess I am sort of a kid here," he laughed. "In a manner of speaking I was just born here a little while ago."

"I'm glad to see you're doing well in your new home, Bob. And Nancy, it's good to see you again. You're positively beaming! Hey, look, I'd better get back to work before the boss thinks he's caught me sleeping!"

"You come and visit me any time, Bruce. We'll be glad to see you," Bob said, extending an invitation.

With that, Bob and Nancy Monroe left. I opened my eyes and went back to work, happy that Bob's transition had gone so smoothly. Happy for both of them.

A short time later, I heard from Rebecca again. She'd gone nonphysically to be with Bob as he was entering the Afterlife.

She talked about how wonderful it had been to visit with Ed and Nancy and Bob after she'd accompanied him There. It was hard for her, she said, to come back here to this world. Rebecca let me know there'd be a memorial service for Bob at the Institute.

A trip to Virginia for Bob's memorial service was a little beyond my financial wherewithal at the time. So, I decided to attend nonphysically. It seemed a fitting way to pay my respects. At the time the service started in Virginia, I lay down on my waterbed in Colorado. I closed my eyes and relaxed with the intent to visit Bob at the service. In a minute or so, he and Nancy came into view. Maybe it was the effect of the emotions of those attending his service, but I sensed Bob felt very somber as I approached where he and Nancy were standing. There was someone else there on Bob's right, a man I couldn't see or get a fix on, but I felt his presence. "Hello, Bob, good to see you again. I couldn't afford to fly to Virginia for your service, so I came to see you this way instead."

"That's quite all right," he replied in a soft, somber tone.

"I just came to express my thanks and gratitude to you for what you brought into this world. It's enabled me to learn to explore places most people would deny exist."

"Thanks, Bruce. I appreciate that you came, and you're more than welcome."

I moved back a short distance away from where they were standing and could see and feel the smile Nancy directed at me. Then, to their left, high above and way behind them, a small ball of multicolored light caught my eye. It felt familiar, but I couldn't make out what it was. I focused on the ball of light, opening my awareness wide, trying to feel it. Moments later, the familiar feeling of Ed Wilson's presence flooded into my consciousness.

"Son of a gun! Boy has Ed changed since the last time I saw him!" I thought out loud to no one in particular.

The last time I saw Ed, which had been months earlier, his campsite next to the stone building had become a blight on the neighborhood. There were boxes of papers he'd collected at the library, stacked on top of each other next to his campfire. A few papers were scattered around his campstool by the fire where he sat reading. He'd looked like I remembered him when he lived in the physical world, a tall, thin frame and dark hair. I'd gone looking for him a couple of times since then. The first time his campsite looked abandoned. The next time everything was cleaned up and gone. Now he looked completely different. A ball of light with all sorts of different colors pulsating and swirling through it. It looked like Ed had changed big time, but I didn't understand what that meant.

Just before leaving Bob and Nancy, I got their attention for a moment and we said our good-byes. As I pulled out of the scene, Bob still looked somber and subdued. I think his memorial service was having a strong emotional effect on him.

Voyaging Solo

It is true that when the student is ready, the teacher appears. It is also true that when the student is ready, the teacher disappears. So it went with The Mysterious Teacher. There came a time when I no longer voyaged with Rebecca. I could no longer compare notes from mutual experiences with her. From then on, I stood at the helm alone. My voyaging became a solo experience, relying on what I'd learned under Rebecca's tutelage and the assistance of nonphysical Helpers.

CHAPTER 13

Meditating on a Financial Cushion

On numerous occasions, Coach had suggested I meditate more often. It's a sign of my general lack of self-discipline that I didn't bounce out of bed early every morning before work and do so. I had other things to do. I was too tired, too hungry; it was always something. Finally, one Saturday morning, I ran out of excuses. Begrudgingly, I rolled out of bed, put on a bathrobe, and walked, yawning, toward my rocking chair in the living room. I sat down and closed my eyes.

"Thank you, Bruce," I heard Coach's voice say in my mind.

My only meditative training came from my early '70's experience with Transcendental Meditation. I had used TM's method religiously for about six months back then, twenty minutes, morning and evening every day. The mantra I'd used then came back easily and I began repeating it in my mind.

"That method's fine, but I have a suggestion," Coach said, "why don't you just switch on Wahunka instead. Just let yourself feel it in the place at the bottom of your skull where you first became aware of it."

Feeling for that spot and quickly finding it, I allowed Wahunka to build in intensity. When it was a very intense sensation, Coach continued.

"Good, now let that feeling move down your spine so you can feel it all along your back. Then let it build up in intensity there too."

I'd never consciously done that before. So, I was a little surprised that, as I felt for the Wahunka sensation along my spine, it was there. As Coach suggested, I allowed the intensity of the feeling to build.

"Good, very good. Now extend your awareness of that feeling outside your body."

This was completely new ground. In the past, I had intended to project the energy of Wahunka outward to play Hot Tub Modified Charlie with a group of people. But I'd never even considered it was possible to actually feel the physical sensation of Wahunka outside my body.

"Are you sure this is possible, Coach?" I asked.

"Just intend to feel it in the space near your physical body and see what happens."

Groping around in the space near the back of my neck, I tried to feel Wahunka.

"You're right! I can feel it in the air! Feels like it extends maybe an inch or so out into the air. If I really feel for it, I can tell it extends out into the air all along my spine. I can actually feel it there. That's amazing!"

"Now feel it a little farther away from your body."

What the hell, I thought, *let's see how far out I can feel it*. I began trying to feel Wahunka's sensation farther away from my body.

"Amazing I can feel it at least a foot away!"

"Try farther yet."

In a very short time, I could feel the Wahunka sensation in an egg-shaped space that extended at least three feet outward in all directions.

"Very good, Bruce. Now let it continue to extend outward. See how far outward you can experience the sensation."

The egg-shaped bubble around me began to expand and become more spherelike. I felt the walls of my apartment as the surface of the bubble went through them.

"This is wild! I just felt the wall of the building!"

The surface of the bubble continued expanding outward. I felt an awareness of the building, people and cars parked outside at the new-car dealership a quarter of a mile from where I was sitting. Still, the size of the bubble continued to expand. As unbelievable as it might sound, in a short time I could tell that the entire planet Earth was inside the bubble. It was while marveling at the feeling of the entire planet within the bubble that I felt its surface pass through the moon. The image that came to mind as it did looked like someone was blowing a soap bubble and its surface had just passed through a stationary, hovering marble, the moon. When the surface passed the opposite side of the moon, the marble was then inside the bubble too. The sun and planets in our solar system felt the same way, as the surface of the Wahunka bubble passed over them. As it did, I could have easily pointed in the direction of each planet and named it. Still it kept expanding outward.

"While you allow that expansion to continue, I'd like you to think about something you desire," I felt Coach say.

What came to mind was the anger I'd been feeling for several days at being poor. Odd jobs had been my source of income for months, and I was getting tired of worrying about where next month's rent was coming from. I felt the desire to have enough money so that I didn't need to worry about it so much.

"I'd like a big cushion," I thought out loud.

Almost immediately, in my mind's eye, I saw a huge sofa cushion floating in the air.

"To be more specific," I corrected, "I'd like a big financial cushion. Say 10,000 dollars; that's what I desire, a financial cushion of 10,000 dollars."

"Okay, feel that desire within you, just like you feel for Wahunka. Locate where the desire is within you," Coach instructed.

Surprised, I found I could actually feel that desire's location within my body.

"Good. Now, let the desire expand outward, just as you did with Wahunka. Let it join with the feeling of the expanding Wahunka energy."

At Coach's suggestion, I let my desire for a 10,000-dollar cushion join with the continuing expansion of the Wahunka bubble. It began to expand outward into the universe also.

"Be attentive to your perception of that desire-bubble surface," Coach suggested.

Its surface encountered objects just as the Wahunka bubble had. As it did the experience was different. Once in a while the object encountered by the surface of the desire-bubble resonated with the desire. The two were compatible; the object could play some part in fulfilling the desire for a financial cushion. When that happened it felt like the energy of the object was turned until it pointed to the center of the bubble and accelerated in that direction. Only objects that resonated with the desire I'd expressed were affected, and they were accelerated toward the center of the bubble where I was sitting. I knew that as this desire-bubble expanded outward into the universe, everything it contacted that could act in some way to fulfill my desire would be directed toward that center. I realized that at the center of that desire-bubble . . . was me.

"Very good, Bruce, glad you caught that perception! Now, just relax and allow both bubbles to continue expanding for a while. When you feel complete with that process, you can stop meditating and go about your business."

Gradually, I lost touch with awareness of the surface contacts of each bubble. I figured that meant I was done, so I got up and poured a bowl full of cereal and milk, and ate breakfast.

Sunday morning I decided to check the paper for engineering jobs. As much as I liked the flexibility of my odd-job schedule, getting my finances in order seemed a more pressing need. One of the ads caught my eye. It had been placed by a company a friend of mine worked for. A couple of hours later, that friend called to let me know where our men's group would be meeting that night.

"By the way, I saw your ad in today's paper for an engineering position."

"Ad, what ad? I don't have one in the paper right now. Must be someone else in the company who put it in. But, I have been looking for someone to do some work on a contract basis. You interested?" my friend asked.

Within four days I'd signed a contract to do a specific engineering job where my friend worked. Multiplying my hourly rate times the hours the job was supposed to take came to 10,000 dollars, exactly. I was flabbergasted! In the time since that Saturday morning when I ran out of excuses, good things have continued to happen. I still don't meditate as often as I should, but when I do, the results still astound. I used to doubt what everybody said about the universe providing for their needs. I'm now beyond doubt on that one.

CHAPTER 14

Sylvia's Retrieval

While picking up my mail on a cold, snowy day in April, I saw a notice posted on the bulletin board next to the apartment complex mailboxes about a *Celestine Prophesy* study group. That's how I met Rosalie, a woman who's been a friend since we met. Her phone number was on the notice, and it turned out that I was the only one who'd called with an interest in discussing James Redfield's book. We visited several times, talking about the book, about our interests, and about things going on in our lives.

During one of our get-togethers, Rosalie mentioned her mother had died about nine months earlier. She also mentioned that her dad, Joe, had been having trouble sleeping since Mom had died. Curiously, it only happened when he slept at home, in the house where his wife, Sylvia, spent her last days. It was odd, Rosalie thought, that he'd had no trouble sleeping during a vacation she and her dad had taken together recently. On the road trip to visit relatives, he'd slept through the night just fine. In motels and the homes they visited, he slept just as well as before Sylvia died. Rosalie wondered out loud if it was possible that her mother was somehow disturbing Joe's sleep.

Recognizing a pattern I'd seen before, I shared with Rosalie a little bit about what I'd learned to do in the Lifeline program. Explaining the process of retrievals, I told her about locating and assisting people who become isolated and stuck after they die. From her description of her dad's sleeping difficulty, I offered that it was possible her mother might have something to do with it.

Later that evening at home, I idly thought about looking for Rosalie's mother just as I started drifting off to sleep. A small, frail woman appeared briefly. There was something unusual about her face, but I didn't get a clear impression of what it was before I decided I was too tired and sank into a deep sleep.

Since there were just the two of us in the study group, and it's easier to cook dinner for two than for one, Rosalie and I got together again the following week for a home-cooked meal at her place. As we talked, I suggested that, if she didn't mind, I'd check in on her mom to see if I could get a feel for her situation. It was okay with Rosalie, and I was delighted she didn't think the idea was too strange. From that conversation, I knew Sylvia had died after a long illness that required extended treatment with the steroid, prednisone. Near the very end, Sylvia had needed morphine to control pain.

In my usual pattern, I put off looking for Sylvia for over a week while my still-active doubts made me worry that I wouldn't be able to find her. As it happened, I was having dinner with another friend, Dan, when I got around to looking for Sylvia. Dan is a Gateway Voyage graduate who's interested in Lifeline retrieval work. He wanted to see if he'd be able to follow along and perceive any of what might happen. Feeling nervous about whether or not I'd be able to do it, I went into the bathroom to contact Coach and asked for his assistance in locating Sylvia. That might sound a little silly, but I find a bathroom is a nice, quiet, private place where a person can be alone. It's less distracting than sitting in a room with other people and a much easier environment in which to be open to receiving information.

Coach showed up with Bob and Nancy Monroe, who suggested they were interested in assisting me also.

"Don't worry, Bruce, everything will be fine," I felt one of them say.

So I moved into the living room and lay down on the sofa. Dan had suggested using a Free Flow Focus 10 tape he had, which was fine with me. After setting up the tape and dimming the lights, Dan took his place in an overstuffed chair. We put on our headsets, and I closed my eyes, letting the Focus 10 sounds deepen my relaxation for a minute or so. I felt the shift in my perception, and then realized I was peering into that special, grainy, 3-D blackness. Then, I turned my attention to Sylvia. I said her name in my mind with the intent to find her, and then waited.

That special blackness has a uniformly random quality such that any shape within it stands out from the background and draws one's attention. I usually just peer into it, waiting for something to appear that looks distinct from the rest of the uniform field of grainy blackness. Sometimes it's just a small patch that looks different from its uniform surroundings, or has some movement or motion in it. So I just peered into that blackness, waiting for something to get my attention. A small, solid, black swirl appeared a little to the right and in front of me. I focused my attention on it, and then felt movement toward it. Moments later, the large, round, smiling face of Dopey, one of Walt Disney's seven dwarfs, popped up into view directly in front of me. I laughed inside, thinking, *what a perfect image for someone with the moon-face side effect of prednisone who needed morphine to control pain before she died! The image of Dopey is perfect. I must be in the right place to find Sylvia!*

Dopey's face dissolved and disappeared, and Sylvia came into view. She materialized, standing in blackness, facing me from perhaps ten feet away. At first I just watched Sylvia to get a feel for her present situation, and to avoid jumping in before I had any idea how to approach her. Jumping into situations and taking control is something I've learned to refrain from doing. Looking at her closely, what stood out most prominently was the dense, grayish-white fog surrounding her. It had the appearance and feel of a large, loose, cotton ball around her body. It was cocoon-like and perhaps twice her body length in diameter. She was a rather small, frail looking woman, and when I mentally reached out to feel her state of mind it was very groggy. She didn't feel confused, as Marla's grandmother had been, sitting on her kitchen chair. Sylvia's thinking ability just felt dulled and muted. Like you might experience as you wake up with that groggy, not-enough-sleep feeling—very clouded with a vacantness in her face and body movements. It reminded me of the facial expressions and movements of a mentally retarded person.

After observing her for a minute or so, I decided to find out if she was responsible for her husband Joe's difficulty sleeping. Approaching her and then getting her attention, I asked Sylvia to show me how she interacted with Joe. At that, she obediently turned and walked a short distance, stopping next to where I could see Joe sleeping. She evidently didn't think it was at all strange that she had walked right through the bed to get close to him. Maybe, in her dulled state of mind, she didn't notice her legs passing through the mattress. Standing next to the left side of Joe's chest, Sylvia turned, faced his body, and reached down through the mattress to get her hands under his back. In a scooping motion, she lifted her hands and arms upward, passing them through Joe's body. As she repeated the motion, I could see it had a rippling effect throughout the entire length of his body, as if the rippling was similar to what you'd see if she had been moving her arms through the still water in a bathtub. Each upward, scooping motion through his body made the ripples get bigger and stronger. After six or seven scooping movements, Joe began to move his body. The ripples were irritating and uncomfortable. By his body movements, I knew that if Sylvia continued, he would wake up very soon. It wasn't clear if he'd wake up physically or nonphysically into a dream, but I was certain Sylvia's movements were disturbing his sleep.

Thanking her for showing me how she interacted with Joe, I told Sylvia she could stop now. She did so immediately, standing numbly, her legs through the mattress and her arms hanging limply at her sides. Observing the ripples she had generated in Joe's nonphysical body, I noticed they didn't seem to be settling down at all. They continued to pulsate like wiggling Jell-O at the same intensity as when she stopped. Joe was still squirming slowly on the bed from their effect.

I took a moment to stop and check nonphysically on Dan to see what kind of luck he was having following along with the events as they were unfolding. Watching him I felt like I was looking at myself several years ago. He'd seen glimpses of what Sylvia, Joe, and I had been doing. Dan seemed busy trying to figure out the meaning of a glimpse of information he had grabbed and focused his attention on. Just as I remembered myself doing earlier in my learning, his attention was focused on analyzing the small bit. All the while, the vast majority of the experience continued on without his awareness focused on it. Then I felt the voices of Bob and Nancy.

"Bruce, you need to continue focusing your attention on what you're doing with Sylvia. She and Joe need your assistance now; you can help Dan later."

"He sure reminds me of myself not so long ago," I remarked.

"You let us attend to Dan; he's doing just fine. It's best if you attend to Sylvia."

So, I turned back toward Sylvia, got her attention, and reestablished our link. It was time to explain to Sylvia just what her situation was. This is always a dilemma for me. Just to come right out and tell someone she's dead can be a shock. To do so seems a little crass and unfeeling to me at times. Perhaps it's not important to tell them. Perhaps I should just go ahead with their retrieval. Surely someone up the line will inform them of their status. Or maybe they'll just gradually catch on to the fact they're dead in their interaction with people they meet in Focus 27. Then again, some people need quite a shock to be sure you get your point across. It's always a dilemma for me, tell them . . . don't tell them . . . ? Those who know me would tell you I'm often blunt to a fault and at times not very diplomatic. They might even volunteer that I'm not as empathetic as someone should be who does this sort of stuff. Oh well.

"Sylvia, I've got something to tell you," was my opening line on the subject, "I know why you're having such difficulty trying to wake up your husband."

She hadn't said a single word so far, and didn't start now. She turned and looked at me through the eyes of a dull, vacant stare.

"You're no longer living in the physical world, Sylvia; you died almost a year ago."

For just a brief moment, I watched as a billowing cloud of confusion passed across her face. I could tell that at first she thought I was nuts. Then her mind passed over some of the inconsistencies in her experiences. Things like her legs passing through the mattress and her arms through Joe's body. Then it felt like I was watching the sun, in all its dazzling brilliance, coming out from behind a thick, gray cloud. The grayish, cottony cocoon surrounding her vaporized and disappeared in the sun's warmth. All the dullness left her eyes and body. She was radiant! Clear and bright, her face was shining, beaming a warm, beautiful smile at me! In that moment she realized and knew exactly where she was and understood exactly her situation.

In the next instant, I could feel her thinking clearly, for the first time since I'd found her.

"Well, if I'm dead, then I know what's supposed to happen next," she thought out loud, looking directly at me.

She was gaining strength with each thought she experienced. She hadn't noticed it yet, but there was a very bright, glowing oval of Light beginning to move toward where we were standing. It stopped quite a distance away as if waiting for Sylvia to notice it.

"If I'm dead, then Jesus is supposed to come for me and take me with Him!" As she said it, her face looked like that of a young girl in love. She was happy and expectant, and she knew without a single doubt He was coming for her.

As she finished with her thought, I could see by the look on her face that she'd caught sight of the Light in the distance. It began slowly moving toward her. As her feeling of recognition of who the Light was grew, it began to change its appearance. No longer just an oval ball of light, it was taking the shape of a Man surrounded by the Light He is. By the time It was twenty feet from where she was standing, It had metamorphosed into the best likeness of a Sunday school Jesus I've ever seen. His radiating Light shone down and illuminated Sylvia. She was positively glowing!

Floating gently toward her in a warm cloud of brilliant yellow-white Light, His appearance adjusted to match her belief in what she should see. She eagerly moved toward Him. Unafraid and reaching out, she took the hand of the One who had come for her. He spoke to her briefly, and then smiling, turned back toward the direction from which He'd come. Then, slowly, they began floating upward and moving away together.

I turned around, again focusing my attention on Dan to see how he was doing. He was intently picking away at some other small bit of the experience, trying to understand the whole of it by analyzing this little piece. He again reminded me of myself, early in the process of learning to do this Lifeline work. I too had spent too much time analyzing and too little time being open to the experience. I know I still have a long way to go, and I could feel that as I looked at Dan.

"Bruce, we'll watch over Dan, your attention needs to be focused back where you were," I felt Nancy say.

Now I was a little confused as to what to do next. Typically, when I find and retrieve someone, I escort them to The Reception Center in Focus 27. Usually they're met There by someone they know and recognize. I had the feeling I was supposed to do something more, but everything seemed to be taken care of. Partly out of curiosity, I decided to follow Sylvia and the One who'd come for her to see what would happen next. It feels a little irreverent to admit, but I almost burst out laughing at what I saw.

Sylvia's clothes had been changed. She was now wearing a long, flowing, white satin dress. She was lying down, on her side, in a beautiful, sunlit, open area with tall, lush, green grass all around her. With a quizzical look on her face she was listening as a deep, bass, male voice intoned, "He maketh me to lie down in green pastures." She knew that somehow this was as it was supposed to be, but to her, it seemed incongruous. Horizontal on the ground in such a beautiful, expensive dress seemed a little out of place. Her position suddenly changed. She was sitting up, looking down at a large, pottery chalice she was holding in her hands in front of her. It looked like a small bowl, sitting on top of a stem with a large round base. A clear, bubbling liquid was continuously overflowing the sides, running down over her hands and spilling down onto the ground. This too seemed familiar to her, but a little out of place as she listened to that same male voice intone, "My cup runneth over." At this point, I decided Sylvia was in good hands and, curiosity aside, my assistance was no longer necessary. I spun slowly around in a circle feeling for where I'd last seen her husband, Joe. I locked onto his signal and headed back to find him.

When I found him, Joe was still lying on the bed, squirming and moaning softly. The pulsating Jell-O-like rippling effect Sylvia had started with her hands was still very active. It hadn't subsided at all since we left him. His movement and moans indicated he was still being disturbed by its effects. Not knowing exactly what to do, I watched and waited for something to occur to me.

As I waited, I began to remember the energy work Rebecca had shown me during many of our nonphysical travels together. I remembered watching how it looked when she did it during some of our retrievals together. After asking in my thoughts if that's what I should try to do, I waited for some indication. It came quickly with an emphatic feeling like, *go ahead, get at it*! Standing next to Joe, with my legs sticking through the mattress to the floor too, I began to pass my hands slowly back and forth above the length of his body. Mentally I held the intent that the ripples be smoothed away. They immediately began to subside. I continued moving my hands until all evidence of the rippling went away without a trace. I could feel Joe relaxing, and then he drifted back into a deep, comfortable sleep. Everything seemed to be finished, so I turned my attention once again toward Dan, wondering what to do next. It didn't take long until something completely unexpected began to happen.

Dan was still there, in a sitting position and surrounded by a ball of bright, golden light. He was analyzing more bits of what had just transpired, trying to fit them together with the other bits he'd gathered. There were so few bits of information and the gaps between them were so wide, there was little chance he would get the whole picture.

As I watched him, I was waiting for whatever would happen next. Suddenly, an older man I somehow knew to be Dan's father moved toward Dan in a rush from my right. He moved up very close to Dan and got his attention. Dan registered surprise at seeing his father. His father began to talk with him about something he wanted to resolve between them.

For a moment I thought about focusing in on their conversation. If he remembered any of the experience, by listening in, perhaps I could verify its content for him later. As I began to focus in on their conversation, I felt both Bob and Nancy suggest otherwise.

"You don't need to listen in to what they are saying. Just back away a little and assist us in surrounding them both in a ball of light."

I moved back, perhaps 15 feet away, and placed my intent on adding to the ball of light I could already see surrounding the two of them. I continued to watch for a short time, and noticed Dan beginning to feel agitated as his father talked about whatever he wanted to resolve. There seemed to be a wall building up that made it increasingly difficult for the father to reach his son. In a short time Dan's agitation and restlessness had the effect of closing off their channel of communication. Seeing this, his father quietly left. I waited a short time longer, and then thanked Bob, Nancy and Coach for their assistance. Opening my eyes, I returned my awareness to the sofa and the living room.

Dan and I moved to chairs at the dining room table and talked for a while. I wanted to give him the opportunity to verify any mutually shared experience. He had little conscious memory of what had taken place.

"I remember bits and pieces, but I can't make any sense out them," Dan summed up.

I should have left it at that. What was between Dan and his father was a private matter and none of my business. That should have been obvious to me from Bob and Nancy's actions, but I made a mistake I could learn from. I felt some hesitation at bringing up his father's arrival, attributing that to not knowing if he was "dead" or "alive." That feeling of hesitation should have been my cue to leave this alone. I didn't take my cue. I opened the conversation by asking how his relationship was with his father. Dan talked about some issues between them that his father (alive) wanted very much to resolve, in what I took to be a loving, fatherly way. A forgiveness, if you will, which Dan was having a very hard time accepting from his dad. Several days later, Dan told me his father had called the morning after his "visit" and they'd set up a time to get together and talk. I don't know what they talked about. By that time I'd realized this was all theirs to work out and none of my business. It was a mistake for me to interfere by telling Dan about his father's visit. If I've learned from this mistake, I'll remember it, and next time, try a different way. People deserve the opportunity to take care of their own affairs.

When Rosalie and I got together over another home-cooked meal a day or two later, I told Rosalie what I'd experienced when I retrieved her mother. She showed me a photograph of Sylvia, taken some time before she entered the Afterlife. The similarities between her image and the cartoon image of Dopey surprised me. Both have the same roundness of the face with prominent, chubby cheeks. Both have a bright smile that would warm anybody's heart.

Within two weeks of the retrieval, Joe decided it would be all right to begin sleeping again in the bedroom he'd shared with his wife, Sylvia, through the years of their life together. He hadn't slept there since she had died, said it just didn't feel comfortable. Rosalie reported that, except for a pretty typical geriatric pattern, Joe's sleep was more restful and not disturbed. That was the only real evidence that anything I did was real, other then the vague similarity between the faces of Dopey and Sylvia. Not very flattering perhaps, but it was there.

Yet it all fit a pattern I had seen in my Afterlife explorations before. Spouses who die are sometimes unaware of their condition. They stay around the comfort of old, familiar surroundings and people. Some of them are confused or even angered at being ignored and by the inattention of their physically living spouse. Often, attempts at interaction with the loved ones they've left behind have tangible affects. It's a fairly common pattern.

When I've told this story to some people, their reaction is to strongly question whether it was really Jesus who came for Sylvia. I guess to some it seems irreverent or sacrilegious that a person they see as a heretic, such as I, would be witness to such a happening, even if it really did occur. I certainly have no proof. I don't really know, and frankly it doesn't matter much to me. Sylvia is no longer stuck, and Joe's sleep is no longer disturbed. That's enough for me. For all I know, it could have been Jesus or just a Helper taking on His appearance as a way of fitting in with Sylvia's beliefs and expectations. Helpers can easily take on the appearance of someone the person will recognize. I do know her transition from the house in which she died to the place she was to go was made more easily because of His appearance. Besides, I think He would have approved of the Helper's use of His likeness. I didn't go looking to check on Sylvia again after she left with the One who came for her. I always had the feeling she was doing just fine.

CHAPTER 15

Bob Monroe Visits with a Proposition

Almost two months after he died, Bob Monroe paid me another visit, one night as I was about to drift off to sleep. It was three weeks after the Oklahoma City bombing, and I'd fully recovered from nonphysically being there. Those of you who've read *Voyages Into the Unknown* may recall that its first chapter recounts my experience there and the aftereffects. I bring it up now just to give you a sense of the timing of this journey I'm on.

It was late at night, and, as I drifted off toward sleep, I was seeing those fleeting little images of faces and things you sometimes see before you zonk out. Then I felt Bob's voice call my name and realized I was looking at both him and Nancy, standing before my mind's eye.

"Well Hi, Bob. Nancy, I can see you too. Nice of you to stop by."

"Good to see you again, too," they both said.

"Glad to see you're still writing. Remember, you keep at it, and I'll keep working on my side to help get it published as a book," Bob reminded me.

"Yeah, I'm working on another article to send to Dar at the Institute. I retrieved a Bible study friend's grandmother a while back."

"Yes, we know," Nancy remarked. "That went really well."

"I suppose you've noticed an increase in your overall energy level lately?" Bob questioned.

"It's amazing! I get home from a full day's work, turn on my word processor, and write nonstop until two in the morning almost every day. Four hours later I'm up, ready, and leaving for work. I should be absolutely exhausted, but I feel great! Glad it's happening since working a full-time job doesn't normally leave much time to write."

"Well, as I told you while you were writing about Oklahoma City, you keep writing and I'll do what I can from my side."

I didn't realize at the time that Bob was telling me that I'd be supplied with all the energy I needed to help me continue writing. I had attributed the abundance of energy to the fact that I really enjoy writing. Throughout my day at work, I always looked forward to when I'd get home and be able to work on whatever I was writing at the time.

"Say, we didn't stop just to chew the fat, I've got a proposition for you."

I felt my guard go up instinctively. When Bob was living Here he had a way of involving a person in some project or another, and it usually started in just such an offhand manner.

"What sort of proposition, Bob?"

"I . . . that is . . . we, could make some minor *adjustments* that would make it much easier for you to connect over here. Depending on what you chose to do with it, it could improve your communication ability."

"That sounds great; why don't you just go ahead and do it?"

"Well, we . . . ah... we need your permission to make the adjustments."

"Why is that?"

"Because the adjustments are something we'd do directly to you," he replied.

"I . . . see."

Now my guard was definitely up. I felt all sorts of things rolling around in me, and needed a few minutes to let them settle down so I could be sure what the implications were.

"Could you guys wait here? I'd like to think about this and maybe check in with Coach. I'll be back in a minute," I said.

"By all means. We'll wait right here for you."

I did a one-eighty and shifted my awareness to Coach. I found him immediately and told him what Bob was suggesting.

"Got any suggestions, Coach?" I asked.

"It's entirely your decision. It's not something I want to influence in any way."

Typical! People call folks like Coach guides! Hardly ever do you get a straight answer out of them for things like this!

"Maybe if you thought about your concerns it would help you come to a decision," Coach suggested.

"Well, physical pain is something I dislike intensely. I'd want to be sure it isn't going to be painful. And I want to know any potential downside to agreeing to these adjustments Bob is suggesting."

"Those seem like reasonable concerns," Coach remarked.

For the next half a minute or so, I let all the vague feelings rattling around inside me float into my awareness. When it felt like everything was back to being smooth inside me again, I asked Coach to accompany me to talk to Bob and Nancy. He readily agreed.

"Is there any physical pain involved, Bob?" I asked. "That's one of my biggest concerns. My pain threshold is a negative number, and you know it."

"There might be some very mild, short-lived discomfort. Not painful. At least I don't think so."

"What will these adjustment do? What abilities will they affect?"

"That all depends on you. They may improve your ability to communicate in nonphysical worlds. There may be a lot more to it than that. The effects might be very far reaching in other parts of your life too, but that will be up to how you utilize the effects of the adjustments. It has the potential to be an opening on many different levels, but that's up to how you respond."

"Is there any other downside to my agreeing?"

"Bruce, I'm going to make sure this is all done with compassion for your situation," Nancy said, sensing my implicit trust in her.

I had pretty much decided to agree when I noticed Darlene come into view. I'd trust her with my life. She is as loving, compassionate, and honest a human being as you'll ever find in any world. If she was also a part of this, then I had nothing to worry about.

"Bob, I'll be happy to accept your gift of these adjustments. Go ahead, I'm ready."

"There are a few things we need to do before the actual adjustments can be made," he replied. "It isn't something we would do right now. As soon as everything is ready we'll go ahead, with your permission."

"How will I know for sure when it happens."

"Don't worry, you'll know," Bob said, laughing as he did Here when he knew something you didn't, but you might soon find out.

"Anything else I should know about what to do after the adjustments have been made?" I inquired.

"Yes, it would be a good idea to increase your intake of water. After the adjustments are completed, drink excessive amounts of water for three or four days."

"Excessive amounts?"

"Quarts!"

"Anything else?"

"No, that's all we came for tonight," he said. "I'm glad you decided to go along with this. I know it took some courage to take the risk. We'll be going now so you can get your rest. Good night."

And with that, Bob, Nancy, Darlene, and Coach all faded into the darkness of sleep.

For the next several weeks, I noticed occasional mild disorientation and "almost headaches." That's what I call it when I feel dull, sluggish, and almost achy. It feels like a headache might be in the offing, but it never quite arrives. I wondered if this might be a result of the adjustments Bob talked about, but it might have been just a very, very mild case of the flu.

Three weeks after their visit, the adjustments Bob and Nancy asked my permission to make made their unmistakable appearance. A little after 1:30 in the afternoon, the Friday before the three-day Memorial Day weekend, I was at work sitting in my cubicle. These "adjustments" started with an extremely loud, audible tone emanating from a point at the base of my skull about an inch below the surface of the skin. Very close to the same place I feel the energy I call Wahunka. It had to be very close to the point at which the skull and spine are connected. The single-frequency tone was so loud that it drowned out all other sounds around me. I couldn't hear the voice of the person sitting next to me talking on the phone or any other sound except the incredibly loud tone. It lasted for five to seven seconds. Taken completely by surprise, all I could do was sit in my chair and wait for it to subside. Then its level dropped and tapered off to zero.

The tone was then replaced by the sensation of heat in the same location in an area half the size of a pea. Very quickly it went from warm to hot to very hot and then searing. Like a white-hot BB had been placed there. I remained fully conscious throughout the experience. In a few seconds, the searing, burning sensation subsided to just tolerable. A slight aching accompanied the heat. From the instant the process started, I had absolutely no doubt that this was part of the adjustment Bob and Nancy had talked about. If I hadn't been prepared for the experience, I'd have panicked. It was that intense. Instead, as soon as I realized I could tolerate it, I got up out of my chair and quickly made for the door to get outside.

Sitting at a picnic table, I calmly rolled a cigarette and waited, observing the sensation closely. Within four or five minutes, the size of the hot area had expanded to that of a golf ball. Ten minutes after it started, now the size of a tennis ball, the intensity of heat had tapered down to an easily tolerable level. After butting out my second cigarette, I went back to my desk to call Rebecca. She has the ability to remotely view medical conditions, and I wanted to hear her opinion.

"My sense is that it's not a stroke or any medically dangerous condition," she said after I explained what I was experiencing.

"Thanks, that confirms my feeling about it. I think it's something Bob and Nancy talked to me about three weeks ago."

After explaining Bob's proposition and my agreement, Rebecca concurred.

"Did he mention drinking lots of extra water?"

"As a matter of fact he did!" I responded.

"If I were you, I'd start right now and continue for several days," was her advice.

I did as she suggested. Three hours later, when I got home from work, the sensation of heat still filled an area the size of a tennis ball. It remained that size and just a little above warm for most of the Memorial Day weekend. It was nice of them to pick a time frame with three days in a row I didn't have to be at work.

After the heat at the base of my skull subsided to a gentle warmth, I noticed an ache in the center of my chest. This went on for over a week. At times intense, and at other times mild, I knew it wasn't physical, but chest pain still has a way of causing concern. Five days after it started, I called Rebecca again for a second opinion.

"You're right, it's not a problem with your physical heart. The whole process of the hot spot and the ache in the center of our chest is a call to open your heart chakra. That's an intelligence which is not a rational kind."

After finishing our conversation, I felt relief at confirmation of my feeling that this wasn't a physical problem. From the day the tone and hot spot started, my life has never been the same. In the weeks and months that followed, I began to understand what it meant to open your heart. I began to experience feelings I hadn't felt in so many years that I'd forgotten there were such things. Joy, sadness, glee, depression, the list went on and on. I discovered that as a young boy I'd done my best to close my heart as a defense against emotional pain too harsh to bear. It had worked for the forty years since then. Emotionally, I had seldom moved too far from either side of a flat, dull, stable isolation. Now I learned to gradually allow myself to experience an ever-widening range of feelings. My life took on tasting the flavors of feelings like a kid samples ice creams. Some I enjoyed, some I didn't care for, but I kept myself open to all the flavors I could find. I was building trust in a new area of myself. Trusting that it was okay to feel whatever I experienced. Grandma and the skunk had taught me how beliefs can block perception. The adjustments I'd given my permission for were beginning to teach me a new language with which to know, the language of feelings. Rebecca was right; the heart is not an intelligence that would be classified as rational. It's not learning through logic and reason.

It is, instead, an intelligence that comes purely through feelings. It doesn't need reason or logic to justify or explain how it knows. Knowledge comes through the heart just in the knowing.

It feels like I'm having a hard time explaining the effect Bob's and Nancy's adjustments had on me. Maybe that's because it's a process I'm still learning from. But I know it's important to understand, especially for us men who seldom have the foggiest notion of what it means to know through the heart. Knowing through the heart does not require reasoning. In fact, we often use reason to discount and obliterate the knowledge that comes through the heart. In the little more than a year since this process started, I've learned to trust heart knowing. As I continue to allow myself to feel, heart knowing and the improved perception it brings continue to dissolve my doubt.

CHAPTER 16

Afterlife Recuperation

The circumstances in which a person enters the Afterlife can affect their experience There. Marla's grandmother illustrated an aspect of this. The following story of George's recuperation after his death, and why it was necessary, illustrates another. His story shows how one's state of mind at the moment of death can influence Afterlife existence. It also illustrates how Helpers in the Afterlife deal with this situation.

This opportunity to continue learning about and building trust in the reality of human existence beyond the physical world came through my association with TMI. Graduates of its programs are among the few people in the world who realize it's possible to know the circumstances of a departed loved one. From time to time, TMI receives requests from such people, and some of those requests are forwarded to me. Such was the case with Tom, and, since he's connected to the Internet, I received via e-mail his request to check on his father, George. The following is an edited version of Tom's email request.

"Re: Lifeline Request
Hi Bruce,
My name is Tom. I am a member of TMI, Gateway graduate, and DEC member. Your name was suggested to me by Shirley, with regards to a Lifeline request. My father just passed away yesterday, Friday the 16th of June. His name is George and he lived in Ottawa, Ontario, Canada. My request to you is to assist him to reach the appropriate level, if he hasn't already done so. I am hoping you have the time to fulfill my request, and I am thanking you in advance.

All The Best.
Tom"

After receiving Tom's request, I e-mailed back my condolences and told him I'd check on his father within the next two weeks. Still unable to shake my last bits of doubt, I gave myself extra time to check in on his dad in case I tried and failed a couple of times. Up to this point, my attempts had never failed. I always found the person I was looking for, but my doubt kept assuring me that someday this whole made-up-in-my-mind charade would come crashing down. A lack of confidence breeds avoidance, and so it was also a way to put off actually having to try, at least for a little while. A week and a half later, I decided I couldn't put it off any longer, so I lay down on my waterbed to look for George. Coach was there almost immediately.

"You might want to consider trying a method of retrieval you haven't used in a long time."

"Hi, Coach. What are you suggesting?"

"Remember what Shee-un taught you?"

"Yes. I learned to focus on a spot in the center of my chest and sort of see into the Afterlife through it. Boy, I haven't thought of doing that in quite a while."

"In view of the changes you're experiencing from Bob's adjustments, this might be a good time to try it again," Coach suggested.

"I get it! Seeing through the Shee-un spot and opening of the heart chakra are related, aren't they!"

"You might say that, yes," Coach replied.

"Let me see now, I feel for where my awareness is centered . . . in my head as usual . . . now feel it move to the center of my chest. . . ."

"That's what Shee-un taught you, yes," Coach interrupted, "next time, you might try just focusing your attention through your heart and see what happens."

"Okay, Coach, thanks."

"Happy hunting."

While intending to focus my awareness through my heart center instead of my head, I'd felt the gentle, fuzzy, buzzing feeling move back and forth from one location to the other. Then that feeling stayed in the center of my chest. Relaxed, with the intent to find Tom's dad, I just waited for whatever would happen next. Moments later, I found myself standing in a room.

Visually, I was seeing a holographic image in the familiar, grainy, black and white. The room had the feel of a hospital. There was a man in front of me, lying on his back in bed, sound asleep. On the right side of the bed, a woman sat in a chair, as though she were holding a vigil. She turned her head to look at me just as I arrived, acknowledging my presence with her eyes. Very thin and frail looking, she had light-colored hair. The way she was watching over him, attending to him, gave me the feel of a mother or perhaps a grandmother. My strongest impression was that she was George's mother. She motioned toward the man with her eyes, indicating I should go ahead and try to wake him. Assuming he was George, I moved closer to the bed and called his name.

"George . . . George," I called out firmly.

He stirred slightly in the bed and groaned softly, but didn't wake up.

"George?" I said, a little more firmly.

Grumbling incoherently, he stirred a little more.

"George, I'd like to talk to you."

He sat straight up and peered at me through the groggy eyes of sleep. The old woman beside the bed was watching him very closely. Then, all I could see was his face. It had a long, oval shape and looked heavy, as though he might be a little overweight.

"Who are you?" George asked through a yawn.

"My name is Bruce."

"Why'd you wake me up?" He didn't seem too pleased by the tone of his voice.

"Your son, Tom, asked me to come and check to see how you're doing."

"Oh."

He seemed to be very tired and planning to talk as little as necessary, only answering questions, not volunteering much. His sleeping seemed to be part of a recuperation process connected with how he'd died. He wasn't stuck in Focus 23; he knew the woman beside the bed was there. George just needed time to rest from the experience of his dying process. He lay back down and drifted back asleep. After my brief exchange with him, the woman interrupted any further queries. With a look from her eyes, she told me that he really needed his rest, and suggested I come back later if I wanted to talk to him again. I told her I'd check back later to see how he was doing. She assured me that he was just recuperating, and that once he was fully rested, he'd be more alert.

Based on my previous experience, I felt George was doing well. Sometimes the people I check on are unaware of those around them, there to assist. This was definitely not the case with George. As I stood there looking into the old woman's eyes I saw flashes of images that told the story of their interaction. Whenever he woke up on his own, or at her prompting, he was aware of her presence and what she said to him. Sometimes he'd answer her questions and sometimes he'd just listen before going back to sleep. Since he was aware of his surroundings and able to communicate, I knew he'd be just fine where he was. There wasn't any need for me to try to move him anywhere else.

The thing that stood out in my mind about using the heart method, as Coach had suggested, was my communication with the woman. She'd never said a word the whole time I was there. By just looking into my eyes, she communicated everything I'd gotten from her. She'd answered every question I could have thought to ask, but neither of us had said a word.

I sent an e-mail back to Tom and described what I'd found out about his father's situation, assuring him that his dad was doing well. I also told Tom I'd check in on his dad again in a couple of weeks and report whatever I found out. He responded via e-mail with:

"Re: Thank you
Hi Bruce,
Thank you for getting back to me so soon. It is reassuring what you have told me of how dad is doing. I'm not surprised that he is recuperating, it's been a long haul. I won't go into any

details at this point as to his condition when he died. I am chronicling this information you send me, so the more you receive from my dad the more authentic it will be. I think you already know this. The woman could very well be his mother, not sure at this point. I would think that more will be revealed once he is more alert. Your ability and gift in this endeavor is more than appreciated. Thank you again, Bruce, and I wait for your next encounter. Take care.

ALL THE BEST.

Tom"

Over a period of the next two months, I continued checking on George to watch the progress of his recuperation. Each time I used the method Coach had suggested, just focusing my attention on my heart center and expressing my intent to visit. Gradually, my process of finding George changed. Instead of peering into 3-D blackness and waiting, I'd find myself in his hospital room moments after expressing my intent. It took me a while to feel comfortable with the idea I didn't have to go through the process I'd been using before. More than once I got to George's room so quickly, I decided it couldn't be the right place. I'd pull back out and start over, using my old, "peer into the 3-D blackness" method. It took longer, and I always ended up back in the same scene in George's hospital room. Gradually, the doubt about this new technique dissolved, and I used it almost exclusively. There were still times it felt too easy, and I'd go back to doing it the hard way. Building trust, for me, seems to be a slow process that requires testing and assurance that everything is still *real*.

Several weeks after my first visit, I went back to see how George was doing. He was still sleeping much of the time, and the old woman was still at his bedside. As I looked into her eyes, I got an update on the high points of his recuperation since my last visit. He was spending a little larger percentage of his time awake. Watching the interaction between him and the woman, I realized her role. While he was asleep, George was in a state much like dreaming, though his dreams were pretty empty. There was not much going on in his mind while he was asleep. He just seemed to be waiting for something.

Each time he woke up to his surroundings in the hospital room, the woman was there, communicating with him in any way she could. She'd wipe his forehead with a damp wash-cloth and talk to him. She'd tell him about events that he'd missed while he was asleep. Mostly, these were things about his family and what the doctors had supposedly said about his condition. She always assured him that he was getting well. George didn't say much back to her. He mostly focused on the sound of her voice and heard everything she said. When-ever she'd talked about his prognosis, I could tell he didn't believe her. He thought she was just telling him he'd recover and get well out of kindness to a dying man.

By talking to him, she was building up a level of coherence in the time he was awake. She was there every time he awoke, and, over the period of the last several weeks, he'd come to expect to find her there when he did. He was in and out of consciousness between empty delirium and awareness of her presence. The woman was specifically working at building up the percentage of time he was awake and his expectation of finding her there when he awoke. As I realized how important it was that she was building a bridge of conscious communica-tion with him, I felt strong gratitude toward her.

A couple of weeks later, I returned to check on George's progress again. Since I hadn't fully comprehended the implica-tions of his sleeping earlier, the change I witnessed came as a surprise to me. Looking into the old woman's eyes, I was again given a synopsis of his progress along with an understanding of the reasons for the change.

George's dying process had been a long ordeal. When he first entered the hospital, he held out the hope that somehow he'd beat the long, slow-acting disease that was trying to kill him. He'd held onto that hope for a long time, but, as the disease continued its progression, there came a time when he realized he wouldn't beat it. Finally, he gave up all hope and accepted that he was going to die. At that point, he mentally gave in to the inevitable, framing that with the idea that he was never going to recover, never going to leave the hospital, and never going to regain his health. The way he had framed the acceptance of his approaching death was responsible for his present situation in the Afterlife. He accepted that his disease would continue to progress *toward* death and that nothing could change that fact. Most likely comatose near the very end, he had not been aware of his actual transition into the Afterlife when he left his physical body for the last time. The way he'd accepted his impending death had left him *waiting* for it to happen. Even though he was no longer physically alive, in his mind, he was still *moving toward* death. He was still waiting to die, and I hadn't understood any of this on my first two visits. All I knew was that he needed to rest and recuperate, and so he was sleeping.

Peering into the old woman's eyes, I was then shown the exact moment when George changed his mind. It was what the old woman had been working toward since the moment he arrived. It was the moment he reframed his existence.

The expression of complete capitulation on his face changed into a brightening smile of hope as he thought, *I'm going to get well, I'm going to recover!* Still unaware of his death, he was thinking completely in terms of physical recovery. He saw himself regaining his health and strength. He saw himself leaving the hospital, returning to his home, and living life again. In the expression of hope on his face, I could feel him reasoning; *I don't know how it happened, something must have happened while I was unconscious. It doesn't matter how it happened! I've beaten the odds, I've beaten this disease, and I'm going to get well!* He was beginning to see himself in a future beyond his hospital stay and no longer waiting for his approaching death. This change of mind was the event crucial to his real recovery.

What I hadn't realized during my earlier visit was that his sleeping was a state of unconsciousness induced by accepting that he wouldn't recover before he died. It left him no future in which he could picture recovery and being alive again. His belief about death was that he would be in a state of complete unconsciousness. Any awareness of anything around him meant he wasn't dead yet; to him that meant he had to wait a little longer to die. After changing his mind, deciding he would live after all, he was eager to work his way through convalescence and regain his health. All the woman's communication with him during the brief times he was awake had been aimed at instilling this belief. He was the only one who could change his mind. She was there to do everything in her power to assist him in doing so. That was her role. Wordlessly thanking her for the update on George's progress, I expressed my gratitude for the work that she was doing. I left the room feeling her beaming smile in return.

It was several weeks later when I went to visit George again. So much had changed, I wasn't sure I'd ended up in the right place. I backed out and used my old method, again arriving at the same scene. It was a hospital room, but this time George was up pacing. In a light robe, over pajamas, he was wearing slippers, and walking back and forth from one end of his room to the other. He seemed to have fully recovered, and was in the process of regaining his strength. The woman I'd expected to find there was not in the room with him. As I watched him pacing the floor, I saw a review of his activities since my last visit.

Once he'd changed his mind and began to focus on his recovery, other people had been introduced into his routine. Physical therapists, doctors, and nurses had begun to assist his rehabilitation in a manner that fit with his physical world expectations. In his eagerness to leave the hospital and go on with his life, he had been very cooperative. His recovery had moved along at a pace faster than he believed possible. That was one source of the puzzlement that had him pacing the floor. Things about his environment puzzled him also. Everything seemed to be just too perfect. His previous experience with hospitals always had its difficulties, and here, nothing ever went wrong.

Each person he'd interacted with had dropped gentle hints about his true situation. Though never intrusive, and always supporting his conception of what recovery meant, they nevertheless were moving him toward his own realization of his death. They were giving him every opportunity to make the realization that he was no longer physically alive and to begin living his new life beyond the physical world. He felt fully recovered from the effects of the illness that killed him, but he was beginning to understand that going home from the hospital wasn't going to be quite what he expected. His suspicion about that matched reality. He suspected he'd physically died, and that where he was was whatever came after death. The pacing and thinking process he was undergoing was his way of fitting all the hints together with his experience and accepting that this might be true. That was the last time I went to check on George. It was obvious he was headed toward fully adjusting to the new reality in which he lived.

In a long e-mail, I related to Tom all information I'd gathered in the last three trips to check on his dad. I thanked him for the opportunity to learn more about our existence as human beings. It was my first experience of finding someone who was in an active process of recovery from an illness that had killed him. The power of George's belief when he gave up and began waiting to die had persisted beyond his physical death. Until he changed his mind, he would be locked in the power of those beliefs. But instead of finding him alone and isolated in Focus 23, he was in a place where people were attending to him. It felt more like Focus 27. He was aware of the old woman's presence and able to cooperate with her. During my experiences with retrievals before, I'd always assumed such contact provided an immediate change in which the person began conscious adaptation to their new existence in the Afterlife. I hadn't fully understood the power and implications of a decision like George's as he approached certain death. Through Tom's simple request that I check on his father and assist him if it was necessary, I'd discovered more about the existence of human beings beyond the physical world. The internal consistency of the whole episode made sense and contributed to my process of building trust and resolving doubt.

CHAPTER 17

Grandma Meets Bob and Nancy

The pager I carry everywhere but into the shower is a tool of my business, but clients aren't the only ones who use it to contact me. It went off late one evening, showing my ex-wife's phone number on the display. In my mother's grief and confusion, she'd dialed the number I hadn't lived at for almost two and a half years. My ex-wife relayed my mother's message. My grandma Winnie, Mom's mom, had died just a few hours before she called. It was just as well that she'd called the *wrong* number. I was visiting at Pharon's apartment—my fiancée, and wasn't at home to answer the phone. The only way anyone could have reached me was by pager. My ex and the kids knew how to get hold of me; they use my pager all the time.

Winnie had come to America from England in the early 1920s, and still carried a bit of British accent in her voice into her nineties. A sweet lady with never an unkind word to a living soul, she'd outlived two husbands, and was a clear-thinking, conscious, loving human being to the day she died.

My mother's voice told me she was emotionally distraught when I reached her a few minutes later. We talked for a while, sharing our feelings about Winnie and her death. Mom filled me in on the details.

Winnie was ninety-six years old when she died. In three months, she'd have been ninety-seven. For a person her age, she'd been in very good health up until the previous week. Then a slight cough, a little fever, and she died in her sleep between 4:00 and 4:30 in the afternoon. The only fear of death Winnie ever had that I knew about was fear of suffocation. She knew too much to fear leaving this world. She had too much experience with the Afterlife to worry about where she was going. For most of her life, my grandma Winnie talked to the dead. She never said it that way, of course. She would only describe these *strange dreams* she had.

As people get old in this country, our culture tends to congregate them together. Subsidized housing for the elderly, nursing and retirement homes, these are places where the old folks get gathered together before they die. Part of the experience of living in such places includes making friends with other old folks who die sooner, rather than later. Widowhood in her sixties qualified Winnie for a slot in a nice subsidized-housing building in North Minneapolis. Lots of old folks lived there. Lots of Winnie's friends made their last trip out the back door of the building on a cart, headed for a mortuary.

As a kid, I heard one or two stories about Grandma Winnie and her strange dreams. My aunt or my mother must have been visiting Grandma, and I overheard their conversation as one told the other the story. One story in particular I remember quite clearly. It seems a man down the hall had died a week or so earlier. He and his wife, now a widow, had lived in the building together. My aunt had gone to visit Winnie and she'd described one of her strange dreams. She'd been awakened in the night by the sound of a man's voice in her room. When she opened her eyes, the neighbor man who'd died was standing in full view at the foot of her bed. He'd come to ask Winnie a favor. His widow had been trying to locate his life insurance policy since he died, and still hadn't found it. The man asked Winnie to tell her where it was located. The next day, Grandma walked down the hall and told the widow about her strange dream. The papers she had been looking for were right where Grandma said they would be. My grandmother thought nothing about it. It was just another one of her strange dreams. As I said earlier, Winnie knew too much to be afraid of death. She had too many experiences to be worried about such a trivial matter. Her only fear as she approached dying had been that fear of suffocation. As my mother and I talked about Grandma's death, Mom was at least thankful that Winnie had gotten her wish, and died in her sleep. It was a small consolation to which my mother could cling, while feeling the grief of her loss.

"You just want to hang on to them here forever, but you just can't," my mother said as we continued talking. "They've got to go sometime."

We talked for a while longer, and, as my mother expressed her grief, she began to calm down and feel better. We'd talked in the past about the retrieval things I do, so she knew what I meant when I told her I'd check in on Winnie. After we'd finished, I decided to take a short walk in the parking lot so I could be alone.

As I stepped through the doorway into the cool Denver evening, I placed my intent on finding Winnie to check on her condition and help her if she needed it. I held my awareness in two places at once. Part of me was focused in the nonphysical world to find her, and the rest of me was focused in the parking lot so I could walk to my Jeep. I needed to get my tobacco tin and refill my pouch. Within a few steps after closing the door, I could feel a slight acceleration into that grainy, 3-D blackness, and then could feel Winnie coming into view. As I approached her she turned, looked in my direction, and smiled at me warmly. She was sitting in an overstuffed chair, and there was a long, low table in front of her. She greeted me in her ninety-six-year-old voice and manner, jolly, clear, bright, and alert. I could feel she was still under the influence of living in a very old body. I knew right away that this was a habit she'd soon be out of.

"Oh, you dears have no need to feel worried about me," I could feel Winnie say, "I'm just fine."

She wanted to make sure nobody spent too much time feeling bad about her death, and wanted that message passed through to everyone who was grieving. Just like her! Always concerned about other people's feelings.

I had to shift my attention away from her for a moment to get the tobacco tin out of my Jeep and into my pocket. As I turned back across the parking lot, toward Pharon's apartment door, I again focused my attention on Winnie. This time I could feel two other people with her as I began to tune into her presence again. As the room where she was sitting came back into view, I could see Bob and Nancy Monroe were there with her. In a scene that had all the outward appearances of an afternoon tea, the three of them were talking. Fitting for her home country, England, where taking tea is part of the custom.

Bob and Nancy had introduced themselves to her as, "friends of her grandson, Bruce." They'd evidently been chatting with her for quite a while. All three were immediately aware of my presence in the room.

"You've got some nice friends living here," I felt Winnie say. "We're having a lovely time together, Dear."

Bob moved off to the side with me for a moment and told me everything was going well with Winnie.

"There's nothing to be concerned about at all," he said. "Your grandmother is in great shape and doing just fine."

From my own observation, I completely agreed. She was fully alert and aware of her surroundings. She knew she was no longer living in her physical body, and was in contact with others around her. There was nothing she needed from me by way of assistance except to pass on her message to those still Here who were grieving her loss. With the purpose of my nighttime walk completed, I went back to Pharon's apartment and we finished watching the HBO movie that was running when I left. She filled me in on the three or four minutes I'd missed.

An hour or so later, I decided to check on Winnie again to see how she was doing. As I focused my attention on moving toward her, I felt the pull of Coach off to one side. Figuring that meant he had something he wanted to discuss, I turned toward his signal and moved in that direction until Coach came into view.

"Hi, Coach! Just on my way to visit my grandmother. She died today and I thought I'd visit again for a minute just to see how she's doing."

He must get a chuckle out of working with me sometimes. Coach lives in the nonphysical world, and has access to awareness of my every thought and action. Yet, when I meet him, I explain that I'm going to visit Winnie as though he wouldn't already know that! In the isolation of living in the physical world, it's so easy to forget that not everyone's awareness is as limited as ours. At least he's considerate enough not to burst out laughing at my way of dealing with him.

"Yes, I know," Coach replied. "Perhaps you'd like to introduce her to me?"

So, Coach accompanied me on the rest of my trip to visit Grandma. As we approached the room where Winnie, Bob, and Nancy were sitting, we materialized outside a door that led into the room. Hearing their voices on the other side of the door, I knocked lightly, opened it, and then Coach and I entered the room.

"Oh dear, you're back visiting so soon!" Winnie said. "And who's that there with you?"

I introduced Grandma to Coach, and he sat down in the room, joining into their afternoon tea.

"My, you seem to have lots of nice friends here, Bruce," Winnie said, beaming a smile in my direction. "My goodness, we're having such a wonderful time here! You be sure and let them all know back there not to be worrying about me."

I thanked everyone there, and came back to physical awareness in the apartment. It was getting late and it was time to get some sleep.

The next morning I decided to check on Winnie again. Just after I woke up, I went back to the place where I'd found her earlier. I was shocked to discover she wasn't there, and when I asked, somebody I couldn't see told me she was gone.

"Gone where?" I asked.

Whoever this guy was, I couldn't clearly understand what he was telling me. All I got was not to worry

Winnie was just gone for right now. Feeling concerned for her, I opened up my awareness into a full, spherical shape and reached out in all directions feeling for a sign of Winnie. Nothing. I couldn't feel her in any direction. I closed back down a little to focus on the one who'd told me she was gone.

"Yes, she's gone right now, but don't worry, everything is okay," I could feel him say more clearly this time.

"It's just a shock to me because it's the first time I've experienced someone being gone after having found them before. I'm concerned that perhaps she's wandered off somewhere and is alone."

"No, she's fine, just not available to you right now. She'll be back. Try again later," came the reply.

Indeed, when I checked in on her a few hours later, she was back again, in a jovial mood and happy to see me. After a brief chat, it was time for me to leave. Later in the day I called my mom and relayed Winnie's message. I'm glad my parents have come to accept my Afterlife exploration as something other than weirdness. They don't think it's that unusual that their son, "communicates with the dead," as they put it. It's nice to be accepted by family.

Over the next few days, I checked in on Winnie a couple more times. She wasn't gone again any time I went looking for her. She was just happy to see me and share a little of what she was doing. I was right about her not holding on to the image and feel of the old lady body she died in. I noticed her movements and mannerisms were beginning to remind me of how she appeared when I knew her as a child. As time passed between my visits I began to notice Winnie looked younger and younger each time.

Out of curiosity I inquired about where Winnie had been the one time I couldn't find her. What I got indicated Winnie had been occupied with something it would have been inappropriate for me to barge in on. Somehow her location had apparently been shielded from my probing to insure I wouldn't interfere. It wasn't divulged what that meant exactly, leaving more for me to find out about while exploring on my own. It didn't seem too important to know what she'd been busy with, so I never followed up to find out.

One of the things my grandmother's death made clear to me is just how much my attitudes and beliefs have changed since my voyages of discovery began. Originally I had only beliefs from religious teachings I'd been told to accept on faith as a child. Based on those, I could have only hoped my grandmother had gone to the right place with only vague notions of what that meant. Having learned how to find her after she left and how to help her if she needed it, I wasn't left with not knowing. Through the trust that's built up in my experience, I could accept her death as just a change of her location. A change not much different than if she'd just moved back to England. Probably a long time before I'd see her again on a regular basis, both the Afterlife and England are a long way away. But we can still visit on occasion; she's not lost and gone forever. In fact, years later Winnie was there waiting when my own mother died, and helped Mom in her transition into her life in the New World. How I dealt with Winnie's death seems, to me, indicative of my continuing reduction of doubt.

By sharing her strange dreams with my mother when I was just a kid, Winnie had held open a door of belief. Her one story of the neighbor and his insurance papers is part of the reason I can explore the Afterlife. It was a source of belief in the possibility of such a place. Winnie's story helped hold that door open so that one day I'd be able to pass through it and explore. Thanks, Grandma.

Something else that the experience pointed out quite clearly was the effect of Winnie's attitude toward death. She had knowledge of the existence of the Afterlife through the experience of her strange dreams. For her, a visit from a neighbor who had died a week ago was a normal, accepted part of her reality. She had no fear whatsoever of what would happen to her or where she would go after she died. Her death was just a natural process of human existence as far as she was concerned. Winnie had acquired Afterlife knowledge during Thislife, and it made all the difference when she entered the Afterlife.

THROUGH A HURRICANE, ALONE

Teachers don't always have to be flesh and blood human beings, or even human beings at all. When the student is ready for the teacher to disappear, a time of testing begins. Gaining proficiency as a sailor can give you a false sense of security while voyaging the open sea. You've learned a lot and gradually come to feel you can handle anything. My next voyage started innocently enough. A few people began asking for assistance in moving ghosts out of their homes. No big deal, I could handle it. Then suddenly I found myself in the midst of an Afterlife hurricane with gale force winds and gigantic waves coming at me from every direction. In such a test, there is no way out but to hang on and sail through it.

CHAPTER 18

Ghost Busting

In July of 1995, I got the first response to an advertisement Rebecca and I had placed in the Boulder, Colorado, *Nexus*, a New Age newspaper. Our ad ran from January to March of 1994, and solicited inquiries about our latest brainstorm, ghost busting.

We'd been sitting at breakfast, drinking coffee and trying to come up with ways to financially support ourselves using skills developed during Afterlife exploration. It was a typical, sunny January morning in Colorado, and we were laughing our way through some of the more outlandish ideas. One we both found intriguing was to advertise ourselves as "The Real Ghost Busters." We fantasized about taking frantic calls from ritzy hotels and resorts whose guests were scared out of their wits by some ghost's shenanigans. We delighted in imagining the hotel manager's bewilderment when we showed up with our pillows and blankets instead of fancy Hollywood hardware. We'd lie down on the floor where the ghost had last been seen, and dispatch it forthwith. Ghost busters to the stars! Oprah would grill us on national television with satisfied customers sitting on stage to extol our prowess. We fantasized on and on with all different kinds of schemes. Each one was more hilarious and ridiculous than the last. It got to be so funny we both laughed until there were tears rolling down our cheeks! At some point we stopped laughing and said, *Why not?* So we put together some advertising copy and placed the ad in the *Nexus*. One such ad read:

"Ghost Problems?

Ghosts are just people, no longer in physical bodies, with their awareness still strongly focused in the physical world.

Some, recently deceased, confused about or unaware of their situation, may stay close to a person who's familiar or connected in some way. Or a ghost, long ago drawn to the comfort of familiar surroundings, stays in a place we now call haunted. For all involved it's most always best for ghosts to move to a place with more and better choices. We're experienced in contacting and communicating with ghosts to facilitate re-establishment of their communication with their own nonphysical family, friends, guides, and other helpers who are trying to reach them. For information or to make arrangements, call my pager number—"

The only responses we ever got while our ad was running were from other newspapers trying to sell space in their paper for our ad. By March of 1994, we decided Boulder, Colorado, just wasn't ready for The Real Ghost Busters. That was the last time the ad appeared in any newspaper. It was a blast to play with the idea. Fun while the fantasy lasted.

Then, over a year later, I returned a page to a woman in Colorado Springs who was responding to the *Nexus* ad. She'd called several metaphysical bookstores in the Denver area trying to find someone who could help with her situation. It turned out that the Nic-Nac-Nook, my favorite metaphysical bookstore in Denver, had clipped out the ad and saved it for future reference. When the woman called the store, Candy, the owner, gave her the pager number that was printed in the ad.

The woman and her family had recently purchased a house in Colorado Springs, and it wasn't long before they all started to see the ghost. Catching glimpses of him occasionally, they'd become intrigued with the idea of finding out who he was. They wanted to identify him and research records of the house's previous owners and occupants to verify that what they were seeing was real. Using her name and the house address, I went nonphysically to investigate.

During my first two trips there, I found him easily. He seemed to be just a very confused old man. In deference to the family's desire to research his identity, I left him in their house on those first two trips. Each time I tried to get a fix on his name, but doubted he would tell me, so he didn't. On my last trip, I discovered he was an old alcoholic, who'd died in the house years ago. He was in a drunken stupor and showed what a mean, violent, belligerent guy he could be. Since there were children physically living in the house, and they could be frightened by his presence, I decided it was time for him to move on. I rather unceremoniously grabbed onto him and hauled him off to the Reception Center in Focus 27. There he'd be in contact with people who could help him, and he would no longer be bothering the children.

Two days later, the woman called to tell me that the ghost seemed to be gone. No one had felt his presence or seen him in two days, and she wondered if I knew what had happened. She seemed a little disappointed at not being able to verify his existence, but agreed that if he was the one responsible for her children's agitation, it was okay that I had removed him. That was the end of my first Real Ghost Buster adventure.

By the time the next call came in November, I'd spoken to Candy at the Nic-Nak-Nook and told her it was my pager number in the newspaper ad she had saved. I gave her my home number to pass along to anyone she felt had a genuine need. The next call turned out to be interesting, but it wasn't really a problem with a ghost. The guy who called kept hearing noises in a closet, and thought it was a ghost. When I went to investigate, I found it wasn't a ghost haunting his closet. Instead, it was an aspect of himself wanting out of the closet. He'd split off a part of himself and kept it hidden away, even from himself. That aspect of him made noises in the closet trying to get his attention. I'd never come across this type of thing before. He listened to my report of what I'd found in his closet with mild disbelief. I couldn't blame him, I wasn't certain about it myself. I'd gone looking for a ghost in his closet, and that aspect of him introduced itself and explained the situation. I was genuinely surprised when he called back a week later and told me he understood what it all meant. A part of himself he'd been denying for a very long time contacted him during a quiet moment. The last I heard, he was in the process of reintegrating that part of himself back into in his life.

Then, at 3:55 P.M. on November 13, while getting ready to leave my day job as an engineer, my pager went off with a number I didn't recognize. I dialed it, and the female voice that answered was the third person to respond to the old ghost buster's ad. This one turned out to be very complicated. You know how people say that when the student is ready the teacher will arrive? This teacher arrived with a pop quiz that was an extreme test of trust in my nonphysical abilities. She announced the start of this test in a frantic voice that grabbed my attention. "Thank God, you called back! I don't know if I'm going crazy or what, but I've got to talk to somebody!"

For the next twenty minutes I listened to the woman I'll call Helaina. At times, she could barely rein in the anxiety and fear in her voice as she poured out her story to a total stranger, me, over the phone. It was more than a little disjointed and hard to follow at times. She wanted to blurt out everything, all at once, and jumped back and forth so fast through times and places that I had a hard time making sense of it all. There were times I had to deliberately stop her, asking questions just to calm her down and understand the chronology of events. She was doing her best to keep it coherent and tell me her story in the order that things had happened. The strain in her voice told me this was not an easy task for her. She was excited, frightened, anxious, and nervous all at the same time, barely maintaining a grip as she babbled out times, places, and events. The thing that stood out through all of it was her biggest fear. She was afraid that she was going crazy, or, worse yet, already too far past the edge of insanity. With the advantage of time since Helaina told me her story, I can organize it into an understandable chronology of events.

The morning that she called me she'd walked past a picture on her bedroom wall at the foot of her bed and something white and flimsy had flown through the air between her and the picture. She didn't know what it was, but it frightened her witless. It was the last straw in a string of bizarre events that drove her to try to find help. So much had already happened that she was constantly nervous and jumpy. She was running scared most of the time. Two days earlier she'd called the Nic-Nac-Nook and tried to explain her problem to the man who answered. She was scared then, too, and had opened the yellow pages to try to find help. The Nic-Nac-Nook was the first and only place she'd called. She liked that their ad said they were "the friendly metaphysical bookstore." That's what had attracted her attention. The guy had suggested an appointment with a psychic, but the earliest available one was almost a week later. She'd made the appointment, but after what had happened this morning, she couldn't wait any longer. Something had to be done NOW! Just before she'd called me she'd phoned the store again. The woman who answered, Candy's sister, had listened to Helaina's story and told her she had the home phone number of someone she thought might be able to help.

"I got your pager number from the recording on your answering machine," she said. "I couldn't bring myself to leave a message on your machine. They never sound that good, and I was afraid you would think I was a nut case. I had to page you so we could talk in person."

Things had been happening in Helaina's apartment, scary things. She told me about them in staccato snippets in a voice filled with agitation and fear. Radios turned on by themselves at precisely 6:00 every morning whether their alarms were set or not. TVs went on and off regularly with a mind of their own. The blinds on her apartment window went down by themselves just before she was going to let them down herself. And the bowl! She had a set of four bowls, bought them herself, and had lent one to her brother. He took it to school and lost it. It had been gone for weeks. All her bowls were dirty and in the dishwasher one morning, when she needed one for breakfast cereal. She had looked in the cupboards trying to find something to use. When she looked back down, the missing bowl had materialized out of thin air and was sitting on the counter.

"I know my brother didn't bring it back! I asked him; he told me he lost it and had no idea where it was. He wouldn't lie to me!" she screamed, the strain sounding in her voice again. "There's a ghost in my apartment too. He followed me from the house I lived in right after I moved away from my husband, when we started our divorce. The things this ghost is doing are past just scaring me witless. I'm afraid I'm going to completely freak out! Do I sound crazy to you? Does any of this make sense to you?"

"Helaina, what you're telling me is making some sense to me. No I don't think you're crazy. You sound very frightened by things that are happening around you that you can't explain."

"You're not lying to me, are you? You really don't think I'm crazy?"

"I'm being honest with you, Helaina. What you're telling me so far fits in with my experience and understanding. Please continue."

"Okay," she said, a sense of some relief in her voice. "It started at my friend's house, I moved in there right after we started our divorce. I was feeling lonely one night and thought it might be fun to have a ghost around to talk to, somebody really old. I asked for one to come. A few nights later, I was in bed. I woke up and couldn't move. I was completely paralyzed. I looked over toward the door, and there was a face, a really big face, floating in front of the door. I was a little scared, but happy too. I've always had an interest in ghosts. I'd asked to meet one, and there he was. But the more times I saw him, the more frightened I became. Not long after the ghost came, my cat was so nervous that she licked off most of her fur. She was licking herself all the time. I took her to the vet, and he thought she was suffering from some kind of constant anxiety. I had to give her drugs to calm her down enough that she stopped licking off her fur. Can cats see ghosts too?"

"Yes, and probably even when you can't see them, cats still can."

" Well, I thought maybe this ghost was someone who'd died in my friend's old house, so I decided to move out. I threw out everything: furniture, dishes, my wedding dress, everything. I sold my wedding ring to a girl friend, got a hundred bucks for it. When I moved to my own apartment, all I brought with me were my clothes. I bought all new stuff, adding to it as I could afford to. But it didn't work; I think the ghost followed me here. He lives in my closet. It can be ninety-five degrees in my apartment with the closet door open, and it's still just freezing cold in there. I see him some-times in the bathroom mirror. He's, maybe, thirty years old, very handsome, and there's a woman too. She's young and very beautiful. I think he did something very bad to the woman. I see them down by a river, and he's carrying a boat oar. I think he did something awful to her with a knife; maybe he killed her." Helaina's voice was starting to tremble with fear. Almost crying. "He keeps trying to show me what he did to her, but I don't want to see it. I always stop looking at the mirror just before he shows me what he did to her." Her voice started sliding toward hysteria. "Sometimes, when I see him in the closet, I can feel he's pulling something out of my chest."

I stopped her story for a moment, "Helaina?"

"What?"

"I'd like you to take a couple of deep breaths, relax, and give yourself a moment to calm down."

I heard her inhale deeply over the phone, then, in a little calmer voice, she continued.

"Someone's got to help me make him go away! I don't know how much more of this I can take before I run out of this apartment screaming and never come back. I can't live in this place with him here anymore; it's driving me crazy. I can't spend one more night in this apartment with him here. I'm really afraid that I'm going to run out screaming into the night and everyone will think I'm crazy. Do you think I'm crazy? Do you think I'm making this all up?" Then in a very firm voice, almost yelling at me, she said, "Tell me the truth!"

"Helaina, I've heard similar stories from other people," I assured her. "You don't sound crazy to me. I believe you're telling me what you've actually experienced. Please go on."

"I'm afraid he's going to do to me whatever he did to the woman. He can make all these radio, TV, and window blind things happen. I just know he's going to do something terrible to me, too."

"He can't physically harm you; he can only make himself known to scare you," I replied. "I'd like to hear more."

"I've been feeling like something really big is going to hap-pen in my life! I've been feeling like this for quite a while now. I don't know what it is that's going to happen, but I know it's something really big. And I know I have to be ready for it, but I'm not sure how to prepare myself. The dream I had last night feels like it has something to do with whatever it is that's going to happen, something really big."

"Would you like to tell me about your dream?"

CHAPTER 19

Helaina's Dream

"Before I went to sleep last night, I was thinking it might be really cool to try to visit my grandmother. She's dead now, and I never met her when she was alive. My family told me she was a crazy woman, but I thought it would be neat to try to contact her. When the dream started out, I was standing next to my husband on a street corner. We were under a street light, and there was another man and a woman there too. They were all saying really mean, evil things to me, trying to scare me. I was feeling more scared, and bad, and worthless the longer I stood there listening to them. Finally, I couldn't take it anymore. I escaped from them and ran across the street to my little pickup truck. I don't have one really, but in the dream I did. I sped off in my truck and just kept driving and driving real fast down these narrow old roads. I had to get away from them before they did something really bad to me.

"I stopped in front of an old house where I knew I lived in the dream. I went inside and walked up the stairs to go to my room. At the top of the stairs, I heard this old woman behind me say something. She was at the bottom of the stairs and walking up towards me. She was saying really mean, evil things to me, too. When she got close she tried to give me something evil she was holding in her hands. She was scaring the shit out of me!"

Helaina's voice was moving up in pitch, and I could feel the fear and anxiety building up. Her voice was beginning to shake.

"Helaina, would you do me a favor again please?" I interrupted.

"What?" she asked, the feeling of fear in her voice dropping off slightly.

"Would you take another deep breath or two and a moment to allow yourself to relax?"

Again I heard her inhale deeply, and felt the tension gone from her voice as she continued.

"Well, I pushed the old woman down the stairs and I meant to kill her. But she just got up and came back at me. I pushed her down the stairs again and again, lots of times. I'm really a bad person. I was actually enjoying pushing her down the stairs, trying to kill her, to stop her. Then, suddenly, I was on my back in a bed, and I couldn't move a muscle. I couldn't say a word or even scream. Something was holding me down, and I was powerless to overcome it. It was like I was paralyzed and I could see the door to the room in front of me, at the foot of the bed. Behind the door, there was this really bright light. I couldn't see the light actually, just where it was coming into the room through cracks and under the door. I was afraid it was going to punish me, kill me and take me away forever, because I'm bad and for what I did to the old woman. I couldn't speak; I was so terrified I could barely think. I never learned how to pray as a kid, but I was screaming out my thoughts to God, praying he'd come and save me from this terrible light behind the door. I just knew, if that door opened, I'd be a goner. No one would ever see or hear from me again. I'd be dead and gone."

Fear was shooting out through her voice in all directions like exploding bursts of antiaircraft fire, not hysterical yet, but thoroughly afraid.

"I think my dream has something to do with whatever this really big thing is that's going to happen in my life. Anyway, I kept struggling to move and screaming my thought prayers to God to save me."

"What religion were you brought up in?" I asked.

"None, my family never went to any church."

"Have you had any metaphysical training in your life?"

"I don't think so, what exactly does that word 'metaphysical' mean?" she asked.

"It means studying about what some people might call the 'supernatural'," I explained.

"Well, I really like scary horror movies, and two days ago a friend gave me a book called, *The Eagle and the Rose*. I read the whole book already and some of it really made sense."

"Tell me more about your dream, if that's all right with you."

"There's not much more to tell. I was finally able to open my physical eyes. I broke free and escaped from that terrifying light. I just know that light would have put an end to me if it came through the door. Look, I'm too afraid to go to sleep in this apartment tonight; is there anything you can do to help me?"

I explained that I was still at work, just getting ready to leave for home when I'd answered her page. I didn't say out loud that my cubicle is right outside the open office door of the fundamentalist Christian owner of the company I work for. Remembering that fact, however, was beginning to make me feel uncomfortably nervous about continuing this conversation at my desk.

"If it's all right with you, as soon as I get home, I'll call you back and we can talk some more. If traffic's not bad, I will be there in about thirty or forty minutes. Is that all right with you?"

"I'm sorry I didn't realize you were at work."

"That's quite all right."

"I'll be here at home, the same number you called to get me this time. I'll wait right by the phone until you call," she told me.

"I'll be happy to do whatever I can to help you. I'll call back as soon as I get home."

After hanging up, I turned off my computer workstation and put away a few papers. Then I left the building, climbed into my Jeep, and headed for the entrance ramp toward my half-hour, freeway drive home. When traffic allowed time to think, I tried to assimilate what Helaina had just poured out to me.

What am I supposed to say when I call her? I wondered. *How on earth am I going to talk about this in a way that will make sense to her?*

What worried me most was wondering if she was at risk of veering off some psychological roadway and going over the edge. *And, why do I find myself drifting off into erotic attraction toward this woman I've only spoken to on the phone?* These and many other questions ran through my mind as I negotiated my way through relatively light, rush-hour traffic.

It was clear to me that somehow she had opened a portal into the nonphysical world, but this was not just a peek behind the curtain! She had opened her perception to awareness beyond the physical world not in small, measured baby steps as I had. She'd taken one big, giant step. Silly me, later that evening I would see what a real giant step was. Furthermore, she'd opened this perception with no religious, spiritual, or metaphysical training other than Hollywood horror movies and one book she had read. As a result, some very strange things had begun to happen around her.

My mind kept drifting back to the fact that she was in the grip of such a powerful state of fear that she might run screaming from her apartment while I was talking to her. That really worried me! The things she would say to someone who might find her in that state of mind would most likely qualify her for a ride to a psych ward and powerful drugs to make those things go away. People responsible for prescribing such drugs have their medical licenses to worry about, and will most always err on the side of caution. If I said the wrong thing, or something beyond my control pushed her over the edge, she could get caught up in a medical whirlpool that might keep her drugged and incarcerated for a very long time. The phrase they use is, "until she's no longer a danger to herself or others." There were worse possibilities to consider, but it scared me too much to think about them. I'd just have to trust that I'd get the help I needed to assist her through whatever happened. It gave me pause just thinking about the risks involved in working with her and what might happen to her if I didn't. So, I decided to pay more attention to freeway traffic for a while and let this simmer in my mind.

Some starting points in the coming phone conversation came to mind by the time I neared my apartment. Like the concept that "thoughts are things" and how that might fit into her situation, and that "fear and love cannot coexist." By the time I pressed the button on the remote control to open my garage door, I was feeling more than a little nervous.

Pharon, then my fiancée, was at my place when I got home, working on letters and her resume. I told her very briefly what was going on and that I needed to lie down and check in with Coach. We'd been together long enough by then that the things I do didn't spook her. She's a wonderful, understanding woman, and great support. I left her in the computer room, and walked down the hall to my bedroom. After closing the door, I lay down on my waterbed to contact Coach.

I let myself relax until I felt I could get a clear connection with Coach and begin. I was just starting to formulate my request to him for information, when I felt him nearby.

"You'll have to relax more, Bruce."

Fine, I let myself relax a little more, and got ready to start again.

"I mean relax *a lot more*, Bruce," I felt Coach say again.

I let the petty cares of the day drift through my mind and be on their way, sinking deeper into relaxation. Four or five minutes passed, and then I realized I could only feel the barest hint of contact with the waterbed beneath me. My body had taken on the shape of a huge egg. As I reached out and felt it, I could sense every bit of this egg shape, inside and out. It was maybe four or five feet in diameter at the waist and seven or eight feet long. It had a solid, not hollow, sturdy feeling with a slight energetic buzzing throughout.

"I think I'm relaxed enough now," drifted gently through my thoughts. *All my energy channels are clean, clear, open, and functioning perfectly. Any energies I encounter pass through me with no effect.*

I started using that affirmation at Rebecca's suggestion, after my episode in Oklahoma City the previous April. While doing retrievals there, after a terrorist bomb killed 168 people, I'd picked up strong, energetic, emotional baggage. It took me five days to drain off that energy in order to feel normal and emotionally stable again. I'd learned from that experience that the best protection from emotional energies during my nonphysical travels was not really protection at all. To paraphrase *The Course in Miracles*, any defense is just an invitation to attack. I'd since found that allowing such energies to pass freely through me without effect was the best way to deal with them. Hence, the affirmation.

"Go ahead and ask your questions; I think we'll do just fine," Coach thought to me.

"I want to receive all the information which will be most beneficial to Helaina for her situation," I said, placing my intent with the thoughts in my mind.

Focusing my attention on my heart chakra, I found myself peering at a very agitated jumble in the 3-D blackness in front of me. Waiting for whatever would happen next, the jumble transformed itself into a woman. I saw only her face at first, young and beautiful. The smooth, dark complexion of her face was beaming me a gorgeous, alluring smile. Moving backward a short distance, I could see she was dancing. She loved to dance, and her body movements, so sensuously rhythmic, were made all the more seductive by her arms gently swaying outstretched over her head.

Then, her appearance suddenly changed. Standing farther away from her I saw the same young woman rigidly frozen in front of me. Her entire body was encased in thick, hardened, black, tarry plates of fear. Almost instinctively, I began moving my hands up and down in the air in front of her, energetically loosening the fear. When I could see the black stuff beginning to shimmer slightly, I used *seeing it not there*. Moments later, the black plates of fear were completely gone from view. Then, I continued to energetically massage, loosen, and lighten her field. In less than a minute she was dancing, happy, and smiling again. While working on her, I got the impression that she was the one causing all the poltergeist activity in her apartment, as she called it. For a few moments more, I watched her dancing, waiting for more information. Then I felt I had enough to go on and decided to check in on the ghost who lives in her closet.

This guy was not so nice. He was the kind of guy who would terrorize a woman in the slow, brutally torturous process of killing her, just to feed upon her fear. He'd extend her torture and dying as long as possible so he could suck every last drop of fear from her veins. While living in a physical body, he'd used that method of feeding before. He used the boat oar Helaina had seen him carrying to club and stun the woman by the river. Then sitting on top of her, looking into her face, he waited for her to regain consciousness before slowly carving her to death with a knife. The delight he took in the stark terror she felt was sickening. He reminded me of stories of Jack the Ripper, another fiend who fed on women's fear.

Now that he was living in the nonphysical world, he needed a victim in the physical world who could see him. There was no way to terrorize a victim unless he could show her what he wanted to do and make her think he could do it to her. He had an insatiable hunger that only a woman's horrified terror could satisfy. Helaina's desire to contact a ghost had been answered by a very, very nasty guy.

Enough of this jerk, I thought to myself, letting the image of the ghost in the closet fade into the blackness. *Time to check out Helaina's husband.*

Her husband (I'll call him Mike) was obviously a mean-spirited man who often chose to take out his pent-up rage, anger, and frustration on the woman he'd married. He didn't physically beat her. His assaults came in the form of venomous words and mental energy intended to inflict maximum pain, fear, and humiliation. It was his way of maintaining total control of Helaina.

Isn't it amazing, I remember thinking, *the mates we choose to fulfill our subconscious beliefs about what we think we deserve in our lives.*

I'd seen enough of this guy, too, and decided I was ready to get out of bed and phone Helaina. When I stopped to talk to Pharon about what I'd found, she pointed out something I hadn't considered. The energetic link between Helaina and Mike had played a part in her connection to the ghost. Mike kept her in a constant state of fear and humiliation that kept her expecting punishment for being so bad. It was while in that energetic state she'd asked to meet a ghost. The one who showed up matched the state induced by her husband in some critical ways. Mike and the ghost had a similar bond with Helaina. That made her connection to the ghost much

stronger, since it matched closely with her everyday experience with Mike. I told Pharon my phone conversation might
take a while

Little did I know!

CHAPTER 20

The Phone Call Starts

After a trip to the kitchen to fill a large glass of water, I went to the living room and sat down on the sofa. Feeling very nervous about what I was going to say and what would happen for Helaina as a result, I picked up my portable phone. Before dialing her number, I checked in with Coach.

"Coach . . . I'm really scared about doing this."

"If you need any input from me, I'll be right here to help," I felt him say, "just remember to ask!"

"What if this woman ends up in some horrible situation because of something I say? I'd feel terrible to be responsible for that."

"And if you do nothing?"

"That's why I feel so nervous! I know I have to do this, but what if I screw up? She's going to suffer the consequences."

"And if you do nothing?"

"A rock and a hard place, that's where it feels like I am right now!"

"It's your choice to do or not do this, Bruce."

"And Helaina's choice?"

"She called you," Coach pointed out. "She made her choice."

"Well, I'm going to call her and do what I can to help. It just scares me to think about what could happen. I'm no expert. I'm still learning about this stuff myself."

"Need I remind you that trust is always the first issue?"

"Just be here with me and connect me with whatever is the absolute best for Helaina, okay?"

"I'll be here, just ask."

Before dialing Helaina's number, I took a few deep breaths to calm myself. I thought about the lines our conversation would follow, my thoughts driving home from work, and the ghost's energetic connections. Moving the ghost out of her apartment was no problem, but, if her fear and self-loathing didn't change, it would be a brief respite. It wouldn't be long before some other ghost with a similar taste for fear picked up the scent, moved in, and started the whole process all over again. Something would have to happen that would cause Helaina to change her whole way of relating to herself and to the world. That troubled me, as I've become very cautious about pointing out a person's faults and taking on any responsibility for the changes they must make. That's been my pattern at times in the past. I had no idea how to handle this part of the problem. It turned out to be the least of my worries.

Asking Coach again to be with me and provide all the information most beneficial to Helaina in her situation, I looked down at my pager display for her number.

"Okay Coach, here goes . . . "

The phone rang once, and then I heard Helaina's voice say, "Hello?" I casually looked at the digital clock on my VCR. It said 6:04 P.M.

Years ago, old-fashioned wind-up alarm clocks were used to make time bombs. When the alarm went off, a string wound tighter and tighter around the wind-up key until it pulled the switch and set off the bomb. Crude, but effective. The safety switch was the little lever on the back of the clock that sets the alarm. It makes a soft, metallic sliding sound and a gentle clunk as you move it to the armed position. Once that safety is off, when the time runs out, the bomb explodes. If I'd been listening carefully enough when Helaina answered the phone, I'd have heard that metallic sliding sound and the gentle clunk. Or at least the sound of a ticking clock. I didn't hear either as I shifted into our conversation, feeling anxious and nervous. Some part of me perhaps was aware that a bomb had been planted and the safety was off. It was just a matter of time before I found out.

"Hello, Helaina, this is Bruce. We were talking on the phone a little while ago. I'm at home now, so we'll have as much time to talk as you'd like."

"Can you hang on for a second?"

After a few brief interruptions to turn off her TV and settle in comfortably on her sofa, we started to talk. I'd rehearsed my opening lines driving home in the Jeep. We'd start out talking about the boundaries between the physical and non-physical worlds, about how these boundaries could thin out for a person under strong emotional stress. I'd ask about her stress level early in her divorce process. We'd talk about the concept that thoughts are things in the nonphysical world, and then with the ice broken, we'd go with the flow.

"Before I called you, I did a check-in to get some information about your situation."

"What do you mean by a check-in?" she asked.

"Well, first I relax and let myself get into a meditative state. Then I kind of mentally get in contact with your situation to get information that might be helpful."

"What did you find out?" she asked, simple inquiry in her voice.

"Well, for example when I checked on you, I saw a beautiful young woman with a dark, smooth complexion. She was dancing. She had very dark, smooth, shoulder-length hair, and she was positively beaming a strong, beautiful smile. She gave me the impression she was happy and enjoyed her dancing."

I answered her question, but didn't give her any detail about the rest of what I saw. Something told me not to—Coach, I think.

"I do dance for a living, and I love dancing. My hair is black and just below my shoulders but it's curly, not smooth. I'm Indian, Portuguese, and Irish and my complexion is dark. I know I'm pretty, maybe not a *Cosmo* cover girl, but pretty. Just how much of me could you see?" she asked, with a note of alarm in her voice. She was obviously concerned that I might have peeked at more than decorum would allow.

"I saw only the woman's face at first, and then I could see her dancing. Don't worry, it was more of an impression, not actually seeing your physical body. For me, it's like a real grainy black and white image," I replied with a laugh, trying to dispel her concern about a peeping Tom.

"How is it that you could find me? I mean there are lots of people, how did you know it was me when you found me?"

"Well, I could tell you a story about someone else I found and maybe that would illustrate how I do it. Are you up for a story?"

"Yeah, I'd like that."

Relating the story of retrieving Marla's grandmother from the wooden chair in her kitchen, I explained I had only needed her name to locate her.

"All you need is a name to find anybody?" she asked incredulously.

"Yep. I don't know how or why it works, but it never fails. Of course in the grandmother's case it was an unusual name, Gwendilyn Eudora Winterlax."

"That is quite a name," Helaina responded, giggling.

"Her granddaughter, Marla, confirmed all the information I'd gotten about Gwendilyn, including that everyone, even Gwendilyn, called Margaret, 'Maggie.' "

"Okay, but how do you know for sure that you found me when you were checking? How can you be sure you didn't find someone else?" she demanded.

"While I was watching the woman that I saw dancing, I didn't know for absolutely certain that it was you. But I've done this so many times and it's been verified so many times, I'm beginning to trust it. In your case, except for the fact that I saw your hair as smooth instead of curly, I'd say it was pretty accurate, wouldn't you?"

"Well, yeah, I'd say it was all pretty close." It didn't make sense to her how it was possible, but it was, after all, accurate.

"I'd like to talk a little bit about how you were feeling as your divorce was approaching, if that's all right?" My plan was to lay a little groundwork for talking about the first appearance of the ghost.

She didn't talk about the abusive nature of her marriage to Mike. I'm not sure she recognized her husband's behavior as abuse.

"Well, the most important thing to Mike was which power tool he'd buy next. He had no interests beyond things like that. I felt so far beyond him that I was bored out of my mind. We had nothing to talk about or share. I felt so neglected and bored I just had to leave. I struggled with the whole idea of splitting up, and it really stressed me out."

From Coach, I was reminded that, in her stressed state, contact with a ghost would be easier. In that state of mind, she'd expressed a desire to contact a ghost. The one who'd come was scaring her, causing even more stress. In a vicious circle of fear, she'd moved into a space where boundaries between the physical and nonphysical worlds became progressively thinner and thinner. Stress made it easier and easier to connect to this ghost who induced more fear and caused more stress.

"Sometimes people under great stress have a much easier time seeing into the nonphysical world. Have you heard of anything like that?"

"Yeah, I've heard of that. Like when people who almost die see their dead relatives? You mean stuff like that?"

"Yes, that's the idea! When people are under great physical or emotional stress, the boundaries between the physical and nonphysical worlds sort of get thinner. The thinner they get the easier it is to see through them. I get the feeling that's what's going on in your case. Your divorce put you under stress. That made it easier to see the ghost the first time. Now the ghost scares you and you're under more stress. It's a vicious-circle thing."

"That's really making some sense to me," she said. Then she suddenly changed the subject. "Can you see something like energy in a room, like it's full of something moving around? I mean, I can still see my things in the room, but the air is full of something you almost can't see, but you can feel it."

"Yes, sometimes I sense something like what you're describing, why do you ask?"

"My living room looks and feels that way right now," she said with a little edge to her voice.

She switched subjects again. She talked about a new, growing feeling of power in her chest.

"Like a sort of pressure that extends outward from my chest," she described. "Have you ever heard of anything like that before?"

"Sounds like what I've heard called a heart chakra opening. Where in your chest is it located?"

"It's centered on my breastbone and extends out into the air a ways."

"Do you know much about chakras?"

"No, what are chakras?"

"They're centers of different kinds of energies within the physical body. The heart chakra is the center through which we love. The energy of connectedness with all life flows through it. There are seven major chakras in the human body arranged along a line that coincides with your spine. The energy of each chakra has different characteristics. There are lots of books about chakras in places like the Nic-Nac-Nook bookstore. I could recommend some if you like?"

"Maybe sometime later I'd like to do that."

Her talking about a heart chakra opening reminded me of my earlier intent to discuss Helaina's dream. I wanted to pass along what I knew about love and fear, specifically that they can't coexist. My hope was that she'd understand and be able to use the technique I'd learned whenever her fear began to build up to freak-out levels. "You know, there's a way you can use heart energy that might be helpful. You might be able to learn to use it to dissipate the fear you feel in your dreams and other situations. Would you like to hear about that?"

"Sure."

"To illustrate what I mean, I'd like to tell you another story from my experience."

"Okay."

I related the story about the Banshee and how it was actually Marty's own fear taking form. Explaining what Rebecca taught Marty about extending his love toward the Banshee and making it disappear, I hoped she would get the connection to her own fears.

"By extending his Love, the Banshee would always disappear because it's like a law of nature in the nonphysical world; Love and Fear can't be in the same space at the same time. I suspect some of the things you see might be your own fears taking on form. This can be particularly true in your dreams. You can extend your Love from the center of your chest towards scary things in your dreams or anywhere else. If they're made out of your fears, then they'll disappear.

"What if they're not made up out of my fears?" she asked, a genuine sense of curiosity in her voice.

"If they're not something fabricated out of your fear, and they still seem scary, then it might mean your fears have kind of masked or covered over what they really are. In that case extending your love can remove the masking of fear. It might let you see more clearly who or what is really there."

"Could you give me an example?"

"Let's take the dream you had last night. You wanted to visit with your dead grandmother. Because of what happened earlier in the dream with Mike, you were already in a fearful state of mind. As long as you were afraid, everything from then on in your dream might have been masked over or colored by your fear. It's entirely possible the woman you saw coming up the stairs was your grandmother. She might actually be the sweetest old lady you could ever meet. She might have come to meet with you and give you something wonderful. But, with your fear overlaying everything you saw, she appeared to be an evil old woman saying evil things and trying to make you take something evil from her. If you had extended your love toward her in that dream, one of two things probably would have happened. If she was made of your fear, she would have disappeared into thin air and that would have been the end of her. If it was really your sweet old grandmother, trying to contact you through the mask of your fearful state of mind, the mask would have dropped away. Then you would have seen her as she really is. For all we know, she might have then been there to give you an incredible gift. Who knows, she might have been trying to help you with your problem of the ghost. But in your fearful state of mind she looked evil and nasty," I explained.

"The same goes for the light behind the door you were terrified of. Extending your love to that light might have made the fear mask drop away from it too. You were screaming with your thoughts for God to come and save you. If you extended your love to that light, maybe God Itself would have come through the door to answer your prayers."

"Do you believe in God?"

"Yes I do."

"Do you believe he's a big guy who sits on a throne and rules over us?"

"No, I don't see God that way. For me, God is Everything and Everything is God, for me God is Love and Love is God."

"Do you believe there's a Hell? A place God sends really bad people to punish them for doing evil things when they were alive?"

I could feel this was a fear she carried about her own future.

"No, I don't. I've explored all over everywhere in the non-physical world, and there's only one place I've ever found that I could call Hell. But it was not like people say, fire and a devil and all that."

"Really?"

"Are you up for another story?"

"About the Hell you found? Sure."

For the next few minutes I described Max and the kind of life he lived in the physical world.

"You're right, he sounds like not a very nice guy."

Then I described the place where I found Max after he died, what he did there, and what others who lived there did to him. I talked a little about why I felt Max had been attracted to his Hell.

"That sounds like an awful place to be," Helaina remarked, a sense of disgust in her voice.

"And the funny part is that Max will have to stay there until he can forgive himself and the others, and decide to change the way he is. Then he'll be able to move on to a much better place. His only punishment is to live his life exactly like he wants to and live with the consequences. It's all self-in-flicted. The instant he changes his ways, he'll be free to leave."

"You're right, it's not the picture of Hell I've heard about. Yet it seems like the perfect way to deal with people who've been evil in their lives."

"The best part is we don't have to wait until we die and are living in our own Hell to change. We can decide to change anytime."

Helaina then changed the subject again.

"How is it that all this stuff can be happening to me when I don't know anything about it? I dropped out of school in the ninth grade to go to work and earn money for my parents. I was never raised in any religion. How can these things be happening to me?"

"First, let me say that there are people who study for a lifetime trying to have happen to them what is happening to you. I mean the heart chakra opening and awareness of the nonphysical world. I know it may not seem like it to you right now, but in so many ways, what has happened would be a blessing beyond most people's dreams."

"You're right, that's hard to believe."

"As for why it's happening to you . . . Actually your lack of training makes it easier for you to directly experience such things, because you have few contradictory beliefs about them. A person's beliefs can make it virtually impossible for this stuff to happen."

"Really, why?"

"Someone with strong beliefs that it's impossible to see a ghost almost never sees one. Their beliefs against it prevent them from seeing anything they don't believe in. Their belief that something is impossible puts up a kind of curtain that they can't see behind. Lots of our beliefs come from something we learned in school or church or studying about metaphysics. To me, that explains, in part, why these things are happening to you, not all the reasons, but part of them."

"How?"

"You probably have fewer of the beliefs against these things than most of us. You left school early, never went to church, and never studied metaphysics. Those are the places most of us picked up beliefs that prevent the ability to see into the nonphysical world. Does that make any sense to you?"

"Yeah, it does in a funny kind of way; I feel I'm getting what you mean. It's kind of like I don't know it can't happen, so it can."

"Exactly, yes, that's what I mean," I replied.

She backtracked a little more, talking about her childhood.

"In my life, a lot of bad things have happened to me. Some

of my friends wonder why I haven't jumped off a bridge a long time ago. Like I tell them, it's all just made me stronger."

CHAPTER 21

Helaina's Poltergeist

"Can we talk for a minute about the poltergeist things that have been happening in your apartment?" I asked, prompted by Coach to broach the subject.

"Sure, that's really scary for me to think that these ghosts could do something to me, and I can't stop them. In fact, something spooky happened when I called the Nic-Nac-Nook. The first time I called them, I had just changed channels on my TV, and the movie *Poltergeist* was just ending. That scared me! I mean here I am calling to see if anyone can help me with poltergeists in my house, and that movie is just ending. I was calling because I was so afraid the ghost in my house was going do something really bad to me. Just when I'd finally had enough and worked up the courage to do something about it, that movie is ending on my TV."

Looking back now at Helaina's remark, I can't help but marvel at the timing and synchronicity of events in our lives. She took this event to mean *they* were reminding her of *their* power to do her harm just as she started taking action to eliminate *them*. From my perspective, it has an entirely different meaning.

"First of all, to my understanding, ghosts can't do anything within the physical world by themselves. There has to be a physically living person involved in order to affect the physical world. During my check-in earlier tonight, I got that you are the one doing these poltergeist things. It might be subconscious, but it's you who is making these things happen."

"That's ridiculous!" she yelled. "How can that be? I don't know anything about how to do this stuff!"

"Take it as just my opinion. You shouldn't automatically believe anything I say just because I say it's true. You've got to

173

find out the truth for yourself. But, that's the understanding I got from my earlier check-in."

"Is there any way you could explain how it could be possible?"

"Could you hang on a second? I need to check on something," I interrupted.

"Sure."

It was time for Coach to provide some information. After listening to his answer to Helaina's question, I translated and repeated it back to her.

"In the nonphysical world, bowls appearing on a kitchen counter, window blinds going up and down, radios and TV's going on and off are not any big trick. In the nonphysical world, thoughts are things and just thinking about something, picturing it, can make it happen. In the nonphysical world, picturing a bowl on the kitchen counter causes one to appear. By contacting a ghost, you opened a door into the nonphysical world. As you've been passing back and forth through that door, you've learned that thoughts are things. You've brought that concept with you and applied it in this world. You may not even be conscious of bringing this understanding with you. Since even our physical world is not as solid as it seems, you might be subconsciously exercising your new understanding in the physical world."

"So that somehow explains the blinds going down by themselves?"

"Let's use that as an example to illustrate what I mean. Tell me again about when it happened. Start just before it happened and tell me everything you can remember, especially what you were thinking and feeling."

"Well, let's see . . . I was lying on the sofa before it happened. I was feeling really tired and lazy. People can see into my place at night if the blinds are open, and it really bugged me that I had to get up, walk across the room, and lower them. I was feeling angry that I had to get up and close the blinds. People shouldn't look into my place just because they can. I was feeling really irritated, and, the closer I got to the blinds, the more irritated I was feeling. When I got a few steps away from them, I stopped and looked up at them, feeling really irritated. Then, they just came down by themselves! I never touched them; they just came down all by themselves."

"I see."

"It really scared me! If the ghost can do a simple thing like that, I'm afraid he could do something really bad to me!"

"Has something else happened all by itself, when you were feeling really irritated?" I could feel we were onto something.

"Well, the TV goes on and off mostly when Mike is over. I was irritated at him because of something he said to me. The TV just turned on by itself! We could both see the remote control thing sitting on the nightstand. Nobody was touching it, but the TV just kept going on and off by itself. We had to pull the plug out of the wall to make it stop!"

"Are there any other times something like this happened?"

"Yeah, right after the big face of the ghost appeared that first time, I was so excited I just had to tell somebody. I went to see the marriage counselor Mike and I were going to. I thought that since he was into psychology, he would know about this stuff. But the longer I talked, the more I told him about the ghost stuff, the more I could see he didn't believe me. I could tell he was thinking I was a nut case. I was really irritated by the time I left his office, and wanted to show him I was telling the truth and I wasn't a nut case. As I was leaving his office, now you have to realize his office is in a five-story building in Cherry Creek, just as I touched the doorknob all the lights in the entire building went out. The power went out in the whole building! I turned around and said, 'See, I told you this weird stuff is happening around me,' but I still don't think he believed me."

"Do things like this ever happen when you're not irritated or angry?"

"No, only when I'm really irritated."

"Are you noticing a pattern here? Is there another feeling that happens at the same time you're irritated? Do you see a connection between them?"

"You're right! In all the weird happenings, I can remember I had a feeling like I really wanted something to happen! I wanted those blinds down! I wanted to show that marriage counselor I wasn't a nut case, but I still don't see how I could be doing it if I don't know anything about it."

"Each time, there's a pattern of strong emotion, feeling irritated, coupled with a strong desire to make something happen. I've seen this pattern around weird happenings before, but like I said, it's only my opinion. You'll have to find out if it's true or not for yourself."

CHAPTER 22

Is That an Alarm Clock Ringing?

I could sense Helaina was focusing into the teeming field of energy in her living room that she had mentioned earlier.

"What are you feeling right now," I asked her, "what's going on?"

"I'm kinda looking into that energy in the room, trying to see what it is," she said with a childlike curiosity in her voice.

If I'd been paying attention right then, I'd have been alerted to the impending bomb detonation by the ringing alarm of one of those old, wind-up clocks. I'd been unaware of the time bomb Helaina was carrying, and time had just run out. I felt her sense of tension streaking upwards in the instant before her scream announced the explosion.

In her shrieking voice I could just make out, "There's a hand, a hand, a person's hand! It's floating in the air right in front of me."

In what had been the Veil between the Worlds, she'd blown a gaping hole so big that I couldn't see the Veil in front of me anymore. Through the phone I'm hearing her crackling, screeching voice screaming.

"The hand . . . the hand . . . it's waving at me."

Joining impressions of Helaina's experience, I turn slightly and see the edges of the hole, like tattered, shredded silk flapping in the breeze. Strangely calm, I feel my attention turn back to Helaina. Standing firmly on the ground, I feel Coach fold into me. Through me, his voice reaches through the hole, grabs on to her, and pulls Helaina back to my side of the Veil.

"Helaina, how does seeing that hand make you feel?"

"I'm really scared," squeaks out of her. The waving hand is freaking her out. I can feel her grip on the real world loosening. If Coach can't hang on to Helaina's mind, she's gone.

"Helaina, would you like the hand to go away?"

"Yes!"

She is screeching like a terrified little girl, in a voice three octaves above humanly possible, and very loud.

"Repeat, out loud, after me," I say, "You don't belong here."

Through the phone in her crackling voice, I hear her say it.

"Now say, 'I want you to leave right now,'" in the firmest voice I can muster.

She repeats the phrase, and I can feel her moving back toward my side of the Veil. She's calming down.

"It's gone; it just disappeared," a note of calm seeping back into her voice.

"Very good, Helaina, you can have control in this situation. Nothing can harm you, you're safe."

I feel a huge release of tension, both hers and mine. Then I feel her peering into the energy in her living room again.

"Oh . . . my . . . God! The room is full of them . . . men . . . my living room is full of men! Where the hand was . . . there's . . . there's a man standing in front of me," the pitch of her voice is climbing. "I don't want to see him. He's scaring me! I don't want to see him!"

She's screaming so loudly that it's distorting her voice, and I'm having difficulty understanding her words. I feel the fear that I might lose her welling up in me.

"Helaina, would you like the man to leave?"

"Yes, yes!" and, as she's screaming, I can feel tears coming to her eyes. She's moving swiftly toward a mental break.

"Helaina, repeat, out loud, after me," I feel an unaccustomed force going through my voice, tightly gripping her attention as I say, "You don't belong here."

With more anger in her voice this time, emotion coupling to her desire, I hear her repeat the phrase.

"Now say, 'I want you to leave right now,'" my voice still flowing with unaccustomed force. Then, like turning off the heat under a whistling teakettle, I can feel her tension drop as she's saying the words.

"He's gone!" I hear her say with genuine surprise in her voice.

"What are you feeling right now, Helaina?" I hear my voice ask for a reality check.

"I'm feeling almost calm, kinda peaceful actually."

"What have you eaten today?" comes from me out of the blue, but I immediately know where this train of thought is headed.

"Let's see, this morning I had some kind of snack and just tonight I had maybe, a cup of ice cream. Why, what's so important about what kind of food I eat?"

"It's not so much what you ate today as it is how much. Remember when we talked about stress making the boundary thinner between the physical and nonphysical worlds?"

"Yes, I remember."

"Not eating or eating very little does the same thing. The longer you don't eat, the thinner the boundary gets. In the Bible, it talks about prayer and fasting as a way of making it easier to communicate with Spirit. Since you haven't eaten much today, it's even easier for you to see into the nonphysical worlds. When you eat food, some of your consciousness has to focus on all the processes necessary to digest it. That leaves less of your consciousness available to be focused anywhere else. One of the things you can do if things are getting too hairy is to eat something. Make any sense to you?"

"I guess I'll just have to take your word for it," she replied, calmly.

"Something else to know is that alcohol and other drugs can thin that boundary too. Using them to excess or under certain conditions can accentuate the effect."

"I don't drink, do drugs, or smoke," she replies indignantly, then she shifts subjects again.

"You know I don't mind seeing fragments. Just seeing little pieces of these guys would be okay, but I don't want to see their whole bodies. I can kinda see little bits of them all over everywhere in my living room."

Like a spiking fever, I can hear her tension rising fast toward a peak. She's been caught so off guard that her first words come out as she's still inhaling.

"There's another man, he's standing in my kitchen. Oh God, make him go away!"

"Helaina, do you want the man in your kitchen to leave?"

"YES!" I hear conviction in her voice this time.

"Look at where he is and say, 'You don't belong here,' and after a short pause, 'I want you to leave right now.' "

"He's gone!" and her fever drops just as quickly as it rose. "I don't have to say it out loud, I just, sorta like, thought it to him and he was gone."

"That's right, communication in the nonphysical world can be done by thoughts. Thoughts themselves are nonphysical too, sort of made out of the same stuff. The language of the nonphysical world is the language of thoughts and feelings. You *felt* your message to him. In his world, that thought or feeling was just as real as a bulldozer. You directed it at him, and he couldn't avoid it. Your thought was a real thing that pushed him away. Remember earlier when we talked about thoughts being things and what that meant?"

"Yeah."

"Being able to use your thoughts to communicate with these people you're seeing is an example of that. Your thoughts are real things, just as real as your voice, and they have real effects. In my opinion, sometimes it's a good idea to physically say your thoughts as a way of focusing your intent and cementing it in physical reality."

"Do you think I'm making all this up?" comes out of nowhere. "Do you think I'm crazy, that I'm just imagining all this, and it's not really happening?" she demands.

"Helaina, everything you've told me so far I've either experienced myself or heard about from friends I trust. I don't think you're making this up and you're not crazy. What I hear you telling me is that very unfamiliar things are happening and you're afraid."

"You're not lying to me are you?" a mixture of fright and relief in her voice.

"No, Helaina. I'm not lying to you. Maybe it might help if I told you about when weird things started happening to me and I thought I was going crazy. It was a long time ago, and I got lucky. I found a book, early on, written by someone who'd experienced the same things. Reading about his experience let me know I wasn't the only human being this happened to and I wasn't stark raving nuts."

"Yeah, two days ago one of my girlfriends gave me a book called *The Eagle and the Rose*. I read it all in two days, just finished it," she remembered out loud. "A lot of it made sense to me. Tell me about when you thought you were going crazy."

"Over twenty years ago, I had a lucid dream in which I saw someone who really terrified me."

"A lucid dream?"

"A dream in which I knew I was dreaming. I was wide awake in the dream and could do anything I wanted to."

"Oh."

"The guy in the dream wasn't doing anything that should have made me afraid. But, as he moved closer and closer to me in the dream, I kept screaming, each time louder and more terrified, 'Who are you?' I kept screaming, *'Who are you?'* at him until he disappeared. Two weeks after the dream, I was in a library looking for a book on hypnosis, a hobby of mine at the time. I could see the book I wanted on the shelf. I reached for it, pulled it down, opened it up at random, and started reading halfway down the left-hand page. I was reading a description of the guy in the dream from two weeks before. It wasn't the book on hypnosis that I'd reached for. I grabbed the one next to it by mistake."

"Who were they, I mean the guy in the book and the guy you saw in the dream?"

"The best way I can describe the whole experience is that I was guided to grab the wrong book by what some people call a 'Guide' or a 'Guardian Angel.' That's who both guys were, Guides. They were trying to help me understand that I wasn't going crazy. They led me to the book that explained what was happening in my life. Do you have any beliefs or knowledge of Guardian Angels in your training or background?"

"Well, I know there are supposed to be something called 'angels,' but not much about them. I didn't go to church as a kid, and never learned much about that kind of stuff. Does everyone have a Guardian Angel?"

"Well, in my opinion, everyone has at least one Guardian Angel."

"Do you think I have a Guardian Angel?" she asked, the sound of disbelief in her voice.

"I believe we all do."

"Are you sure it's all right that I called you? It's okay with you? You don't mind?"

"It's perfectly all right that you called me. In fact you were probably guided to call me."

"You mean, you think my Guardian Angel guided me to find you?"

"I wouldn't be the least bit surprised to find out that's how you found me."

"Why wouldn't that surprise you?"

"Tell me again how you were able to get in touch with me."

"I had to talk to someone; my friends thought I was crazy. I had to find someone who knew about this stuff. I picked up up the yellow pages, opened them up to bookstores, and looked at the ads. There was one that stood out from the rest on the page. It felt friendly, like its ad said, *The Friendly Metaphysical Bookstore*. It felt friendly so that's the one I called."

"Is that the only one you called?"

"Yes. It was the only one that felt friendly."

"And you found me through them?"

"I talked to a man that answered. He seemed to know something about what was going on with me. He suggested an appointment with a psychic on Wednesday. Then, today, when the picture thing happened, I couldn't wait any more. I called back and this time I got a woman who listened to my story, and she said she had the number of a man she thought might be able to help. She gave me your number."

"Let me tell you how she happened to have my number. Over a year and a half ago, she saw a strange little ad in a monthly newspaper and clipped it out. That ad was only printed in three issues of the paper at the beginning of 1994. It was never printed again or in any other newspaper since then. As far as I know, The Nic-Nak-Nook is the only bookstore in Denver that saved a copy of that ad. Theirs is the only number in the Yellow Pages you could call and reach me, because she saved that strange little ad. Think about it. Think about the odds against your picking that one and only number out of the entire yellow pages and reaching me."

"I see what you mean. There's lots of phone numbers in the Yellow Pages. Those are impossible odds. So, you're sure it's okay I called you?"

"Absolutely. As I see it, you were guided to me. In fact, I was worried about talking to you before I called. One of the reasons I felt all right about it is because of the way you found me. Do you feel okay about calling me?" I asked, bringing us back to where she'd started with her question.

"Yeah, I feel okay about it."

"Good, I'm glad to be here working with you."

Coach popped in and asked me to go over a point about communication again.

"I'd like to emphasize something that just came to mind," I shifted. "The way you just thought toward the guy in your kitchen. You communicated with him by thinking what you wanted to say."

"Yes?"

"You can communicate with anyone or anything in any world I know of by using that method. You can ask questions and hear the answers. You can use it anywhere."

Our conversation provided a brief respite from the appearance of ghosts in Helaina's apartment. Just talking had a way of pulling us both back to the physical world. From time to time throughout our conversation, I intentionally broke her nonphysical world connection with a story or remark, pulling us both back to the physical world side of the gaping hole in the Veil.

CHAPTER 23

Jack the Ripper Takes a Seat

Our conversation calmed Helaina down, and I could feel her relaxing and beginning to intentionally focus into the energies in her living room.

"Hang on, Bruce," I clearly heard Coach say in my mind. "Hang on and don't let go of her."

"Oh no," came through my phone in a voice filled with the sound of the willies. "There are people all crowded into my living room."

Then, the telltale sign of freaking out pushes into her voice.

"One just sat down on the sofa next to me. I can feel the cushions next to me moving just like someone is sitting down there."

The fear is suddenly so strong her voice comes in a gasping sound. There's almost no breath behind it. She's so scared that her diaphragm and chest are paralyzed. Without moving air, her voice is made of pure terror.

"It's him . . . it's him . . . It's the one I see in my bathroom mirror . . . the one who lives in my closet . . . He just sat down next to me."

Her body can't wait any longer; if she doesn't breathe soon, she's going to pass out. On automatic pilot, I hear her body suck in a long, deep breath. She holds it as long as she can, and then her voice comes screeching out of the phone at the top of her lungs.

"I can feel it, he's sitting right here. Oh God!" comes screeching out of my phone.

"Helaina! . . . Helaina!"

". . . What!"

"Do you want him to leave?" I ask in a loud, flat, direct voice. I can feel I'm losing her. She's close to running out the door. I know any second now she could be gone. All I have is her first name and phone number. Fear is pushing its way into my awareness.

Shrieking, "Yes, yes, yes!"

"Tell him, 'You're not welcome here; you must leave right now!'" my own voice betraying concern that she's about to throw down the phone and run screaming into the night.

She's not bothering with sending him her thoughts. She's blaring out loud like the air horn of a freight train approaching a crossing. Emotion coupled to desire.

"He's gone . . . and I don't know how I know . . . but he's never coming back." I can feel relief and calm moving back into her voice just as quickly as it left.

"You're right. After a sendoff like that, he'll never be able to come back again. What are you feeling right now?" My question was meant to let her hear that she's fully back with me again.

"Peaceful, I'm feeling peaceful and calm." I can hear it in her voice. "They're all gone now, I don't see any of them here with me right now."

"I'm not surprised."

Happily, I can feel that we've both moved back to the physical world side of the hole in the Veil. I'm relieved just to know we can still do that. I'm hoping that was the worst of whatever we have to face tonight. I'm feeling like the whole thing is almost over.

"I knew you could do it, Bruce," I heard Coach say, "but pay attention. We're just getting started. She had to face her fear and learn she could be in control. She had to be the one to send that Jack the Ripper type out of the situation. She's doing very well. Now we can get on to the real reason she made the connection to the nonphysical world in the first place. Remember? She told you something big was going to happen in her life? She knew she had to prepare, but didn't know how? You just watched her prepare! Now stay on your toes and pay attention."

"It's going to get worse?" I asked Coach, mentally.

"If I had told you what was going to happen, it might have affected your choice to continue."

"I seldom get a straight answer out of you, Coach."

"There's a reason for that," he replied. "We all learn best from our own direct experience. This is your experience, so pay attention. I'm right here if you need me."

CHAPTER 24

The Eye of the Storm

Helaina changed the subject again.

"I can tell what people are really like just by looking into them," she says calmly. "It's something new for me, like a new ability or something."

"Tell me what you mean by that, if you don't mind," I asked.

"Not at all. I can just look at a person, and I know if they're friendly or not. I can tell if it's okay to be around them or if I should stay away. I don't know how I know. I just know. I've tested it out by talking to both kinds of people, and my feeling about them is always right. I can tell if I can trust them or not. Some people, in one look, I know to stay away from them, because they can't be trusted. Other people I know I can trust won't hurt me or use me or lie to me. I can just tell by kind of looking *into* them. Have you ever heard of that before?"

"Yes, I've heard of that; sometimes I'm able to do it. Friends of mine always have that ability turned on and available to them. I suspect it's connected to the opening of your heart chakra that we talked about earlier. When the heart opens, we're connected to everything in a special way. Do you remember when we talked about that?" I asked, wanting a memory reality check by hearing her answer.

"I remember, and I think I get the connection," she said, almost surprised at herself. "That's why I don't like being around my husband. You know, he makes me feel like such a bad, evil person. We went horseback riding just the other day, and Mike's hat blew off. He started yelling and screaming at his horse, kicking and hitting it. He was yelling that the horse was so stupid it didn't know how to do anything right. I turned to him and said, 'Mike, stop hurting your horse; it's not his fault. The reason you think your horse is such a stupid, know-nothing is because of the way you treat him. You blame him for everything that happens to you. Screaming and beating him for everything that happens is confusing him. He doesn't know what you want him to do about things only you have control over.' I don't know where that came from, but it was absolutely dead on. I could tell by the way what I said hit him. It was right to the core! I told him I didn't want to ride with him anymore today, and took off to ride by myself. I wanted to get as far away from him as I could. I rode miles off into the middle of nowhere. Riding back to the stable we crossed paths, and I didn't even look at him. We still see each other sometimes, but afterwards, I always feel so bad, so evil and worthless."

"It's none of my business, but I'm going to say this any-way," responding to a prompt from Coach. "In a sexual rela-tionship between two people, there are energetic connections made between them. These connections provide sort of open channels for feelings, thoughts, emotions, desires, intents, and other things to pass back and forth between them. It's such an open channel that it can be difficult to tell whose feelings are whose. It's easy to get confused into thinking that the other persons' feelings are your own, and start reacting to them is if they were. A simple example would be if your partner were feeling very hungry. Even though you weren't the least bit hungry yourself, because your partner is feeling hungry, you might start eating without even questioning why you're doing it. I've learned to be careful about who I'm willing to join with sexually for this reason. It can get really confusing, and, with the wrong person, it can become quite tiresome to have to constantly question whose feelings I'm having. Sometimes it can lead to real trouble when the feelings that pass between you are more complex and hurtful than a simple thing like feeling hungry. Is this making any sense to you?"

"Yes, it is!" she said, with feeling like a light bulb had just turned on for her, "Yes it is! There's another man in the room with me now," she says, her voice rising just a little.

"What does he want?" I ask, casually.

"I can't see them all, but I know there are a lot of men in

my living room. They all want to talk to me. They all want to tell me something, just like the one I can see. He wants to tell me something, but I can't quite get what it is. He has some problem he wants to tell me about. I don't know how to help him with his problem."

"Do you want him to leave?"

"He might as well leave; I can't help him," she says, more exasperation than fear in her voice. "I thought to him that he should leave and he's gone now."

"Very good, Helaina, you're handling this very well," I say with a genuine sense of praise. "You're in control of the situation, and you're doing great."

"Why are all these men here? Why do they all want to talk to me?" she asks, curious once again.

I wish now, writing this, I had thought to have her single out one of the men and listen to what he had to say. Maybe Coach was asking me to do that and I didn't feel him say it, or maybe I'm just Monday-morning quarterbacking. I don't know. For some reason, the thought of asking her to do this didn't come to mind. Looking back, it might have opened a part of this experience for Helaina with answers to questions she'll have to find some day. My mind was more on the fact that I had only a phone connection with her. If she freaked out and ran away, I'd have no way to find her. I didn't want to be reading about her in tomorrow's newspaper.

"One possibility is that these men recognize that you can see them," I conjectured. "They might have questions to ask or things to say, and you're maybe the first living human they've come across who can see them. Did you see the movie *Ghost*?"

"Yes, I did."

I could feel her anxiety about where my question might lead.

"Remember that the Whoopi Goldberg character was a fake medium until after the Patrick Swayze character contacted her?"

"Yes, I remember that."

"He had a message he wanted to get back to his girlfriend, and Whoopi was the only person he could contact to get the message through to her. Once Whoopi was able to communicate with him, she was able to communicate with lots of others. They flocked to her seance room because they knew she could hear them. She could relay messages back into the physical world for them. That is what attracted them to her room. You opened your perception to the world of ghosts when you saw the big face of the ghost at your bedroom door. It's kind of like Whoopi after she heard Patrick Swayze. One possible reason that all these men are in your living room is just that they know you can hear them, and they have something to say. These men are just ordinary people like you and me, except they don't live in physical bodies anymore. So, they can't communicate with anyone here unless the person has the ability to see or hear them. They're no threat to you. They're just ordinary people with something to say. Does that make sense to you?"

"Yes, I understand what you're telling me. I'm still afraid about it, but I understand it."

After two more men appeared and were dispatched using direct thought communication, the next one shows up standing in a corner of her living room. There's almost no fear in her voice. She's still scared, but the element of shock is gone as she tells me he is there.

"What's the man in the corner doing?" I can feel a welcome shift in Helaina as she takes in the question.

"He wants to talk to me. He's trying to tell me something. I don't want to talk to him; I don't like the way he's looking at me."

"Do you want him to leave?" I asked, in an almost conversational tone.

"I don't know. He really wants to say something to me. He's got a problem, too, a big problem. No, I can't help him with his problem; yeah, he can leave. I told him to go and now he's gone."

CHAPTER 25

Who's that Poltergeist in the Bathroom?

"What are you feeling right now?"

"I'm feeling peaceful and calm again. I don't feel afraid at all."

"Helaina, you're really doing great! You're handling this really well." No sooner do the words leave my mouth than I feel her fear zipping back up toward the top of the charts again.

"There's one in the bathroom," she yells out, "He's standing behind the door!"

"What is he doing?" I ask, in a pattern that's developed in our conversation that seems to cushion her shock.

"I'm afraid to look, but I have to. He's peeking at me from behind the door," speaking a little more calmly. Then she's shrieking, screaming into the phone, "He just opened the door; the bathroom door just opened all by itself." We're quickly back to the edge of Helaina running away, screaming, into the night.

"No, Helaina, you opened the door! A physical body is needed for that!" I'm surprised at the low volume, calm flatness in my voice, "You opened the door, not him."

There's a pause that lasts about ten seconds. I can feel Helaina taking in what I said and rolling it over in her mind.

"You're right!" she remembered out loud. "Just after I saw him behind the door, I wanted it open more so I could see him better! You're right! I opened the door farther to see him better. I did it with my thoughts! It felt the same as sending my thoughts to these men. I was feeling scared. I was feeling desire to open the door. I opened the door with my thoughts!"

"Sounds like now you know the truth about poltergeists," I suggested.

Thank you Coach or whoever said that through me, thank you; I thought after all we'd been through we were going to lose her.

"He's gone now, I sent him away. He was like the others; he wanted me to help him with his problem. I can't help him with that problem! And I don't really see them with my physical eyes, I know they are there, where I'm looking, but I don't really see them. Do you know what I mean?"

"Yes, I know exactly what you mean. Some people might say they see them in their mind's eye. Sometimes their image overlays the world you see with your physical eyes. We'll just have to call it *seeing them* for now, but I know exactly what you mean."

"Now there's another one, he's over by the front door." This time her voice doesn't register any shock. She's still frightened, but she's staying with me.

"What does he want?"

"Just like the rest, he wants to talk. He's Amish, all the men here are Amish. They all lived in the same town, and they all died there a long time ago. I don't mean they all died at the same time, just that they all lived and died in the same town a long time ago. They're all very old. They're all dressed in kind of formal black suits, and they're wearing big black hats. I don't know how I know this, I only know it's true and I just know it somehow. How can that be?"

"Communication that comes through the heart doesn't need words. It doesn't have to be verbal to be real. It's kind of like when you know about a person by looking into them. I don't know how to explain it, except to say that it's a way of knowing that comes directly, all at once. It doesn't necessarily come to you through your head, more than likely it comes to you somewhere else, and you just know. And it doesn't have to come like thoughts, one little bit at a time. It can come all at once, suddenly you just know it, all at once."

"Everyone here in my living room, they're all men; there aren't any woman here, only Amish men. I just know that, too."

"I understand what you're telling me. There are only Amish men in your living room, no women." I repeat back to her calmly, just verifying her report.

"Somehow . . . I'm getting . . . I don't know where this is coming from . . . I'm feeling someone tell me to send them to the light. That sounds silly to me, but that's what I'm getting from somewhere."

I'm feeling that Helaina's finally in touch with whoever it is that's choreographing this whole experience. It feels like we're taking a new turn.

"Good. Helaina, remember when we talked before about extending your love from the center of your chest? Can you feel what I mean by that?"

"Yes, I can feel what you mean."

"Good, when you say to the man in the corner what I'd like you to say, say it through the feeling you have in the center of your chest. Not from your head. Do you understand what I mean by that?"

"Kinda . . . yeah . . . I get it. It's like thinking it in my head, but I kinda feel it in my chest instead of my head." I can tell she's got the concept more by her acknowledging tone of voice than her by her words.

"Look at where you feel the man is standing by the door. Extend your love outward from the center of your chest as you say, 'Look for a light.' "

I hear her say it out loud and wonder who asked her to do that.

"Now, say, 'When you see a light, go to it.'" I hear her say it out loud and wonder again. "What's he doing now?"

"He's standing there, looking all around in the air with a puzzled look on his face. Now he's looking at something . . . he's smiling . . . he just disappeared." She reports this calmly, a little surprised perhaps, but she says it like this stuff happens all the time.

"What are you feeling right now, Helaina?" I ask again, checking in on and letting her feel her own state of mind.

"Very calm, very . . . peaceful; I'm not feeling any fear at all right now. This is great, I'm feeling so strong." She replies in a soft, flowing voice that bespeaks strength.

"Bruce," Coach cuts in to chat for a moment. "For the rest of this experience, it's best if it ends only after Helaina feels complete with it. Don't try to cut it off or stop it unless something really weird happens and you feel like you are going to lose her."

Silly me, I thought we were almost there.

CHAPTER 26

Another Clock Alarm?

KA . . . BOOOOM. Without any warning, another bomb goes off. We're both caught completely by surprise. Helaina's trying to talk while she's still inhaling. She's so excited that her first words are formed from sucking sounds deep in her throat. I can't understand a word she's saying until, finally, she starts to exhale. Then, she's loud, and on the edge of her seat.

"There's light! There's light! It's coming out of a picture on the wall in my bedroom; it's lighting up my entire bedroom. Oh God, what's happening?"

"What color is the light?" I ask, calmly.

"What?"

"What color is the light in your bedroom?" This is all happening very fast. I ask, and she answers with almost no space between our words.

"It's white, real bright white, and it's got some yellow, bright, clear yellow in it, too," calming down only a little as she speaks. "It's kinda glowing in a cloud or a fog close to the picture, it's brightest there, close to the picture."

"Where in your bedroom is the picture, Helaina?"

"At the foot of my bed. When I'm lying down in my bed, I can see it from there. It's on the wall at the foot of my bed! It's the same picture where I was freaked out this morning."

"How does it feel, how does the light feel to you?"

"How does it feel?" she questions.

Now there's a silence on the phone. I can feel she's extending something out from the center of her chest. Then, cautiously, she's touching the light. I can feel when she makes a solid connection. She doesn't say a word for at least fifteen seconds.

"That's the most powerfully loving thing I've ever felt in my life."

Her voice is flowing out slowly and smoothly, like warm, sweet honey. Then it registers mild alarm.

"I can see Amish men in my living room again. Some of them are turning toward the hall. I think they can see the light, too. One of them is moving toward it. He's in front of the picture . . . he's looking into the light." With a startled sound, "Oh . . . my . . . God! The light just sucked him into the picture! That was so . . . so . . . weird! It just sucked him into the picture on the wall. This is so weird! Marilyn Monroe, Bogart, and some other people are on that picture. There's nothing special about it. I bought it at the mall. He was just sucked right up into the picture. A few more of the men are moving toward the light. I'm standing up so I can see better. I really want to go in and look at the light myself, but I'm afraid I'll get sucked up by it, too."

"Helaina, the light is not a threat to you! You are completely safe! Are you on a portable phone?" I'm not sure what to do about her going into the bedroom, but I'm checking our options.

"No, my portable is in the bedroom where the light is, but I'm too afraid to go in and get it."

"That's okay, do you feel comfortable watching from where you are?"

"EEE . . . AH . . . ICK," comes blasting out of my phone with a strong feeling of total disgust. It's so loud my ear hurts. "Stop that! Don't do that!"

"What's happening, Helaina?" This time I'm startled.

"One of them just walked through me; one of the men! He just walked right through me! How disgusting . . . how rude!" Her voice carries more anger than fear.

"EEE . . . AH . . . UCK," stop that, another one walked through me!" This time there's a firm tone of command in her voice. "They have no regard for me at all; they're so entranced by the light, they don't even see me. They just walked right through me; how rude."

"Do you want them to stop walking through you?" I ask, not sure if I need to grab on and pull her back.

"Yes! They have no consideration for me at all! That's really rude!"

"Broadcast outward all around you the message that you are here. Let them know where you are and tell them to see you and walk around." It's the only thing I can think of to say.

"Okay, now they're walking around me. Really, these people have no manners at all!"

I almost burst out laughing at her comment. She was no longer afraid of these ghosts. They were just people to her, and very rude, inconsiderate people at that.

"There are a few more of them walking toward the picture; they get there and look into the light, and then they're sucked up into it. WOW, the colors are changing, streamers of light are shooting out of the picture and into my bedroom!"

"What colors do you see?" I ask, curious myself.

"Red. Red streamers and a fog of bright, clear, blue close to the picture. EEE . . . AH . . . UCK, another one just walked through me. Stop that!"

"You can tell them to walk around again. Maybe that guy just wasn't paying attention before."

"Oh yeah, I forgot to do that," she said it like she was reminding herself. "Where is the light taking them, where do they go? I know they are not going to be punished; it's more like they're returning to God. They were stuck, somehow, and now they got loose, somehow, and they're going back to God. The light is so forgiving, so loving; it's the light of mercy. It doesn't matter what they've done up until now, evil or not, they're forgiven."

"As far as I know, you're right. They won't be punished for anything they've done."

"Where is the light taking them; do you know?"

"In my understanding, they are going to a place I call the Park or the Reception Center."

"What's that place like? What happens to them when they get there? I know they aren't going to be punished." I could feel a sense of relief in her voice.

"I've been to the Park many times. Loved ones, friends, or relatives are usually there to meet the people as they arrive. It's a place to recover from the shock of leaving the physical world. There are lots of people I call Helpers who live and work at the Park. Helpers are people who have lived there long enough to know their way around and have volunteered to assist new arrivals. Sometimes Helpers set up special facilities for new arrivals to make their transition easier."

"What kind of special facilities would they set up?" a sincere curiosity in her voice.

"Well, once I brought a doctor there who had died awhile back. We landed in a doctor's office. We were in the receptionist's area, although she wasn't at her desk when we arrived. There were chairs in a waiting room area and magazines on little end tables for patients to read while they waited. There weren't any patients waiting anywhere, and we could see into the examining rooms. Everything looked and felt just like a doctor's office. Pretty soon two Helpers walked into the waiting room and introduced themselves to the doctor I'd brought there. They were dressed like doctors and acted as though that's what they were. The surroundings of this special facility were so familiar to the doctor that he felt right at home. He just joined right in talking to these two Helpers. The Helpers knew that if they could engage the new arrival in conversation, in the familiar, comfortable surroundings of a doctor's office, they would be able to stabilize him and he wouldn't wander off and get himself stuck again. The Park, or the Reception Center, can be altered to look and feel like whatever would be most appropriate for any new arrival. From what I can tell, this is done to help them adjust to the fact they are no longer alive on earth. Does that answer your question fully enough?"

"Yes, that helps. What do you think will happen to these Amish men when they get to the Park?"

"My guess is that they will be reunited with friends and loved ones and welcomed with loving, open arms. What are you feeling right now, Helaina?"

"I'm feeling incredibly peaceful and calm. The light is gone from the picture, and I can't see any of the men in my living room right now."

"Very good, you're really handling this well."

I was happy my little story had brought her back to this

side of the Veil. She moved easily and I felt confident she was going to make it through all this in great shape.

"Bruce," I heard Coach say in my mind, "we're moving to a new phase. Don't interfere with or stop Helaina's experience for any reason from now on."

"Even if I think I'm going to lose her?" I thought out to Coach.

"Even then. She's got to do this on her own, no matter what happens. You've taken her as far as you can. Stay with her, help where you can, but she has to go on until she feels complete with this, no matter how it turns out."

CHAPTER 27

Helaina's Something Big

"WOW, a really big one, another Amish man. This one is powerful, a leader. He's walking past, right in front of me. He's stopping in front of me. He's saying something to me, but I can't make it out. He's so big, and I can feel all this powerful confidence coming from him. Now, he's finished and walking on past, right in front of me. He's going down the hall. He's stopping in front of the picture. He's looking into the light. It's sucking him in . . . he's gone. Now everyone in my living room . . . they're all moving toward the light, and as each one gets there, he looks at it, and it sucks him in. MY . . . GOD . . . WHERE . . . ARE . . . ALL . . . THESE . . . PEOPLE . . . COMING . . . FROM? I had no idea there were so many dead people just waiting around, waiting for someone to show them the way back. I thought after my living room emptied out that would be it, but they're coming in from . . . from . . . I don't know where they're coming from, but there are so many of them. They all just head for the light, look into it and then they're gone, so . . . many . . . people. It's hard to believe there can be so many. There are little balls of light now, kinda flying and flitting around where the light is coming out of the picture. They're bright little balls of light."

"Sounds like there are more Helpers coming through the Light to assist these Amish guys. I've seen the little balls of light before; they're Helpers coming to our side to help with all the traffic. I'm not sure where all the people are coming from either, but I've seen similar things before. Once a pathway opens up and the Light can get through it to shine out into the darkness, the dead people from within that darkness can see it. I think some are just attracted to the bright light like moths. Others can feel the love, forgiveness, and mercy in the Light that you yourself could feel, and they are attracted to that."

I was barely conscious of the similarities between what was happening on Helaina's bedroom wall and my Lifelines explorer group experience at the earthquake in India. Only now, as I'm writing this, do the parallels stand out. I also hadn't made the connection to Helaina's dream and the light behind the door. She'd been paralyzed, looking at a light coming from behind the door at the foot of her bed. That's where the picture with the light was, on the wall at the foot of her bed where she'd had the dream the previous night.

Listening to Helaina's description over the phone, it sounded like a herd of thousands was passing through her living room on the way to the Light. I didn't ask for a count as they went through; it didn't seem important. I was beginning to feel that Helaina was approaching a point of completion with her experience.

"Coach, it feels like she's just about completed this."

"Yes, you can help her start grounding any time now."

"How?"

"Check her refrigerator," Coach suggested.

"Helaina, do you have any solid food in your refrigerator?"

"Well, let me think. I've got some lettuce, some milk, and some hot dogs. I haven't been to the grocery store for a couple of weeks; I really need to do that soon."

"Good, I think the hot dogs will do just fine. I'd like you to go the fridge, get the hot dogs, and eat them." I could tell my request had taken her by surprise, a sudden shift calculated to start the grounding process.

"How many should I eat?"

"How many have you got?"

"Oh, okay, can you hang on a minute?"

As I had mentioned to her earlier, lack of food tends to thin the boundaries between the physical and nonphysical worlds. She had eaten very little today, and that was part of the reason all this had the opportunity to occur. Eating anything at this point would have the effect of closing down a portion of Helaina's perception to the nonphysical. With all the chemicals and crud in hot dogs, the fact that they were in her fridge was a blessing. Much of her awareness would have to be focused on that junk to digest it. I can't think of anything else that has such a great potential for a fast, physical response. As she returned and picked up the phone, I could hear soft chewing sounds.

"Why did you ask me to eat hot dogs? I don't even like hot dogs!"

"It will help with something that's called 'grounding.' Eating solid food causes some of your awareness to be focused inward on eating and digesting. This leaves less awareness to focus outward into the nonphysical world. It will keep you here."

"How many do I have to eat?"

"How many can you stand to eat?"

"Maybe three."

"That will be fine. Three hot dogs will take care of it."

In what seemed like moments, Helaina had eaten her quota.

"You know, I think I don't need to do this any more right now," Helaina said. "I feel like this has been enough for one night."

I remember thinking, *I thought I'd heard understatement before; enough for one night—lady this has been enough to last me for years.*

"What are you feeling right now?" asking, but knowing what I'd hear.

"It's hard to believe. I'm feeling an incredible sense of peace. So calm, so completely without fear . . . serene. My memory of the experience is fading, kinda like a dream does after you wake up. It seems so far away."

"Helaina, I'm so happy to hear you're feeling peaceful, calm, and in control. You've really handled this extremely well. You're really doing great!"

"Bruce, do you teach classes in this stuff?" Helaina asked, out of the blue. "I'd give anything to be able to take classes and learn more about this metaphysical stuff."

"Well, I don't teach classes. I'm an engineer and have a day job. I could recommend some books that might be helpful."

"Oh, I thought you were a teacher in this stuff," she said; then she shifted gears again.

"I don't feel like a hero or anything like that," Helaina volunteered. "All those people needed to find their way back to God, and I just helped them do that. That doesn't make me a hero. I think it's what we should all be doing for them. Bruce, have you ever come across anyone else like me? I mean, have there been others like me that you've seen or talked to?" she asked, wondering if she was one of a kind.

"I've worked with a lot of people who have experienced the sort of thing you have. Not quite to this degree, I mean not so much all at once. Most people I've worked with have taken smaller steps at a time instead of one big, giant step."

"Did it happen to you this way?"

"No, I moved much more slowly, in very small steps. I'm the kind of person who could only let myself embrace a little at a time. I had lots of conflicting beliefs and ideas about how things were supposed to happen, and I got in my own way a lot. I had some wonderfully patient teachers who helped me learn at my own, slower pace."

"Maybe now that this has happened, I should stop working as a dancer. That's what I do for a living, you know; I'm a stripper. I work three nights a week. Maybe it's not right to keep stripping after this."

When she said, "I'm a stripper," a bunch of things suddenly fell into place for me. It explained some of the erotic images drifting through my mind since our first phone conversation earlier in the afternoon.

"I'm an engineer, you're a stripper; I don't see a whole lot of difference between the two. We're both paid by somebody to do something they want done while we'd rather be doing something else. We both have to earn a living to pay our bills and live our lives. Whatever you do in your future is certainly fine with me. Whether you decide to change jobs or not is entirely up to you and how you feel about it."

"Would it be all right for me to meet you? Would that be okay with you?" she asked.

I could feel the desire for verification in her voice. She was sure, before our phone conversation, that all these strange things that were happening in her life were just made up in her own mind. She wanted to make sure that our phone conversation wasn't made up, too.

"Sure, Helaina, I'd be happy to meet with you whenever we can arrange it."

"Could we meet tomorrow?"

"That would be fine with me. You have my pager number; page me anytime during the day and we can work out a time and place."

"Okay, thanks, I'll page you tomorrow." I could feel a sense of relief and excitement in her voice. "You know, when they were walking through me, it didn't really feel that bad. It felt like a cool breeze passing through my body, that's all, just cool air passing through me."

"That makes perfect sense to me. You were focused quite strongly in your nonphysical body. Since the men are non-physical too, you could feel them. Lots of people describe them as feeling cold or cool."

"It was just so rude of them; they gave me no consideration whatsoever. They treated me like I wasn't even there, that's what bugged me. Can I ask you another question?" she asked.

"Sure."

"Could the ghosts in my apartment see me? I mean, could they watch me in the shower if they wanted to?"

"As far as I know, they can pretty much see anywhere into the physical world that they can focus their attention."

"They can see me?" she asked, a sense of upset in her voice.

"I've come to understand that privacy, even of our thoughts, is a myth," I replied. I could tell this worried her.

" How do you live with that Bruce?"

"I just accept that it's true; that's the way it is. If they want to look at me in my most private moments, so what. That's how I live with it; just accept it."

"Oh, okay, I'll call you tomorrow. Are you sure it's okay for me to meet you?"

"Yes, it's okay, I look forward to hearing from you; get some rest tonight."

"Yeah, okay, bye."

"Bye."

As I pressed the button on my portable phone to hang up, I could feel myself coming back to my surroundings. I realized

Pharon had been making trips into the kitchen, and she had dinner ready. I remember feeling so glad she was there, so grateful. She'd been careful to allow me the space to deal with the ups and downs and sideways of my conversation with Helaina. For Helaina, it had started out near frantic hysteria, moved close to blind panic a few times, and resolved itself in a tranquil, peaceful calm. She'd hung in there and learned that she could be in control.

"Coach, I'm sure glad that's over. Thank you and everybody else who helped."

"You're welcome, Bruce. Everybody here says you did very well."

I looked over at the clock on my VCR, it said 9:29 P.M. We'd been on the phone for three and a half hours. The winds died down. The waves subsided. I'd made it through the hurricane, alone.

CHAPTER 28

Dinner Conversation

Helaina wasn't the only one who needed some food to help come back to earth. I hadn't eaten since noon and that probably made the whole experience easier for me too. I joined Pharon in the kitchen, babbling on about details of what had just happened.

As part of my heart chakra opening, I understand that emotional energies must be expressed, not blocked. In my relationship with Pharon, I've found a loving and safe place to give expression to my feelings instead of blocking them, holding them inside, and letting them build up. While I babbled on, I felt several huge releases of energy.

When I mentioned I'd told Helaina it would be all right to meet with me, I felt a twinge of something flash through Pharon. I could feel myself withholding my feelings about Helaina being a twenty-four-year-old stripper. Something about it felt threatening. I needed a little time to come to terms with whatever those feelings were. After we'd eaten dinner, I asked Pharon how she felt about my spending so much time on the phone with Helaina. She has an interest in the Lifelines activities that I do, and, lacking her own direct experience, maintains a healthy bit of skepticism.

"Well, when we were talking in the kitchen, I felt a little twinge of fear. I mean, you were talking to a woman who shares similar experiences to your own, and I was feeling a little threatened. It only lasted for a moment or two and then it passed."

Rounding up all my courage, I decided to face whatever it was that felt threatening to me. It felt physically like when something gets stuck in your throat, except it was in my heart.

"Yeah, I feel some fear, too, and I'm not sure exactly what it's about. It feels threatening, like I should hide whatever it is, but it's stuck in my heart, and I've got to get it out. When I was checking in on Helaina, I watched her dancing. It was very sensual, seductive dancing. Talking to her on the phone, I found out she's a stripper, so what I saw made more sense to me. It was really hard for me to get that out, hard for me to tell you she's a stripper and that I could feel the seductive side of that."

As I said that, I immediately felt the sources of my fear. I was afraid sharing my real feelings with Pharon would threaten our relationship. I got a sudden blast of memories of withholding such feelings in past relationships, and all the stupid rationalizations I'd used to do so. It had just been so hard in the past to admit having feelings I was sure I shouldn't be having. As memories flooded in, I saw the result of holding those feelings secret, sometimes for years. They always built up until they crowded out other feelings I had within those relationships. Eventually there wasn't any room left in my heart to hold anything but old, unexpressed feelings. That always damaged those relationships. My fear of having the relationship threatened by expressing what I was feeling is what always ended up causing the real damage.

Not this time, I could feel myself thinking, *this time I'm going to accept what I feel and express it right now. I'm not going to hold on to something that I'll have to actively hide forever! This time it's coming out right now.*

As quickly as I made that decision, I could feel all the fear leave me and dissipate. The lump in my heart was gone. I felt clean and clear.

"I was afraid to tell you about what I was feeling toward Helaina. I've always hidden those sensual, attractive feelings away, afraid they would threaten my relationship. Maybe you could come along with me when I meet her tomorrow. I don't want anything to threaten our relationship."

"No, that's not necessary, I know everything will be okay," Pharon replied.

I shared with her how freeing it felt to be expressing the feelings running through me and how much I appreciated the love we share. In this brief exchange between us, fear of feelings I'd carried for years completely washed away. A wonderful lesson in what it means to open your heart and keep it open was my gift from that exchange. WOW!

After we ate dinner, I suddenly remembered I'd need to be drinking lots of extra water for a few days. There's a cleansing, renewing, growing process that often accompanies experiences like what transpired that night. From Coach, I got that I should call and suggest to Helaina that she do the same. I picked up the phone and hit the redial button.

"Hello," I heard a sleepy-voiced Helaina say.

"Helaina, this is Bruce again. Sorry to bother you, but I wanted to suggest that you drink extra water for the next several days."

"Why should I do that?"

"With all that you've been through tonight, you might think of drinking extra water as washing out the old and watering the seeds of the new," came out of my mouth completely unplanned.

"Okay. I've been lying here in bed thinking back over all that happened tonight. Trying to let something settle in and make it all fit together. My memory of a lot of it is slowly fading out. It's like remembering a dream."

"What you're doing sounds like an excellent idea. Letting the experience integrate into your awareness and memory is a very good thing to be doing. Well, I just wanted to pass along the message to drink lots of extra water for the next several days. Get as much rest as you can and I'll see you soon."

"Okay, good night," she said, spoken through a yawn.

"Good night, Helaina."

Pharon and I sat and gabbed for a little while longer, and then tiredness began to overtake me. It was 10:30 P.M. and I definitely needed to rest. I did a short set of Tai Chi, took my own advice and drank a giant glass of water, brushed my teeth, and crashed.

CHAPTER 29

Dream a Little Dream with Me

An hour or so after falling asleep, the giant glass of water before bedtime began beckoning me to the bathroom. I slowly drifted awake, so gently I barely left the dream I was involved in. As I slid out of bed, and went through the motions, I was still half in the dream. Returning to bed, I idly began remembering it. I found I could follow every detail all the way back to when I first fell asleep.

When the dream started, I'd found myself sitting in a full-size pickup truck parked next to the curb on a city street. I was sitting on the driver's side of a big, comfortable, bench-style seat, my hands resting easily on the steering wheel. It was a very dark night, and I was staring out the driver's side window at a young couple standing across the street at the corner. They were under a light post, which made their argument easy for anyone to see who cared to look.

He was doing most of the shouting, shaking his finger in her face as he did. She was just standing there with her head bent down taking his abuse. He stood there berating and humiliating her for a very long time. Then, the woman suddenly broke free of him. Turning away from his tirade, she bolted toward the pickup I was sitting in.

She must not have realized, at first, that I was sitting in the truck. She tore open the driver's-side door and climbed up behind the steering wheel as if I weren't there. After struggling for a few moments to get into position to drive away, she realized something was wrong and slid over to the passenger's side. Puzzled about what was going on, she looked directly at where I was sitting trying to figure it out. A look of surprise swept over her face as I materialized into her view.

We started to talk; or rather I began listening to what the woman had to say. She was a young, dark haired beauty. She told me the man had been saying mean, evil things to her. He'd scared her and made her feel very bad. In the dream, we continued talking from the time she climbed into the cab until I started drifting awake. It's no excuse, I know, but I was only half awake even after I'd finished in the bathroom and drank another big glass of water. It never dawned on me who the woman was. Moments after I laid back down in bed, I was asleep and dreaming again.

By the clock on my nightstand, it was an hour later when I slowly drifted awake again. I was still dreaming. Before I got out of bed to empty the last glass of water, I made a point of recalling the dream as far back as I could remember. I followed every detail of the dream's sequence of events to the point I had previously awakened, and then back to its start, with me sitting in the truck. All the way back to my watching the young couple arguing under the street light. It had been one, continuous dream interrupted only by my first giant glass of water.

After I'd awakened that first time and gone back to bed, I was back in the truck again. I kept an eye on the man across the street, but he never moved in my direction. At some point I started the truck and drove away. The woman continued talking as we drove down a long, narrow road in the dark. She kept telling me about all that had happened to her and asking me questions. I answered her questions and listened to her story and kept driving through the night.

She talked about being hungry, and suggested we stop at a little place she knew. We pulled in around back and parked the truck in an unlit lot behind the building. It was okay to go in the back way, she said; the owner was a friend of hers. We sat down at a table and gave the waiter our orders after looking over the menus. The place felt like a neighborhood tavern filled with regulars. A warm and friendly atmosphere. No sooner had those thoughts passed through my mind than the woman spotted a guy she said was trouble. He looked nice enough to me, though he was leering in her direction. Why not? She was a gorgeous young woman. At her insistence, we got up from the table and made our way toward the door before our food arrived. She admonished me to move cautiously and try not to attract attention. We just made it to the door before a huge brawl erupted behind us. The muffled sounds of men's angry voices, crashing furniture, and breaking glass chased us out of the building. I thought she'd made a very poor choice of places to stop and eat. It was strange, the place felt so deceptively friendly when we first walked in. It seemed like a nice joint. Then, suddenly, its true colors had shown after we sat down to eat. We ran to the truck, jumped in, and sped away, barely escaping the angry, pursuing mob. We continued on our way, driving down a dark, paved road and talking about what had just happened and why.

"You just can't trust people," the woman said; "they want you to think they're nice and then they turn on you. The ones who appear to be the nicest will deceive you the most."

When I climbed back into bed, I was remembering the dream forward again and had just gotten to where it left off. Relaxing into the warmth of my waterbed, I drifted off to sleep again.

Pharon hadn't been feeling well earlier in the day. When she got up to take some aspirin an hour after I rejoined the dream, I woke up too. Half asleep, I began recalling the dream. I remembered it all the way back to first being in the pickup truck and both interruptions for trips to the bathroom. I'd just dreamt another segment of the same dream!

After we escaped the mob at the tavern, I drove until daylight. We stopped in the middle of an isolated, small town in the country. We left the truck parked at the curb near some small storefront buildings. Jaywalking across the street, we headed toward the edge of town.

Up ahead was a bridge that spanned a small river and had sidewalks on both sides of the roadway. From the left side of the bridge, we couldn't see much of the river, so we decided to cross the road for the view from the other sidewalk. Three old people, ancient really, were standing on the sidewalk across the road. They were Asian, kindly old folks, and the years had left them bent and feeble. The oldest of the three carefully stepped off the curb, assisted by the other two. They shuffled across the road together, one on either side of the oldest, holding each other's arms for support. The woman and I stood on the sidewalk waiting, each of us thinking perhaps the old folks would need help when they reached our side of the road.

It still didn't occur to me during the dream who the woman was. The old folks smiled appreciatively as they approached where we were standing, waiting to help them. They shuffled toward us slowly with eager anticipation. Just as we were about to reach out to help them, a big, yellow taxicab roared up in reverse and stopped in front of us. He almost ran over the old folks. As we were trying to help them up onto the sidewalk, they suddenly sprang to life. One quickly opened the rear passenger-side door of the cab as the other two pushed us into the back seat. They all jumped in, slamming the doors shut as the cabby turned, looking at the woman and me.

Through the space between his cigar-clenched teeth, the cabby laughed and said, "We're taking you guys for a ride."

He stomped on the gas, and we sped away from the curb, through town, over some railroad tracks, past grain elevators and out into the country. He turned down a driveway and brought the cab to a stop in front of a big shed. The cabby and young toughs we'd taken for old folks hustled us through a door and into a small room. These four had pulled this scam before, luring unsuspecting good Samaritans into a situation in which they could be robbed. This time, the cabby decided to doublecross his cohorts, so we all stood in line, side by side, waiting for him to rob us at knifepoint. He robbed the first two and then started in on the woman traveling with me where she stood at my right. The oldest looking robber, standing on my left, had decided a triple-cross was in order. From somewhere, he produced a strange looking knife with a blade at least a foot and a half long. I'm not sure how he managed it; dreams have their way of making the ridiculous seem reasonable, but he hid the big knife under a normal size billfold in his outstretched hands. When it was his turn to be robbed, he planned to take everyone's money, including the cabby's, and make his getaway. When it was my turn with the cabby, I almost burst out laughing knowing what the old guy next to me was planning. I pulled out my wallet and opened it, expecting to see a thick stash of bills. It was empty.

Hmmm, that's funny, I thought to myself, *I remember filling this up just yesterday before Pharon and I went out to the movie. Oh yeah, I stuffed the wad of bills in my pants pocket when I left the ATM.*

I reached in, pulled out the stash, and handed it over to the knife-wielding cabby. When he moved over to rob the old guy on my left, I turned to the woman I was traveling with, who was shaking with fear.

"Come on, it's time for us to leave," I said quietly.

In the ensuing confusion of the old guy robbing the cabby, we hit the door running and escaped disaster again. By the time Pharon had come back to bed and gone to back to sleep, I was picking up the dream where it left off. We'd run back into town, found our way to the truck, jumped in, and sped off to escape.

This pattern of waking up every hour and remembering the dream back to its beginning continued all night. The patterns within the dream remained the same also. In every situation, we'd meet people who seemed very nice, some of whom asked for our help. Each time the dream situation would demonstrate that you can't trust anybody, no matter who they appear to be. They'll take advantage of you at the first opportunity. You just can't trust anybody! I'm sorry to say, never once did I realize it was Helaina I was traveling with in the dream. I kicked myself for that.

The last time I woke up and remembered the dream from end to beginning and beginning to end, the clock on my nightstand said 5:30 A.M. It had been a long night without much rest, and I really wanted to go back to sleep. Coach had other ideas.

"Oh . . . no . . . you . . . don't," I felt him say, "you're going to get up right now!"

"Ah come on, Coach, I really need the rest, just let me go back to sleep for a little while."

"Nothing doing! I strongly suggest you get up right now, go to the kitchen table, sit down, and start writing everything you can remember," he said, with an unfamiliar firmness in the feel of his voice.

"Come on, Coach, have a heart! Let me get some sleep."

"Get up now!"

"Oh . . . all . . . right, you probably wouldn't let me get back to sleep now anyhow."

"Count on it," Coach replied, like a drill sergeant hassling a green private.

I really can't remember when he's ever felt so invasively persistent in the past. I was sleepy enough that it was probably necessary.

"Can I go to the bathroom first?"

"Only if you continue to remember your way back and forth through the dream the whole time you're in there! Don't dawdle! And whatever you do, do not start reading anything while you're sitting in there."

"Okay . . . okay, I'm getting up. See, I'm getting up," as I rolled toward the edge of the bed. "Really, I've never seen you this way before, Coach; you're being rude and incredibly bossy."

"Insistent better describes my intent," he returned gruffly. "I might even go so far as to say very insistent if that makes you feel any better."

Something about arguing semantics with Coach suddenly struck me as funny. In the next instant, we both burst out laughing like a couple of kids. Of course, Pharon woke up hearing only my side of the laughter.

"What's so funny this early in the morning?" her sleepy voice asked.

That only made matters worse, and I had to let my hysterical laughter subside before I could answer her question.

"Coach was trying to be very stern about something, and he just blew it. It just struck me as funny, that's all. I've been dreaming all night and I really need to get all this written down."

Boy, I remember thinking to myself, *that kind of talk, spoken to the wrong people, could leave them wondering about my sanity*.

I spent the next five and a half hours filling twenty-eight pages in my journal with notes from the dream and the phone call to Helaina. As I wrote about the dream sequence, I felt strong sadness at not having realized it was Helaina I'd been traveling with. If I had, maybe I could have shown her how to extend her love toward the villains in the dream. Maybe some of them would have disappeared, or we'd have seen who they really were. I blew it, and I didn't feel good about that.

I called my boss, already late for work, at 8:00 A.M., and left a voice mail saying something had happened last night, and I had to process my way through it. A little cryptic, perhaps, but I wasn't sure exactly how much to tell him. Fortunately he's in my men's group that meets every week on Sunday night. I've talked in that group about some of my experiences, so it wouldn't come as a complete shock to him. At a little after 11:00 A.M., I called again, this time he answered the phone in person.

"Everything all right?" he asked.

"Yeah, I'm fine. I'm okay. I'm not sure exactly what to tell you, so I guess I'll go with the truth. I got a call yesterday from a woman with a ghost problem at her apartment. It turned out to be quite an ordeal, and I need to write it all down to work my way through all that happened."

There was a very . . . long . . . silent . . . space in our conversation.

"I know that must sound a little weird to you, but that's what happened. It's already so late in the day I probably won't be in until tomorrow morning."

"Well," he offered, "I used to get calls at three in the morning from people who needed to talk. I was a sponsor in a program, and it made me feel like I was helping out to do it. I guess I outgrew the need for that kind of thing in my life over the years, and I don't do it anymore."

Bless my boss for his willingness to accept that there was something in my life he might not understand completely. I know it made him uncomfortable to have this conversation, but he hung in there with me, trying to relate to it in the best way he could.

"I'll tell anybody who asks that you just needed the day off for personal reasons," he said, "see you tomorrow morning."

"Thanks, I'll see you then."

Interfacing with the rest of the people in this world is not always easy for me. I suppose it's not always easy for them either. I'm sure some think that I'm a little odd; some probably think that I'm totally nuts. Oh well, what's a guy supposed to do when something like this is a part of his life? I've learned to just tell the truth in terms that I hope they'll understand and go on from there.

CHAPTER 30

Helaina, Where Are You?

When Helaina didn't contact me at all that day, I began to feel a little worried. She didn't page to set up a time and place to meet, and it made me wonder if she was okay. At the end of our conversation on the phone, she'd seemed to be doing fine. But a lot of pretty strange stuff had happened, and I was concerned she might have had some kind of bad reaction.

It's probably just as well she didn't call right away. It took most of Tuesday before the occasional erotic, dancing fantasy visions of Helaina faded away. I checked in with Coach several times and always got that she was okay, just trying to put some distance between herself and the experience. It was a big bite to swallow, and she needed time to chew. Coach asked that I consider offering to work with Helaina in a student/teacher role if she desired that. If she wanted to follow through on her desire to take classes, Coach suggested that it could be a learning experience for both of us.

By the time I left work two days after our phone call, no amount of Coach's information could assuage my concern. I'd gone into the experience fearful that something I might say or do would push Helaina over some psychological edge. That fear was coming back to haunt me. Later that evening, I called and left a message on her answering machine, telling her I was concerned about how she was doing and asking that she call and let me know.

The next day at work, after just sitting down outside to eat lunch with a buddy, my pager went off, displaying Helaina's number. At my desk, I dialed it, and, on the second ring, Helaina answered.

"Hello Bruce, sorry I didn't call you yesterday, but I was pretty busy and needed time to think about what happened."

"That's okay," I replied, "a lot happened Monday night, and I was feeling some concern about how it was affecting you. I just wanted to know you're okay. I expect you probably needed some time to sort it through."

"Yeah, I'm trying to put some distance between me and what I experienced. I made the mistake of talking to three people about it, and two of them told me I'm totally whacked out, crazy. My mom and my husband told me that. My girl-friend at least listened and tried to understand, but even she looked at me like I was nuts."

"Most people have nothing in their own experience to re-late it to. I do, and I don't think you're crazy at all. You have just come through an experience that was so unfamiliar that it could look crazy to someone with no way to relate to it. No, I don't think you're crazy."

"Well, at least there's one person who doesn't think I'm nuts," she responded, laughing.

"By the way, did you take the time to write down in your journal any of what happened Monday night?"

"No, I don't want to write it down. I'm afraid someone might find it and think I'm insane," she replied. "As I go over any of it in my mind, I keep trying to explain it away, but I can't."

"It might take a while before you are able to accept what you went through. What I hear you saying is that you're find-ing it very difficult to accept that all that stuff could happen. Yet, you can't explain it away."

"Yeah, that's where I'm at with it."

"If you ever feel the need to go back over any of the details, I wrote notes from the experience and a very long dream later that night."

"Yeah, I don't want to think about it too much right now. It's funny, but now while I'm talking to you on the phone, I can tell there are people and things here in the room with me. I see little bits and pieces, but I don't feel afraid at all. It's okay that they're here, and I know that if I want them to leave, they'll have no choice but to go away. I haven't been afraid at all since after we talked on the phone. I've had no trouble at all sleeping through the night."

My feelings of concern vanished as she told me about her loss of fear and feeling like she was in control of whatever situation might come up.

"Helaina, I'm really happy to hear that you know you are safe and in control of what's happening around you. That feels so good to me!"

"Oh, I tried what you suggested the other night, that thing about communicating from the place in the center of my chest. I tried it at work last night, and I made more money in one night than I've ever made before. I didn't even have to dance for anybody to get it either. I just started looking at men in the crowd with that feeling in the center of my chest instead of with the thoughts in my head. I could tell which ones would pay me to just sit at their table and talk, and which ones I'd have to dance for to get the money. So I only went over to the guys who would pay for me just to sit and talk. After a while, I'd just look around and pick another one out of the crowd. It worked every time. They paid me to just sit and talk! I didn't have to dance for anyone, and I made more money than I've ever made before."

I started feeling a little moralistic at Helaina's use of her gift; *my God, woman, is nothing sacred to you?* Luckily I caught myself before I opened my mouth and managed to refrain from dumping it on her.

"Well, there are certainly many ways to use the gift you have been given. All of our actions have consequences, and, if we can accept the results of our actions, I see nothing wrong with using them in whatever way we see fit."

I was getting a very uncomfortable feeling about how Helaina was choosing to use her gift, but I recognized those were *my* feelings about *my* stuff. I knew it was none of my business how she chose to live her life; after all, I've got enough to handle just trying to live my own. A prompt from Coach suddenly changed the direction of my thoughts.

"Helaina, when we were talking Monday night, you asked if I teach classes. I don't teach classes, but my guidance is that I'm to be available to you. If you want to talk about whatever is happening, you can call on me. I'm not an expert in all of this, but I'm willing to share my experience in whatever way might be useful. I have a pretty good library of metaphysical books. If you want to borrow some of them or ask for recommendations in areas of your interest, just call and let me know. That reminds me, I've thought about book recommendations for you. If I could suggest only one book for you to read it would be, *The Course In Miracles*.

"*The Course In Miracles*, okay, where can I find it?" I was surprised to hear Helaina ask.

"Most any bookstore—B. Dalton's, Barnes & Noble, Tattered Cover, or the Nic-Nak-Nook for that matter. It covers a lot of ground and is really the best all-around book I could recommend to anyone."

"Okay, well I guess that's about all I have to say for now; maybe I'll call again to talk sometime later if that's all right?"

"Of course, any time you want to talk just give a call, let me know how you're doing."

We said our good-byes there on the phone as I sat at my desk at work. That's the last time I spoke with Helaina. I was tempted to call her a number of times to find out where her journey had taken her. Each time I decided it was not my place to interfere. After all, it's her gift, her journey to live, and her path to follow.

Looking back on the experience with Helaina, I realized building trust in my knowledge and abilities is a continuing process dealing with more than just voyages into the Afterlife. The Lifeline program, where I first learned to explore, was billed as a program of service There and service Here. As my confidence in doing retrievals There grew, I was given more challenging people and situations to work with and learn from. At first it had been easy; the people I retrieved were cooperative. Then, I found Bengy, and he refused to go with me. Luckily, others had suggestions I learned from. When I found Bengy again, later, the *angel ruse* worked, and he was reunited with an uncle in Focus 27, much to my relief. To succeed, I had to learn how to handle new situations in new ways. I had to learn how to rely on the assistance of Helpers many times to show me the way.

It never occurred to me that service Here might have the same progressively difficult challenges. Passing on information

I'd received during retrievals to loved ones was one of the few ways I conceived of as service Here. That and talking about my experiences and encouraging others to explore the Afterlife too. Helaina's request for assistance in dealing with a ghost upped the ante with a challenge I wasn't sure I could handle. Coming through it successfully continued building trust in an arena that I'd never even considered. Makes me wonder what sort of hairy challenges await me in the future.

Seven months after Helaina first contacted me, I called to see how she was doing. She must have moved; the phone was disconnected with no forwarding number. I expect that some time in the future she'll call to tell me how she's doing. Maybe then I'll find out what sort of wondrous adventures have occurred along her journey. My greatest hope is that she's building trust.

And, Helaina, if you're reading this and want to know what the Amish leader said to me as he walked by you on his way to the light, I heard him and know what he said. It has to do with one of the purposes you had in living this lifetime. It has to do with who you were in previous lifetimes. It explains a lot. It's something really big.

VOYAGING BEYOND DOUBT

After sailing beyond the horizon many times, each time feeling the anxiety, doubting that the New World you've been visiting will be there, eventually the reality of its existence becomes a known. At some point you've sailed the route so many times, always finding land, you begin to trust that you always will. At that point your doubt about this New World's existence disappears.

Experienced sailors look toward the horizon knowing what lies beyond it; they have no doubt. Somehow, their lack of doubt gives them courage to voyage toward any horizon, knowing there will always be a landfall out There, somewhere.

CHAPTER 31

Thislife Associations in the Afterlife

Some retrievals are difficult for no other reason than that the person you're working with refuses to cooperate. Richard was such a man. When I first approached him, trying to move him to The Reception Center, he wanted nothing to do with me. Experience earlier with Bengy taught me that little kids almost always come along if they know they get to fly. That trick hardly ever works on adults. If you sign on to an Afterlife voyage of your own, maybe this story will help, should you encounter someone like Richard.

A couple of weeks after Richard died, his son, Wyatt, contacted me through The Monroe Institute. The only information I had to start with was Richard's full name, and that turned out not to be enough. The first time I went looking, I found him right away, but every time I approached him he backed away. I got no response to calling his name, other than a brief look of disbelief in my presence. Frustrated, I left him where I'd found him.

On my second trip, I was able to talk to him and get an impression of his surroundings. As I approached, he was standing alone in a small room with flat, dark walls. Overhead lighting illuminated him and a small area of the floor around him. This time, when I made my presence known, he seemed to accept it a little better. When I called his name, he responded by looking at me and asking who I was. After introducing myself, I explained that his son had asked me to check on him.

He was very boisterous in general, waving his hands a lot, gesturing as he spoke. There was something very odd about the way he interacted with me. Like he thought he might be talking to a ghost, and, though he didn't believe in such things,

225

he could still see me. It wasn't that he was drunk necessarily, but something about his mannerisms, his voice, and the look on his face were similar. Like he knew the guy standing in front of him talking was either a product of the DT's or a figment of his imagination. He wasn't taking any of our conversation seriously. In that way, he wasn't entirely aware of what was going on between us. Richard treated me with a glad-handing approach usually reserved for politicians who intend to get your vote and have nothing else to do with you. He used it to cover over the level of confusion he was having either about me specifically or in general. It felt like he was constantly bluffing. The appearance of his face changed during this contact with him. He started out looking like an old Bob Monroe, but with more and curlier hair, and then changed to someone younger looking.

Since I wasn't getting anywhere with Richard, I asked if there was someone nearby who could assist in communicating with him. A rather small woman with bushy, dark hair materialized standing next to me. The expression on her wrinkled face was one of sadness mixed with exasperation. She was Richard's deceased mother. One look at her, and Richard threw his hands up in the air, turned around, and walked away from us. He wouldn't cooperate with her either.

She'd been trying to communicate with him since he died, and wasn't having much luck. To demonstrate the problem, she walked toward Richard calling his name. As she approached, telling him she just wanted to talk, he got the same befuddled look on his face that I'd been treated to. He knew and recognized her, but was in complete disbelief of the possibility of her presence. He just couldn't deal with the fact that his dead mother was there. As she got closer to him, he tried to shoo her away with big, sweeping movements of his hands. When that didn't work, he brought his right hand up to his forehead, turned, and walked away hanging his head. It felt like he just kept wishing he could wake up and be out of this bad dream. With nothing else to go on, and getting nowhere with Richard, I thanked the woman and suggested she keep trying to reach him. I promised her I'd return soon to try again, too.

What little information I had, I e-mailed to Wyatt along with a request for some background on his dad. I was hoping for something I could use to get Richard to accept my presence and come along with me to The Reception Center.

From Wyatt's response I learned, among other things, that Richard had been a Fraternal Freemason and it had meant a lot to him. He wore a man's diamond ring and absolutely loved the music of Neil Diamond.

Wyatt also confirmed Richard's curly hair and use of boisterous mannerisms, in Wyatt's words, "particularly when he was afraid." He'd had his own vision of his father, in a dream perhaps, in which he'd seen him huddled in a squatting fetal position. In his vision, Wyatt's dad had a light shining on him in a room similar to the one in my description.

A few evenings after receiving Wyatt's letter, I went back looking for his dad again. Before reaching him, I encountered his mother, and she told me that Richard's response to her hadn't changed. I continued on to find him on my own. As I approached him this time, and reintroduced myself, he recognized me from my previous visit. He was still quite skittish, so I kept my distance as I reminded him that Wyatt had sent me. When I mentioned I knew he was a Freemason, I could feel pride welling up in him at his association with that group.

"I know a place where many other Freemasons are gathered not far from here," I stated, not really knowing, but expecting one would be provided in Focus 27.

"Really, is there a lodge?" Richard asked.

"If you'd like I could take you there to visit."

"Will any of my old buddies be there?" he asked, a feeling of hopeful expectancy in his voice.

"I'm not sure, but if not, at least there'll be others of your brotherhood to meet and welcome you."

"Can I come back here if I want to?" Richard asked nervously.

"Of course, if you want to come back here you can."

My intent was to reach out and take his hand, as I usually do when I take someone to Focus 27. Before I made a movement in that direction, I got the distinct impression he'd feel odd, holding another man's hand. So, instead, I stood beside him asking if it would be all right to place my hand on his shoulder. That seemed a little too personal also, but he agreed to allow it. It was then that I noticed his mother watching from a discreet distance away. She was smiling her gratitude to me as we left Focus 23 on our way to the Reception Center.

Shortly after we stopped moving, the front of a large, gray stone building materialized in front of us. A group of six or eight men was nearby, awaiting our arrival. They were standing at the foot of huge stone steps that led up to the doors of the building. All the men greeted Richard casually, and we stood there a few moments while he looked around. Then, one of the men stepped from the crowd and approached Richard directly. I could feel apprehension build up. He wanted to be certain this was a Freemason facility. The man who approached reached out and shook hands with him. He did it in a way Richard recognized immediately as a Freemason handshake. With that recognition, he immediately calmed down. I noticed his mother unobtrusively standing where she could watch all that happened.

As the two men, now friends, stood and talked, the man invited Richard to tour their lodge. I followed them up the stone stairs and through the huge wooden doors. Once inside, I had the impression of symbols on the walls and wall hangings. I didn't get any clear visualizations of their appearance, but they seemed to be everywhere. Richard's new friend asked if he'd like to change clothes. When he answered, "Yes," he was suddenly wearing a robe. He seemed very pleased and happy to be where he was, so I decided to leave him in the building with his new friend. Once outside, I found his mother and asked for her name. Wyatt had asked me to get it as evidence of who she was. The best I could hear as she spoke it, the ending sounded like "reen." It could have been Irene or Maureen; I honestly didn't know.

Satisfied Richard would be fine at the Masonic Lodge in Focus 27, I decided to leave. Sometimes one little bit of information, like Richard having been a Freemason during his life, can be used to assist in a retrieval. Associations that people value during their physical lives carry over into the Afterlife.

Special facilities exist at the Reception Center, set up and maintained by Helpers. It's just one more way people living There try to ease and assist people Here in their transition to existence beyond the physical world.

CHAPTER 32

Last Voyage with Doubt

There was not much on television worth watching one Monday evening in early December of 1995. Is there ever? Seemed like a good night to retire early and read in bed for a while. On my way to the bedroom, almost as an afterthought, I fired up my computer to check for e-mail messages. There were several; one from my friend Rosalie was entitled "A favor?" I opened and read it first. You met Rosalie in an earlier chapter when I recounted her mother, Sylvia's, retrieval. Sylvia had been unaware of her death and was disturbing her husband, Joe's, sleep. Now, eight months later, Joe was dead. Rosalie's e-mail said:

"This has been a weekend I'll never forget. My dad was crossing a parking lot and was hit by a pickup truck. This happened Friday afternoon. He died at 12:45 this morning. I would appreciate your checking in with him and helping if he needs any. His name is 'Joseph' and he was known by many who loved him as 'Pappy.' " I was instantly hit with a wave of sadness, and my heart went out to my friend. I immediately sent an e-mail back, letting her know I'd check in on her father at the first opportunity. I collected my other messages and headed off to bed.

Pharon and I read and talked and laughed and giggled until a little after eleven and then, tired, it was time for sleep. Just before drifting off, I remembered Rosalie's request that I check in on her father. I briefly relaxed with the intent to find him, and then waited for something to happen. The transition was very quick, and I shifted to a place where I saw Sylvia, standing in front of me. Facing me, she was beaming that bright smile I'd recognize anywhere. The area around her was so brightly lit in brilliant white and pastel yellows that the image of her face appeared in airy, delicate brushstrokes with outlines almost too faint to see. The transition between her body and the light blended so smoothly into each other I couldn't see a boundary.

It's difficult to tell where Sylvia leaves off and the light begins, I remember thinking.

As I focused all my attention on her, the reason for my difficulty became apparent. Sylvia and the light were one. In the time since I'd seen her last, Sylvia had become a Being of Light.

She has certainly learned a lot living in her new environment. She really knows her way around! flashed through my mind.

Another woman, standing to Sylvia's right, caught my attention. She, too was an incredibly bright white light with soft, clear, pastel yellows. This woman's identity really confused me. She was, without a doubt, Joe's mother, but she was much younger than either Joe or Sylvia. Try as I might, I couldn't change my perception of her into anything else to resolve my confusion. Impossibly, she was both younger than Joe and, at the same time, his mother.

How could this other woman be Joe's mother and younger than both Joe and Sylvia? I kept wondering.

Not being able to distort the facts I was perceiving into something that would fit my expectations, I left this puzzle and focused my attention back on Sylvia. As I did I realized she was standing at the headboard of a hospital bed. I was standing at the foot of the bed, and Joe was lying on it between us. He was on his back, awake and alert, propped up with pillows, bent forward slightly at the waist and looking directly at me. By his appearance he was still a little groggy, but conscious and aware of my presence.

"Hi, Joe. My name is Bruce. Just came to see how you're doing."

"I'm just fine!"

He said it like he really meant it. Like no matter how he was really feeling, he wanted me to think he'd never felt better. In his words, I could feel his elation at being with Sylvia again, and, in her beaming smile, I could feel hers.

Satisfied that Joe didn't need any assistance from me, I decided to check on Rosalie.

As I focused on her, I witnessed the events surrounding Joe's departure and the moment of his death. Joe was just phasing out of his physical body for the last time, and Rosalie was with him. Walking close at his side, she was telling him to go to the light. They continued moving together for a short distance, and then came into the brilliant field of light that was Sylvia. By traveling with her father and talking to him, she'd held his attention until Sylvia came into view for both of them. They were all together for a few moments, long enough for Joe to become aware of Sylvia's presence, and then Rosalie left.

I wonder if she'll retain any memory of this?

I made a mental note to ask when I talked to her later. Returning briefly to check on Joe again, I found him easily. Still there with Sylvia and the woman younger than Joe and yet his mother. Sylvia assured me he was doing fine and would have a speedy recovery from the effects of the accident. She explained that he would need a little time to recover from the relatively brief but extremely painful ordeal, and then he would be in great shape. Looking at the two of them, I got another rush of the feeling of their happiness to be together again. I could feel her enthusiasm to be introducing Joe to his new home, touring the neighborhood and showing him the ropes. I was still pondering the identity of the other woman as I drifted off to sleep.

The next morning, I climbed into my Jeep and headed off to work. As I entered freeway traffic for the long drive, I thought about Joe again. I decided to check on him once I'd settled into the pattern of rush hour. Twenty minutes later, the slow-moving morning jam began to thin out, and I opened my attention to Joe. While keeping an eye on traffic, a portion of my attention began focusing on him. It's not much different than intentionally thinking about anything else as you're driving to work, and, as I see it, no more dangerous. I found him immediately, still reclining, propped up at the waist, on the bed. Sylvia was still standing, facing me, at the head of the bed. She was beaming her smile at me. It was a smile I could feel was filled with love for her husband. Joe was waving one arm and I could see his mouth was moving, like he was trying to say something to me.

In all my Afterlife explorations, I'd never really been able to hear anything a specific dead person had tried to say to me. If the opportunity presented itself, I'd brush it off without making any real effort to hear out of fear of what might happen. I just couldn't shake the belief I still carried that, somehow, I was making all this up in my mind, and none of it was real. If I tried and failed, it would prove the Afterlife to be a self-deceiving farce. Considering what might happen if I succeeded never crossed my mind. Such is the way of doubt. A way of hiding from unknown threats so well you don't even see them.

The look on Joe's face said that he desperately wanted me to hear what he was saying. I told him I couldn't understand him, and listened harder. It still sounded like mumbling the third time he said it. Like a cross between *darling* and *turtle*, it sounded like *dirt-ele*, and I knew it was something he wanted me to tell Rosalie.

"Joe, I can't understand what you're saying. I know it's a message for Rosalie, but I haven't got the word yet," I said to him in my thoughts.

"Pet name," Joe said, "pet name!"

Pet name didn't match the movement of his lips as he said the word.

"Okay, I get that it's a pet name for Rosalie," I thought back to him.

That's it, I thought to myself, *he's trying to give me a pet name for Rosalie!*

His expression told me that he felt like he was talking to a deaf person. He was trying to enunciate as clearly as he could, and I almost had it, almost. But I was missing something. Straining hard to understand the mumbling sound I heard every time his lips moved, I focused more attention on hearing him. If I could get it, then Rosalie would know I'd actually visited with her dad in the Afterlife, and that he was okay.

"Punkin," I heard Joe say, and an image of a big, bright orange pumpkin popped into my mind's eye.

"Punkin. Joe, I heard you say 'punkin'; that's your pet name for Rosalie?"

On hearing "Punkin" my Interpreter pulled from memory the fact that my dad's nickname for my younger sister had been "Punkin."

"I got it Joe, your pet name for Rosalie was Punkin!"

He threw up his hands, exasperated with our attempt to communicate. It was like watching someone playing a game of charades who was frustrated at the attempts of his teammates to understand his clues. I was so close, but hadn't said exactly the right word yet. At that point, rush hour traffic became a little too challenging to maintain contact with Joe. I switched my full attention back to lane changers and brake lights. Any more checking in with Joe would have to wait.

The rest of my day was filled with working for a living, and I didn't think about Joe or Rosalie until after arriving home that evening. I called Rosalie's number and left a voice mail saying her dad was all right and I had more to share with her. Pharon and I left for the Taco Bell drive-through, and made it back to my place 20 minutes later. I was just finishing my Big Beef Burrito Supreme when the phone rang. It was Rosalie.

"Thank you for checking in on my dad. I'm so glad to know he's doing well. It was an absolutely awful time, but at the end it turned out to be all right."

She filled me in on the details of her father's dying. The pickup truck had broken Joe's leg and cracked or crushed his ribs. He was in extreme pain a lot of the time. Sunday he was in and out of consciousness and having difficulty breathing.

Joe was a well-liked man, and people from all over Evergreen, Colorado, where he lived, came to the hospital. It was late Sunday afternoon, and Joe rallied a bit. The Intensive Care nurse said it would be all right if his friends came in briefly to say their good-byes. One by one, they paraded through, each saying a few words and then moving on. After the last ones had filed through, things settled down somewhat, and Joe moved between sleeping and waking for the next several hours. Rosalie hadn't eaten, and now seemed like a good time to have a cigarette and grab a bite in the cafeteria. No sooner did she sit down to eat, than her son came running in to get her.

"I still don't believe how fast I ran back to his room. I've never run that fast in my life, ever!" she exclaimed. "We were there, my son and daughter and I, as his heart began to fail. We were there when he left."

"That reminds me of one of the things I wanted to tell you about. When I first checked on your dad last night, I saw that you went with him as he left his body. You and your dad were together when you both reached your mom."

"I knew it! I knew they were together," Rosalie blurted out. "I remember telling my dad to go to the light, and now that you mention it, I remember feeling like I was moving with him."

"You did, at least that's what I saw happen."

I described the image I had seen as they moved together and Joe had become aware of Sylvia's presence. I explained that by talking to her dad the whole time, she had held his attention and that had made it easier for him to become aware of Sylvia. I described the scene with Joe propped up in the bed and Sylvia beaming her smile.

"When my dad died he was propped up in the bed as you describe. Did you see anyone else there with them?"

"Well, yes, I did, but it was very confusing."

I explained about the woman who was Joe's mother and yet younger than he.

"That makes perfect sense," Rosalie exclaimed. "My dad's mother died when he was twelve years old. When she died she was younger than he is."

"Now it's making sense to me too," I understood. "She would probably appear to Joe in a way that he could recognize her."

"See Bruce, it's as I've been telling you. You're always trying to figure it out instead of just letting it be what it is!" Rosalie said with a laugh.

I've got to admit she had me there. I often spend way too much time trying to make the information fit my expectations. It leads to a lot of unnecessary confusion on my part.

I told her about my contact with her dad and mom on the way to work in freeway traffic. I explained about the word Joe was trying to get me to understand, the word that at first sounded like "dirt-ele."

"He seemed to be trying to tell me something that would let you know he was all right. It felt like he was trying to give me something like a pet name, maybe something he used to call you?" I asked.

"No, that doesn't ring any bells for me," she responded.

"The last time he said it, it sounded like 'Punkin.'"

Through the phone I heard Rosalie let out a deep belly laugh.

"'Punky,' he was saying 'Punky.' It's his dog's name. The one thing that he continuously spoke of and worried about was Punky. Over and over again through this whole ordeal he made me promise I'd take care of Punky."

"I see. Then it was a pet name, but not your pet name. It was his pet's name and the image of a pumpkin was enough to get it across." Misinterpretation and expectations got me again, but 'Punkin' and 'Punky' were too close for comfort.

"Yes Bruce," laughing, "right up until he left he was so worried about his dog. I think this morning he wanted you to remind me of my promise to take care of Punky."

"Sounds like his message served both purposes," I thought out loud into the phone. "It's a message I could deliver without knowing precisely what it meant, and still he let you know he's all right. Amazing!"

We continued to talk and laugh for a while. Several times Rosalie remarked she was so happy to know her dad was all right and back together with her mom, his wife. It brought her joy and relief amidst the sadness at her loss. She told me about the service for Joe to be held a week from Thursday.

"Dad's body will be cremated, and all his friends will gather at the lumber yard where he worked to share stories, remember, and bid him farewell. If you'd like to come you're more than welcome."

"Sure, I'd be glad to be there. Let's get on the phone a couple days before and work out the details, okay?"

"That would be great!"

"I wouldn't be surprised at all to find at least your mom and probably your dad at the service on Thursday," I added.

"That would be so nice to see," she replied. "You know I wasn't trying to find him or anything, but last night, just as I was drifting off to sleep, I got an image of my mom and dad. They were kissing like a couple of young lovebirds. I retreated right away. It seemed like a very private moment. Heavens, I never saw them do that in all the years I was growing up!"

We talked and laughed and laughed and talked some more.

"You know, someone had put all Dad's stuff in a bag that rode in the ambulance with him to the hospital. He'd gone to get some groceries and a bottle of his favorite liquor, Black Velvet, just before the truck ran over him. We picked up the bag, my kids and I, as we were leaving the hospital and going back to Dad's house. We opened that bottle, poured ourselves a drink, and toasted Dad. It really seemed a fitting end to the awful ordeal of our weekend. I think Dad would have liked that."

"I'll bet you're right."

"You know, Bruce, I don't think you understand at all what a wonderful thing it is that you are able to do."

"I suppose that's true. I only do it because I can. I guess I don't understand what impact it has on people. But I'm happy I was able to help out."

We said our good-byes and hung up our phones. I, indeed, felt happy to have been of service There and Here.

Next morning on the way to work, I had an unexpected contact with Sylvia and Joe. The freeway entrance ramp, one of those two-lane, quarter-mile-long parking lots, was crowded as usual. Traffic lights at the bottom of the ramp let two cars enter the freeway at a time. The rest of us moved at a snail's pace. It's almost always a long wait, and that morning was no exception.

As my Jeep slowly crawled toward the lights, I became aware of quite a racket. Not the traffic noise kind, but rather, an internal, jumbling, buzz-of-indistinct-thoughts kind of racket. At first I tried to ignore its distraction and almost physical discomfort. The racket took on an urgent tone so I switched off the jeep radio and tuned into the jumble.

"Okay, who is it that is making all the noise?"

I still feel a little silly about saying things like that out loud. At least it's not too embarrassing when I'm alone in my Jeep. My question was answered immediately by a feeling.

"It's Sylvia. Bruce, I'd like to talk to you before you get into traffic if that's all right."

"Sylvia, of course it's all right. It's just that I didn't realize there really *was* someone there. I thought all that racket was some pattern of my own I needed to become aware of. Imagine my surprise to find out it was you!"

"Just think of it like a ringing telephone. A certain level of irritation is used there, too, to get one's attention," Sylvia thought back to me.

Listening to her voice in my thoughts, I became aware of the image of Sylvia and Joe. She was standing at the head of the bed in brilliant white light, tinted with soft pastel yellows. She was facing me, beaming that *rising sun at dawn* smile of hers. But this time, Joe was not lying on his back in the bed between us. He was standing next to the bed, and, as I watched, he turned toward me and looked directly into my eyes.

"You see, Bruce, Joe's recovering very quickly from the effects of the accident," Sylvia said. "He's learning that things over here are much different from where he used to live. I wanted to show you so that you can assure Rosalie her dad is making progress and doing well."

Looking at Joe, I picked up his astonishment at his exceptionally rapid recovery.

"I'll be happy to call and relay your message to Rosalie."

"Also, I want you to know we all appreciate what you've done so very much. Thank you, Bruce."

The feeling that engulfed me as Sylvia spoke was such a powerful experience of being loved, it brought tears to my eyes. It still does as I write this.

"One last thing before you have to get into freeway traffic. Whenever you are working with others to assist with contact between Here and There, I'll be there to help you. All you need do is ask, and I'll be there to assist. It's our way of expressing gratitude and helping others in the way you've helped us."

Tears wanted to begin streaming down my face as feelings of love, gratitude, and appreciation washed through me.

"Thank you, Sylvia, I'm so grateful to you for your offer. I look forward to working with you," I thought out to her.

"It's time for us to go now, almost your turn to get on the freeway. We'll be seeing you again soon."

She was right, the car ahead of me had gotten its green light and was moving down the ramp.

It was my turn next. When my light turned green, I'd start accelerating down the entrance ramp and merge into northbound rush hour, rejoining the workaday world.

Funny how things sneak up on me sometimes. Communicating with Joe and Sylvia had an unexpected impact. Three days after my last contact with them, my grip on this world began to loosen. At first, it felt very odd, almost scary. I kept expecting the world I'm used to living in would dissolve and disappear. Like I could be sitting in a conversation with someone and everything around us would disappear. A palpable anxiety ran through me continuously. It felt like the sand foundation under my feet was being slowly washed away. When it was gone, my whole world would disappear with it, and I'd be left floating in an empty, formless void. A very unnerving feeling.

Over the next few days, the feeling changed. All of the world I've come to know during my lifetime still felt like it could dissolve like the slow fade to black at the end of a movie. But I began to feel like, when that happened, a new, entirely different world would fade back in around me in its place. Following a practice Rebecca had taught me, I expressed my willingness to receive whatever these feelings held for me. It took several days and talking with a few close friends to sort it out, but at last I've got a handle on it.

I'd been exploring human existence after "death" for a little over three years since Lifeline. Many experiences in this arena had contained information verifiable to some extent. But I had always had a feeling of skepticism and doubt, even in these verifiable experiences. Some part of me was holding out, refusing to fully accept my experience as real. That part of me denied the possibility that I could explore the Afterlife, because it held to the belief there was no such thing. Call it a lack of confidence or just plain skepticism, at some level I'd always carried that doubt.

My experience with Joe was the first time I ever dared to try to get a specific word from someone who supposedly lived in the Afterlife. What had always stopped me before was that I never fully believed it was possible or real. Then, the first time I really tried to do it, it worked! That experience, simply trying to hear a word and getting it, conflicted with some deeply held beliefs. I didn't know what specific beliefs they were, but I knew that they couldn't possibly coexist with acceptance of my "Punky" experience as a real event. Feeling that my entire world might disappear at any moment told me that whatever these conflicting beliefs were, they were at the very core of my world-view. Everything I had come to believe about the existence of the physical world, and me in it, was threatened by extinction.

Continued asking to receive the meaning of these unnerving feelings led to the realization that I was faced with a choice. Either refuse to accept the validity of my irrefutably verified experience with Joe, or form a new set of belief structures to incorporate it. I had to either somehow forget it ever hap-pened, or finally and fully accept the Afterlife as real. There had been other times during my explorations when this could have happened. Many times I'd received information later verified as *real*, but somehow I'd always been able to write it off as a fluke and disregard it. The problem was that this experience with Joe was undeniable.

My world is fabricated, as all worlds are, using beliefs as the most basic building material. Since birth, I've interpreted all experience through my growing set of beliefs, to construct the world-view in which I live. Choosing to accept the experience with Joe, in conflict with deeply held, core beliefs, meant that at least part of the world I'd constructed over forty-seven years was going to crumble and disappear. That was the source of my unnerving feelings. But I had no real choice, *it had happened*. So, it was a fait accompli. I consciously chose acceptance of that Afterlife experience as a part of the New World in which I would live. Like mariners of old, I added the true shape of the earth to my world-view. And, like their belief in a flat earth with an edge one could sail off and die, my old world-view crumbled and disappeared. As with theirs, my New World now extended beyond the horizon forever. Accepting the Afterlife reality of *Punky* has made all my nonphysical experiences since then voyages beyond doubt.

CHAPTER 33

A Voyage Beyond Doubt

By now the Nic-Nak-Nook was passing along my home phone number to those with a real need. The fourth response to the *Nexus* advertisement came from Mai. Her friend, Chelik, had died a year and a half ago, and it concerned her that he was still hanging around. I was at my computer working on a manuscript when the ringing phone on my desk announced her call. She was careful not to give me too many details. Felt like she wanted to hear them from me to be sure that I wasn't a hoax. Fine with me; I now knew the truth about that.

Mai had been living on a kibbutz in Israel when she met Chelik. She gave me no more details about how he died other than that it had been a violent death. She'd felt his presence around her for a very long time. It was neither bothersome nor frightening that he was around. She was just worried for him. Time had healed her wound at his loss, except for a little sadness maybe now and then. But her awareness of his presence always carried with it such powerful feelings of sadness and grief. Mai was concerned that these were feelings Chelik was holding within himself. She wondered out loud if maybe he shouldn't have moved on from them by now. That's why she contacted me, to see if there was anything I could do to assist him, to help Chelik move to where he should be. I agreed to try, explaining the only thing left was for me to be able to pronounce his name. With my Minnesota version of English, she had to repeat it several times before my version at all sounded the same. That completed, I told Mai I'd call her back as soon as I had any news.

A few more paragraphs, and the rough draft of the chapter I was writing was finished. Not bothering to shut down my computer, I got up and headed for the bedroom. After lying down and getting comfortable, I relaxed into the soothing feeling of my body against the mattress. In less than a minute, I could feel Chelik hiding in the darkness in front of me. When I asked how he was doing, he put on a good front of being fine and feeling okay. Then I felt his feelings of sorrow and anguish show through, and knew he was trapped by them in Focus 23. Grief stood out strongly in his voice as we started to talk.

"Who are you?"

"My name is Bruce."

"Why are you here?"

"Your friend Mai asked me to come."

"Why?"

"She can feel your presence and is worried for you," I replied.

"Then she does know I am with her!"

"Yes, she's aware of your presence, but it worries her," I told him.

"What worries her?"

"It has been so long since your death, Chelik, she's concerned because you are still feeling so bad."

"How long has it been, since my death I mean?"

"A little over a year and a half."

"That long? It doesn't seem that long. Then, again, it feels like forever."

"Could you step out into the light so I can see you?" I asked, trying to get a stronger connection to Chelik.

"No, I can't do that . . . I'm too . . . grotesque to look at!"

"I just thought that perhaps I could describe you to Mai, and then she'd know I had really seen you."

"She wouldn't recognize me; not even my mother recognized my body."

"Is it because of the way you died, Chelik?"

"After the bomb went off, parts of my body were scattered all over the street. And most of those were burned badly in the explosion."

The impression of a hot, sunny climate came to me. A young man in a lightweight, loose fitting cotton shirt stood at the curb nearby. I saw a bus drive by in front of me. Chelik was not on a bus when the bomb killed him, but something about a bus was involved with his death.

"I see. Then maybe we can just talk awhile?"

"I have a message I want to get back to my friends," Chelik said, "Mai will know who I mean."

"I'll be happy to deliver it to her for you; what would you like to tell them?"

"Forgiveness is the only way. That is my message to my friends. The only way this madness can stop is forgiveness."

"What madness?"

"The Arabs and Jews hate each other. We both carry that hatred around with us every place we go. It acts like a magnet drawing to itself what it is. Our hatred for each other draws us to horrible acts that only bring more hatred. It is an endless, vicious cycle of hatred that must be stopped! We must change our hearts. Forgiveness is the only way," Chelik said, adamantly.

"Forgiveness for acts of hatred is the only way. That is the message you want your friends to hear?"

"Yes, Mai knows them. They still live in Israel. That's where she met me and my friends."

"Yes, she told me."

"Tell them we pulled our pranks on them just as they pull their pranks on us. God knows I pulled my share of pranks on them."

A large, stake-sided, flatbed truck drove by in front of me. Young soldiers in tan uniforms shouldering automatic weapons had just finished loading it. A light-colored tarp had been thrown over the pile of bodies on the truck. It was tied down tightly around the edges of the truck's flatbed so the cargo wouldn't be revealed. The truck drove away to my left through an opening in a wall made of stone. It passed through a curtain that covered the opening and disappeared from my view.

"I'll ask Mai to pass on your message of forgiveness to your friends in Israel."

"Forgiveness . . . it is the only way," Chelik moaned.

"I'd like to be able to give Mai something that will let her know for certain I've been with you. Can you give me a word I can say to her so she'll have no doubt."

" 'Tekashrou;' tell her 'Tekashrou!' "

My spelling of the word he told me is my best phonetic guess at the sound. His accent and his way of saying it are not within my Minnesota English capabilities.

"That's a tough one for me to pronounce, could you tell me what it means?"

"Tell her 'Tekashrou, Tekashrou!' She'll know what it means!"

There was a short-tempered anger in his voice as he said this. I took a few moments to imprint in memory the sound he made with this word meant for Mai. Then I went back to talking with Chelik.

"Mai asked me to help you move on to where you are to go from here. That's the main reason I came," I said, trying to sound matter-of-fact.

"Leave here? I can't leave here yet! I've not finished what I need to do!"

"She's very concerned for your well-being, Chelik."

"It's out of the question! I'm not finished! I'm not allowed to leave until I'm finished!"

Chelik came into view standing in front of me. He looked like a normal young man, tall and thin, not someone blown to bits. He was getting very agitated. He kept rambling on about not being finished, and then he'd stop for a moment and break into sobbing mixed with a chanting kind of yelling. It was time to ask for help.

"Is there anyone nearby who can assist me with Chelik?" I broadcast out in all directions.

An old man stepped from the darkness behind me. Bearded and long-haired, he was dressed in a long, ornate robe, holding a long wooden staff in one hand and wearing a yarmulke. He spoke to me immediately.

"This boy is impossible! I've been trying to get through to him since he died. I am trying and trying, but I can't get through to this boy! He keeps going over and over the same things, and still he doesn't get it."

This man's voice sounded like he'd spent a long time in

New York and still had the accent. The New Yorker sound was mixed with the clear pronunciation one expects from an educated man from the old country.

"I'm not getting anywhere with him yet either. By the way, I'm Bruce," I said, by way of introduction.

"I've been watching you with the boy; I got your name already! You got a good touch, Bruce, with the boy; I was watching you. You got a good touch!"

He had a no-nonsense, direct forcefulness to his voice and manner that left no question about what he was feeling. I immediately liked his direct approach.

"You can call me 'Ribby!' "

Just then, Chelik walked over and interrupted my conversation with Ribby. Ribby moved close to him and started waving his arms and jumping up and down right in front of him.

"Chelik . . . Chelik . . . " Ribby was yelling the name, "I'm standing right in front of you, and I'm jumping up and down in front of you, and I'm calling your name in front of you, and you don't even know I'm here in front of you!"

Ribby sat down off to the side while Chelik continued rambling on, oblivious to Ribby's comical horsing around. Ribby's voice was filled with frustration.

"Would you look at this boy, Bruce. I'm making such a racket, and I can't get through to this boy!"

I turned my head to say something to Ribby and immediately sensed Chelik felt insulted by my lack of attention.

"Look, Bruce, this is important what I am saying; I want you to listen to me!" Chelik shouted.

Ribby was still sitting off to the side.

"I'm telling you, Bruce, this boy is one tough cookie," Ribby went on. "Frustrated! Frustrated I am getting with this boy!"

I turned back to Chelik and switched on my loud, insulted voice. Pointing it right in Chelik's face, I let it loose.

"Chelik! Can't you see you're interrupting my conversation with Ribby! Wait your turn! When we're done I'll get back to you!"

I turned my face toward Ribby and caught the twinkle in his eye.

"You have a good touch, Bruce, a good touch!" Ribby smiled to me.

"But! . . . But! . . . But there is no one else here. Only you and I," Chelik said apologetically.

Without acknowledging his apology, I turned my insulted voice back on Chelik.

"You're being rude! Or are you telling me you can't see my friend, Ribby!"

Ribby was bent over laughing at my show of gruffness.

"But! . . . But! . . . But there is no one else here!"

"Look, do I have to get rude with you before you'll listen! Please wait until I've finished talking with Ribby! Then I'll talk to you!"

I turned my head, looking at Ribby again, desperately trying to keep a straight face. I finally had to turn around and face away from Chelik so I could let out the burst of laughter I felt welling up inside me. Ribby came around and stood in front of me.

"I'm thinking this is gonna work, Bruce. This is gonna work! Now you put your straight face back on, turn around, and get Chelik to look you right in the eyes while you talk to him. Okay? Oh boy, oh boy, this is gonna work!"

I put on my straight face after letting out the rest of the energy of laughter and turned around to face Chelik.

"Chelik, I want you should look at me! Right into my eyes I want you to look!"

I felt Ribby flowing through my voice and eyes. Standing directly behind me, he was looking straight through my eyes at Chelik. The eyes Chelik saw were as much Ribby's as they were mine.

"I want you should look at me, Boy, when I'm talking to you!" Ribby was using my voice and laying it on thick.

He kept up his stern act for a few seconds. When Chelik was seeing him through my body, Ribby stepped out slowly from behind me to my right. He kept talking and maintained eye contact with Chelik the entire time. I watched Chelik's eyes turn to my right, following Ribby's movement. When he was standing completely out in the open and beside me, a look of shocked astonishment had overtaken Chelik's face. He stood there, open jawed, staring at Ribby.

"Boy! Oh boy, have I been trying to reach you for a long time! And this guy, Bruce, this guy's got a nice touch," he said with a smiling twinkle in his eye as he pointed to me. "Such a nice touch!"

Emotions were blasting through Chelik like fireworks on the Fourth of July. He was happy, he was sad, he was shaking, he was whimpering, he was up and down and all over everywhere at once.

"Come on, Boy, we got places to go!" Ribby barked out to Chelik in a sweet tone.

Chelik started walking toward Ribby, still dumbfounded. Chelik was a tall, thin good-looking young man. Evidence of the way he died didn't appear in the form of his body I was seeing. I watched as the clothes he was wearing changed into a beautiful ceremonial robe, very ornate, gold thread embroidery and very colorful. He was shocked to be wearing such clothes. Chelik felt undeserving of whatever honor or meaning these clothes held for him.

"We're leaving now, Chelik; say good bye to this man. On this day, this man has helped you!"

The last item of clothing that appeared on Chelik was a sash of some kind. It was also very ornate; fancy embroidery and designs were worked into its entire length. It hung around his neck on both sides and at least down to his waist.

"Ribby, where are we going?"

"You'll see soon enough, Boy; you'll see soon enough!"

With that, Ribby stood beside Chelik, holding his long wooden staff in one hand and placing the other on Chelik's shoulder. Then, they started to move away into the darkness of Focus 23. I followed them to see where Ribby was taking Chelik.

It was a village. Low modern buildings surrounded a central plaza in an open, dry-desert setting. I arrived just before they did and saw the people gathered in the plaza to greet Chelik. He and Ribby materialized in the middle of the crowd that erupted into loud welcoming voices. People crowded around him, waving their arms in the air and calling his name. Chelik recognized many of them as they embraced and hugged him in turn. There were tables of food set out around the plaza, and the whole place became a raucous celebration of Chelik's arrival. Ten or fifteen people formed a circle and began dancing the way I've seen Jewish people dance in a circle. Laughing and shouting and singing, they were enjoying every instant of the experience. On Chelik's face I could see the joy of reunion and celebration.

Ribby was standing off to the side of the plaza, and I went over to talk to him. "Bruce, I want you to know that I'm thanking you. That boy would still be stuck there if it weren't for your touch. Bruce, I am thanking you!"

"You're most welcome, Ribby! I'm happy we were able to get through to him. Tell me, what had him stuck there?"

"He was spending too much time in grief and sorrow thinking this was Atonement!"

"Atonement?"

Ribby repeated the word very clearly three more times. He wanted to be sure I got it right.

"These kids! They think they know what Atonement means. They don't know what Atonement means! This boy, Chelik, he thought Atonement meant going over and over his feelings of sorrow and grief at what he had done in his life. Every time he felt the need of Atonement he started going over and over and over his feelings of sorrow and grief. That's what held him in your Focus 23! Enough already! Atonement is about asking forgiveness. These kids today think it means going over and over their feelings of sorrow and grief at what they have done. But that's not it! Forgiveness is what it is; Atonement is forgiveness! That's what they should be learning and knowing; forgiveness, that is Atonement!"

Thanking Ribby for his explanation, I decided to look in on Mai. I found her easily and escorted her to the village where Chelik's celebration was still in full swing. Since she had been concerned enough to seek help for him, I felt it was fitting she had the opportunity to see and talk to him again. We landed just outside the crowd, still dancing and singing with joy. She surprised me by showing no interest in Chelik and his celebration. Instead, after looking around for a moment, she started walking straight toward an old couple who were standing in front of a building at the edge of the plaza.

"I just knew they were together," she shouted back to me as she started running toward the old couple.

The old man was quite a bit taller than the woman, and they were smiling at Mai as she approached them. In a flash of knowing, I realized these were her grandparents, both residents of the Afterlife. When she reached them, there were tears of joy and hugs all around in enthusiastic reunion. Standing close to them, I heard Mai's grandfather tell her not to worry; they'd both be waiting for her when her time came to join them. I left her with them, knowing she'd find her way back. I opened my eyes, stretched my body with a yawn, got up, and made notes in my journal. Half an hour later I phoned Mai and told her all that I'd found out about Chelik and what had happened to him. Then she gave me the details of his story.

Her boyfriend was one of a group of young soldiers living on the same kibbutz as she. Mai explained that after military training, Israelis doing their national service are sent to live and work on a kibbutz. There they work with civilians on any projects needing manpower, and they provide security. Chelik was a natural born leader and people followed his direction out of his innate talent.

When I mentioned his use of the word, "pranks," she knew what he meant. Not that she knew the exact details, but she knew this group of young soldiers well. It would not be beyond them, with their hatred of Arabs, to do almost anything they could get away with. She told me that the day Chelik died was the last day of his national service. He and the group of young soldiers had to return some of their equipment to a military base, and that required a bus ride. They'd walked into town and were waiting for the bus when a terrorist bomb exploded in a kiosk in a big open plaza. They had been standing far enough away from the explosion that none of the young soldiers had been injured by the blast. But there were people lying dead, wounded, and dying on the paving stones of the plaza. His comrades tried to stop him from running out to help them, but Chelik broke free and was running to help some lying near the center of the blast. As he got close to a bleeding body, the second bomb detonated. Chelik was standing so close to the second blast that his body had been literally shredded into small, barely recognizable pieces and scattered all over the plaza. The only way anyone could be certain that those body parts had been Chelik was that his buddies had their eyes glued to him as he was running. They had all seen him disappear in a spray of red fog and pieces. It had fueled their hatred of Arabs and, no doubt, some were later killed in a retaliatory prank. Mai understood the power of hatred and the power of forgiveness. She told me she'd pass along Chelik's message of forgiveness as the only way to stop the madness, but expected little effect.

Mai explained "Atonement" to me much as Ribby had. When a Hebrew does something that oversteps the boundaries of his own sense of ethics, he must ask for forgiveness. The Day of Atonement is a day when all Hebrews are to do this. It sounded to her like Chelik had been attempting Atonement.

When I said the word Chelik had given me for Mai, my lack of familiarity or experience with the Hebrew language made the transfer difficult. My spelling here, "Tekashrou," is the closest phonetic spelling I can come up with. I had to pronounce the foreign sound to her several different times as she tried to make it out. It was like trying to sing a fast-fingered trumpet riff's sound with my voice. My voice is just not trained to make proper Hebrew language sounds. Luckily Mai had experience with such pronunciation; she'd studied Hebrew, as had Chelik. After many attempts, the sound she repeated back to me was an exact match for what Chelik had said, "Tekashrou." She didn't know the exact meaning of the word, and told me she would check with her sources to find out. Later that evening, Mai called back to tell me the meaning of "Tekashrou." She was astonished.

"Tekashrou" means making a connection between or bringing two people together. It can mean facilitating such a connection, or being an outside party who causes or facilitates the connection. The Hebrew word for *matchmaker* has a similar sound, and a similar, though different specific meaning of purpose. Chelik couldn't have chosen a better word to describe the whole experience and the part I played in it. Chelik had said, "Tell her Tekashrou, Tekashrou! She'll know what it means!" The meaning packed into that single word amazed me! That single word, in a language I have no knowledge of and couldn't even pronounce, proved to Mai I'd actually contacted Chelik. That single word described to her what my role was in her receiving it, bringing the two of them together. At the same time, that single word proved to Mai the reality of human existence beyond the physical world. That single word came through me to her from the Afterlife.

As I marveled at Chelik's choice of a word, I realized that for me it was no big deal. It wasn't another piece of evidence I needed to gather to convince myself of anything. The *Punky* experience, when retrieving Joe earlier, eliminated that need. My acceptance of that experience had changed me. No longer did I wait, worrying for days, before attempting a retrieval. Now I just got up from the phone call request and did it! When I asked for a word from Chelik he said it and I *heard* it. Truly, I *am* living in a New World, a world that exists beyond doubt.

CHAPTER 34

The Hounds of Hell

Encountering the unexpected is always a possibility when you sail beyond the horizon into Afterlife. The unexpected presents the greatest potential for learning something new. Retrieving Leslie's aunt was just such an opportunity.

One of my favorite places in the physical world to visit is a little piece of Virginia countryside where my friends Dave and Leslie share their lives together. Tucked out of the way in lush green woodlands, with a stream just right for cooling off in the heat of a summer day, their place is a beautiful fantasy turned real. Two friendlier, loving, more supportive people would be hard to find anywhere.

When her aunt died, Leslie called to ask if I'd check in on her. I've since incorporated the unexpected aspects of that encounter into my retrieval process. It's become especially useful with difficult retrievals and a wonderful addition to the easy ones.

Gloria had died very recently and was easy to find. Relaxing briefly, I brought her name to mind and immediately saw her standing ten feet away in darkness. As I watched her for a few moments, she seemed unsure of where she was. Then, she noticed my presence and took off, running and screaming, trying to get as far from me as possible. I followed her briefly, calling her name. Then I stopped and waited. When she stopped running and calmed down a little, she'd moved so far away that I couldn't see her anymore. I still felt her signal, but it was faint and very distant.

As I accelerated in her direction, she came into view again. She was expecting me and probably still felt my signal after she stopped running. As soon as I could see her again I called out her name.

"Gloria."

She shrieked something unintelligible in my direction in a high shrill voice, then turned and ran from me again, screaming. I followed her a short distance and then stopped, waiting for her to stop running away. This time I tried moving more slowly toward her. Just as she came into view, I called her name again.

"Gloria?"

She was looking in my direction, eyes open wide with fright, when I could see her clearly again. Her shrill, shrieking voice carried the feeling of fear and terror as she ran away again. After ten seconds or so, she stopped running away and became very quiet, like she was trying to hide. Her signal was very faint.

Maybe a little different approach is in order, I thought to myself.

Moving very slowly, I approached to a point where I couldn't see her but she was very close by. Then, very slowly, I moved close to where I could just make out where she was. The moment I could see her at all, she ran off screaming again.

Maybe it's how I look to her; maybe I look like something scary?

This time, after she stopped moving away, I approached very slowly again, stopping out of her visual range.

"Gloria, I'm a friend, I've come to . . . "

That's as far as I got before she pulled away, shrieking in terror.

No, that didn't help. If anything, it was worse! Hearing my voice without seeing me just terrified her more!

Again I approached her slowly, very slowly. Staying out of her visual range, I just hovered there silently for at least a minute, trying to get a fix on what it was about my presence that terrified her. She knew I was nearby, she could sense my presence and it terrified her.

Maybe if I just stay close by long enough she'll realize I'm not a threat?

After waiting another two solid minutes for her terror to subside, I could still feel my mere presence had her on edge. Moving slowly, and just as she faintly came into view, I spoke softly to her again in the most angelic voice I could muster.

"I'm a friend . . . "

"God no! The Hounds from Hell!" she shrieked, and she was out of view again, running and screaming before I could finish my sentence.

". . . of Leslie's; she asked me to come and help you." She was almost completely out of range before my last words drifted out into the air.

Well, at least now I know the problem. She sees me as the Hounds from Hell.

Somewhere in Gloria's beliefs, she had accepted that there was a pack of vicious, frenzied dogs that roamed the Afterlife. They were Satan's minions who would attack a soul and tear it to pieces as they dragged it down to Hell. That's what she thought I was, a horrifying pack of dogs who were coming to rip her apart and deliver her to Satan. I embodied the fears of her worst nightmare! Her fears projected a mask over me that made me look like the Hounds from Hell. No matter how I tried to approach her, I would be like the Banshee in Marty's nightmare that he screamed and ran from every time he slept. This was something I'd never encountered before, on my own. No previous experience came to mind that could help me get around this problem. To show her how to extend her love, I had to be able to talk to her, but her fear had turned me into the Hounds of Hell. If something didn't happen soon, I'd have to leave her there. It wasn't a problem that was going to go away for her. Anyone who came to help her, no matter how bright and shining an angel they might be, would look to her like the Hounds of Hell. So, calling on someone There would have the same effect. She'd be running in fear and terror from anything she saw or heard.

I need help with this; is there someone who can assist me with Gloria, please? It was time for me to stop trying to figure this one out on my own and let Spirit provide the way.

"Bring Leslie here, she can help," drifted into my mind from whoever answered my question.

Leslie, of course! Bring Leslie here! Why didn't I think of that before?

"You've never encountered this situation before, Bruce. New Afterlife territory," the unfamiliar voice said. But at least you remembered to stop trying to figure out the right thing to do. You remembered what Rebecca taught you about allowing Spirit to provide the way. Take it as an example of your building trust in Spirit. Good work."

Gloria had stopped running and was fearfully awaiting her next encounter with the Hounds. Moments after bringing her to mind, Leslie was standing nearby.

"Hi Leslie. I'm trying to retrieve Gloria and I need your help."

"What can I do for you, Brucie?"

I explained what had happened each time I approached her aunt and why she reacted the way she did.

"So, what can I do to help her?" Leslie asked.

"If we move just close enough, she can hear your voice, but not see you. Maybe she'll recognize your voice. If she sees us, no matter what we do, she'll run again. She's absolutely terrified and will see us as the pack of Hounds. She's got a fix on me, and, if I get too close, she'll sense my presence and run. I think it would be best if you go ahead of me and stop way before she can see you."

"Where is she?"

We did a slow three sixty, feeling for Gloria's position. When she was directly in front of us I stopped, pointing in her direction.

"There she is, feel her?"

Leslie scanned back and forth a couple of times across the direction I'd pointed to.

"I got her. She's straight over that way, isn't she?" Leslie said, pointing.

"Yes, you've got her. Let's move real slowly. Don't want to get too close."

"How will I know when I'm close enough that she can hear me?"

"Just keep moving in her direction real slow. Pay real close attention to the blackness in front of you. If you see anything at all, a spot, a swirl, even a little jiggle, back away quick!"

"Oh . . . I get it! If I focus on the little spot, or whatever, in the blackness, it connects us visually. She'll come into my visual awareness and I'll come into hers! This is neat!"

"Leslie, I never thought of it that way before! I've been using that method of finding people for quite a while, and it never occurred to me what was actually going on! Of course, the swirl is a nonphysical, visual experience! Focusing my attention on it connects me visually to the person. Thank you, Leslie, I learned something new! Thanks!"

"No problem, Brucie!"

"I'm going to have to close down as tight as I can," I told Leslie, "and hope it's good enough."

"Close down?"

"Yeah, try to minimize how far away someone can detect my presence," I replied, "turn down my volume control so to speak. It's sort of like a combination between Klingon cloaking in Star Trek and rig for silent running in a submarine."

Leslie let out a laugh. "Okay, Worf, let's go!"

We started moving slowly in Gloria's direction, Leslie ahead and me trailing a short distance behind. After a little while, we stopped. I could feel Leslie thinking about what to say.

"Aunt Gloria. It's me, Leslie," I heard her say softly.

Gloria started running away again.

"Aunt Gloria, it's Leslie, everything's okay," she called out in the direction Gloria was moving.

I felt Gloria's sense of recognition when she realized she was hearing Leslie's voice. She stopped running and turned back, looking in our direction.

"Leslie? . . . Leslie . . . is that you?"

"Yes, Aunt Gloria, it's me. It's Leslie."

"Where are you, Dear? I can't see you."

"I'm right over here," Leslie said softly. "Just follow the sound of my voice. Over this way."

Great move, Leslie! She's moving toward us, eliminates her feeling of being chased. She feels she's in control! I knew she probably couldn't hear my thoughts, but I wanted to tuck it away for future reference.

"Is that you, Leslie, over there?" Gloria asked, pointing in our direction.

"Yes, Aunt Gloria, it's me. I'm standing right over here," Leslie called out, waving her hand.

Gloria moved closer and closer until she was just a few feet away.

"Am I ever glad to see you!" she said. "There were these awful dogs chasing me before. I was so scared! I ran away so they wouldn't get me, but they kept coming back!"

"Everything's all right now; they won't ever come back again."

The two of them chatted for a little while, and I could feel Leslie was doing an excellent job of calming Gloria down. As they stood talking, I surrounded them and silently shifted the three of us off to Focus 27. We landed in the Park on an open grassy field. Gloria hardly noticed the change of scene.

"There's someone I'd like to you meet," Leslie informed her aunt, "he's a good friend and I asked him if he'd come and help us. Would you like to meet him?"

"Okay, where is he?" Gloria asked.

I slowly opened up, allowing awareness of my presence to gradually come to Gloria.

"He's right over there," Leslie told her, pointing in my direction.

Squinting at first, trying to make out where I was and what I looked like, Gloria got a lock on me quickly.

"Oh, he looks like a nice young man."

"Aunt Gloria, this is Bruce," Leslie said, introducing us.

I walked across the grass toward her, smiling.

"Gloria, you have no idea how happy I am to meet you at last."

The three of us made small talk for a few minutes, and then two other people made their appearance. Gloria's mother and brother had come to welcome her into the Afterlife. After she recognized them and they drew her into conversation, Leslie and I said good-bye to her and left.

"Les, wait up a second!" I called out to her.

She stopped up ahead and I caught up to her.

"I just wanted to thank you for coming and for your insight into connecting visually around here. This is the first time I've intentionally called in someone physically living who knows the person I'm working with to help with a retrieval. It worked so well that I'm going to use it more often. Thanks Leslie!"

"You're entirely welcome, Brucie boy! Glad to help out."

After a big hug, we parted company, and I returned from this Afterlife voyage. I'd come back with a great bit of treasure from the trip, and made some notes in my journal. This encounter in uncharted waters was one I wanted to remember. The Afterlife knowledge I gained as a result was something I'd carry with me on future voyages.

Epilogue

At the beginning of my Afterlife explorations, I had a vague intellectual understanding that my experiences could somehow affect my beliefs. I could accept that new knowledge would supersede the old and need to be integrated into my existing beliefs. I never even considered what that really meant, and gave little thought to what going through such changes might feel like. Intellectual acceptance has no room for what things feel like. It's a barren, lifeless substitute for knowing through direct experience. New Afterlife knowledge couldn't always be integrated into existing beliefs; instead it often had to replace them. It was naive of me to believe that wholesale destruction of old beliefs and their replacement could be done purely at an intellectual level.

My naiveté became apparent when I discovered that since childhood I'd come to identify the vast interlocking web of my beliefs as me, as my identity. I came to visualize this interlocking web in the shape of a ball. Each belief in this huge ball looks like a small marble with threads running from it to other beliefs, marbles, that support it. All these beliefs, my identity, are interconnected to each other, forming a self-supporting system of beliefs I use to interpret my experience. If I experience something that conflicts with a belief on the outer surface of the huge ball, and I accept the conflicting experience as real, the belief, or marble representing that belief, dissolves and disappears. Surrounding beliefs, previously supported by the one which disappeared, may now also be challenged by my acceptance of the experience. Until the remaining beliefs can fend off their dissolution by defending themselves with supporting rationalizations or distraction, my very identity is at risk.

In the *Punky* experience, beliefs close to the central core of this huge ball, my identity, were dissolved. These were core beliefs I used to interpret my central understanding of the nature of physical reality, my only reality up to that point in time. Being at the center of my belief structure, these beliefs were at the very core of my identity. Their position at the core meant they were interconnected to a much larger portion of the network of self-supporting beliefs than if they were on the outer surface. When they disappeared as a result of my accepting the reality of the Afterlife from the *Punky* experience, my neatly organized little understanding that reality ended at the edge of the physical world disappeared with them. Threads running from these now dissolved; core beliefs carried the conflict outward to a progressively larger and larger portion of my identity. I went through what a shrink might call an identity crisis.

The beliefs *Punky* conflicted with weren't just some intellectual construct; they were me, they were part of my identity. Core beliefs holding together the center of who and what I knew myself to be were dissolved in that experience. With the center gone, a huge section of me unraveled. It felt as though I were disintegrating. It was frightening, unnerving, and very disorienting. That was the source of my feelings after *Punky* that the world around me would disappear, leaving whatever was left of me floating in a formless void. For days I felt like I was wandering around in a fog. I didn't know who I was any more. I couldn't seem to function in the way that I could recognize as me. At times it felt like I was either about to die or already had. This was a very uncomfortable period in my life.

Over time I realized I was forming a new identity. I realized that by accepting the Afterlife reality *Punky* pointed to, I was no longer the same person I had been. I realized I had to gradually assemble a new identity, incorporating all that I had discovered from the beginning of my Afterlife explorations. This process continued for a long time as beliefs farther out from my core battled to resist the implications *Punky* held for them. But my acceptance of the reality of an existence beyond the physical world was impossible to withdraw; it was verifiably, undeniably real.

As the process progressed I began to see how my belief structures, my identity, incorporated my new reality. I could see how this new me processed information differently. How I came to conclusions in my day-to-day experience that reflected my new understanding of a larger reality. Insights into my experiences and the experiences of those around me now included how they fit into a much larger plan, one that included an Afterlife as an unquestioned reality.

I write about this out of concern for others who wish to begin exploring the Afterlife. This process of identity crisis and reintegration takes time and can be a very disorienting experience. Some I've talked to since I came to understand this aspect of such exploration were fearfully certain they were about to die. Some went so far as to update their wills and begin the process of saying good-bye to loved ones. This can get serious.

Those of you who undertake Afterlife explorations of your own should be aware that feelings of disorientation and loss often follow direct experiences which challenge your core beliefs. It can feel as though you don't know who you are any more. It can feel like you don't know where to go or what to do. It can feel as though you might die soon. It can be very unnerving. I write about this because I want you to know that from my experience these feelings are part of rebirth and growth. They are, in my experience, part of the natural process of change we all go through when we become aware of anything previously unknown. Afterlife knowledge may just be something that effects us more at our core. So many of our beliefs are centered on the physical world being the only "true" reality. As you explore There, and encounter the Unknown, who you are is changing. For me it is a process of growth from which I am emerging as a new, more fully integrated human being, increasingly aware of more and more of our human existence in our physical reality, the Afterlife, and elsewhere. I sincerely hope you'll remember this message as you encounter your own conflicting experiences in the Unknown.

Within a few days of retrieving Joe and the *Punky* experience, another part of me disappeared—Coach. That part of myself that I'd come to rely on for assistance in exploring the nonphysical world was gone. For weeks I tried in vain to find him. White Bear, a guide I'd met during my second Lifeline program, briefly seemed to replace him. Then, after little bits and pieces of contact, he too, was gone. Coach's disappearance marked the beginning of something Rebecca used to call *the dark night of the soul*. I felt completely and utterly alone. I languished in my darkness for two solid months of grief at all the loss. In his books, Bob Monroe spoke of the time his Inspec said good-bye and left. Now I experienced such a loss; now Bob's words became a known to me.

One bright pinpoint of light shone into the darkness of that long, awful night. A few weeks before Joe's retrieval, I'd signed up for The Monroe Institute's newest program, Exploration 27. It was billed as detailed exploration of Focus 27 beyond the Park and Reception Center. An opportunity to take part in discovery and mapping of a vast unexplored nonphysical territory created for, and inhabited by, humans.

There was also talk of exploring deep space at Focus 34/35. This is the area Bob Monroe described as *The Gathering*, in his second book, *Far Journeys*. *The Gathering*, according to Bob, is a focus of attention or level of consciousness where intelligences from other areas of the physical universe are gathered. He claimed that they were there to witness something he called the *Big Show* which people nowadays refer to as the Earth Changes. Before my dark night started, I'd been excited at the prospect of exploring these new unknowns. In the desolation and depression following *Punky*, and Coach's leaving, not much of anything excited me anymore.

As the mid-February start date for Exploration 27 approached, I began feeling hope that it would, somehow, lead me out of the dark night of my soul. Maybe, I thought, the intense focus of the program would somehow serve to reconnect me to Guidance.

The first two days of that program were a frustrating repetition of connection to absolutely nothing. On the third day, the sun rose into my dark night of the soul in a dazzling display, signaling an end to darkness and the dawn of the soul's new day. It arose in the most powerful nonphysical world experience of pure unconditional love my physical body could withstand. Words are severely strained attempting to describe that experience with Rebecca, Ed Wilson, and Bob and Nancy Monroe. In the light of that day, I found new abilities of perception far beyond anything I'd ever experienced.

A surprise also awaited me at my place in Focus 27, the place with the beach hut umbrella roof and hanging canvas chairs around a table high up in the mountains. On every visit since I'd first built that place, I'd been met by a group of people sitting around the table. I'd never seen their faces, and had no idea who they were. When they introduced themselves during Exploration 27, their identities were an eye-opening realization. Coach was there to explain why he'd disappeared and to raise the curtain on a new Guide. This new Guide didn't speak to me in words. To communicate and discover this Guide's identity, I had to learn a new tonal method. In part, it's a universal translator allowing communication with anything, anyone, anywhere. I'm still learning more facets of this method today. It's a marvelous tool that combines words and feelings into a solid knowing. By moving beyond doubt with *Punky*, I became ready to understand and use this tool to learn more about the New World.

Exploration 27 marked the beginning in a new era of Afterlife discovery for me. Previously, I'd used retrievals of people stuck in Focus 23 as a vehicle that taught me about the non-physical world and how to explore There. In Exploration 27, my retrieval training wheels were no longer needed as a means of gathering detailed information about the infrastructure supporting human existence beyond the physical world.

In my next book, third in my *Exploring the Afterlife Series*, you'll read about various Centers of activity in the New World. The Education Center, where all knowledge acquired by humankind is stored and accessible. The Hall of Bright Ideas, where you'll learn how inventions not yet in the physical world are created. The Planning Center, which coordinates activities between the physical and nonphysical worlds. The Health and Rejuvenation Center, where new arrivals recover from the aftereffects of their death.

Several months after Exploration 27, a group of fellow participants and I began making regular trips together to Focus 27 to continue mapping the New World. We were aware of each other There and communicated much as Rebecca and I had during my earlier training with her. After each partnered exploring trip, we compared notes to verify the information we had gathered.

Bob Monroe, now living in the Afterlife, joined our explorations as native guide, giving them the flavor of a Lewis and Clark expedition. Twice a week for months, we trekked across the unmapped territory of the nonphysical New World, led by a guide who knows the lay of the land, the people, what they do, and where to find them. He guided us to meetings and connections with those living in the Afterlife with the information we sought. Sometimes Bob led us to places he wrote about during his physical lifetime, allowing us to observe and learn more about them. These explorations became the source material for the fourth book in my *Exploring the Afterlife Series*.

In that book, you'll read about The Review Center, where workers provide past life information to assist people with their decisions about choices for their future, and about The Scheduling Center, whose function it is to coordinate events within physical world time. You'll visit some more of the Hells of Focus 25 and learn more about what draws people into them and holds them there. Max's Hell is one of these. You'll meet a worker from The Rehabilitation Center who enters these Hells to assist people in getting out early; offering a back door out of Hell is what they call it. You'll go to one of the Hollow Heavens in Focus 25 and learn what they are, and why and how people get stuck there. A worker from The House of God Center tells about his time in a Hollow Heaven, how he got out, and how he now works to free others. In my next two books, we'll visit these and places beyond to learn about the Afterlife that we'll all enter when we die.

As I leave you for now, I want to encourage any of you with curiosity to begin exploring. Explore your beliefs and learn how they affect your perception. Learn to use imagination as a tool of communication. Learn more about who and what you are in your present existence beyond your physical body. If you're an ordinary human being with curiosity, you've got all that it takes to sail out past the edge of doubt and begin discovering the New World of the Afterlife for yourself.

Dr. Ed Wilson's Electromagnetic Theory of Gravity

After Dr. Ed Wilson moved to the Afterlife, he began investigating things he'd been interested in while living in the physical world. Part of the reason he spent so much time building a means of communication with me during that third Lifeline program was to pass along what he found. His Electromagnetic Theory of Gravity is one example of something he thought I'd find interesting. I started my college days as a physics major, so he was right. On December 3, 1993, he downloaded the theory to me during a dream state.

I awoke that morning feeling Ed nearby and talking to me. Two other people were there with him. My impression was that these two were "experts" in the theory Ed had come across in his poking around. For certain, the limitations of my own ability to translate what they told me into physical world terms colored what they were actually saying. After all, any of us can only rely on using words and concepts we already know to describe something previously unknown.

I feel a little pretentious even writing about this. Who am I to suggest the answer to a puzzle which physicists have been working on since before Isaac Newton? Still, I know just enough about the science of physics to find Ed's theory quite intriguing. My translation isn't exactly what Ed's new friends were saying. Though not a complete understanding of the subject, it provides a new way to think about gravity. Ed's gravity theory, combined with present knowledge of the other forces of the physical universe, may point toward a new concept of a unified field theory. As I said, this feels pretentious, but it's an example of the information available through connections with friends in the Afterlife. If some physicist finds a kernel of truth that leads to rethinking the force of gravity, I'm sure Ed would be pleased.

The Theory:

The force we call gravity is the result of an imbalance in electromagnetic radiation pressure acting upon a mass. This imbalance is due to density gradients in an almost incomprehensibly dense field of purely randomly acting electromagnetic energies. The density gradients are induced by localized compression of that field.

Assumptions

1. Existence of an extremely dense Field of purely randomly acting energy which can be conceptualized as electromagnetic in nature. This Field fills, interpenetrates, and extends throughout all of "empty space." It can be visualized as almost uncountable numbers of "beams" of electromagnetic energy of all types (visible light, radio, X ray, infrared, etc.) traveling in purely random fashion from all directions through any point in space.
2. This Field of extremely dense energy, conceptualized as electromagnetic in nature, has the property of internal cohesion.

Available Experimental Evidence

Extremely high-magnification observation of single atoms of relatively low atomic weight reveals a constant, random, "jiggling" motion of such atoms. Modern science has no explanation for this. Ed's friends suggested "atomic jiggling" is an example of the Brownian-Motion-like action of the dense, random Field acting upon a mass, and is evidence of the Field's existence. Further, they suggest quantitative analysis of atomic jiggling will lead to measurements of the Field itself.

Brownian Motion

In 1827, Robert Brown, an English botanist, discovered that grains of pollen suspended on water show continuous random motion when viewed under a microscope. There was no scientific explanation of this "pollen jiggling" until the development of kinetic theory by Albert Einstein in 1905. Brown's discovery led to proof of the existence of atoms and quantitative measurements of their size.

Ed's friends began their explanation by suggesting the use of Brownian motion as a metaphor and model to aid my understanding of the Theory. They further suggested future testing of the Theory could be visualized using this same metaphor. To aid your understanding, I'd encourage you, as Ed's friends encouraged me, to take the time to visualize the images as they are presented.

The Classic Brownian Motion Experiment

First, remember an experiment from your 12th grade physics class that demonstrated Brownian motion. In an experiment in my memory, a small, transparent chamber is placed under a microscope. A small amount of smoke is injected into the chamber through a valve. The valve is closed, thereby isolating the smoke in the still air of the chamber. Since the chamber is transparent, the microscope can be focused on the small particles of smoke inside. Doing so, we find they are not sitting perfectly still as expected, but rather they are jiggling in what appears to be constant, random movement. This movement is given the name Brownian motion, after its discoverer. It's explained as the effect of air molecules in thermal motion bouncing off the smoke particles. Our picture of air molecules in the chamber is that of an extremely large number of very small particles, bouncing off each other, the chamber walls, and the smoke particles in a completely random fashion. They act like the "beams" in Ed's theory, "traveling in purely random fashion from all directions through any point in space." Smoke particles represent single atoms of matter in Ed's gravity Theory.

Since the mass of an individual smoke particle is very small, it gives us the opportunity to observe the effect of random motion of air molecules. As an air molecule impacts the smoke particle, it exerts a force in classic billiard ball fashion. The air molecule transfers some of its momentum to the smoke particle. The force exerted by a single air molecule impact upon a smoke particle is like a grain of sand against a boulder, too minuscule to observe. But with so many billions of billions of air molecules in the chamber, billions of impacts occur in very short spans of time. Since the air molecules' motion is completely random, there exists the probability that, during any single, small slice of time, more will impact one side of the smoke particle than the other side. The smoke particle accelerates away from this point of greater numbers of impacts. It's just like if one hundred billiard balls hit a bowling ball on one side, and only fifty hit the other side. The bowling ball would move in a direction away from where the one hundred hit it. In the very next slice of time, a different side of the smoke particle might receive the greater number of random impacts, thus accelerating it in a different direction. In some time slices, the random impacts are uniformly distributed around the smoke particle so that it doesn't move during that time slice. These random, probabilistic impacts of air molecules explain the jiggling movement, Brownian motion, of smoke particles in the chamber. Brownian motion provides a starting point for understanding the concept of Ed's electromagnetic Theory of gravity.

An Experiment Using Imagination

So far, the Brownian model can be used to explain the atomic jiggling cited as "Available Experimental Evidence" above. A single atom of matter in the Theory's Field would jiggle in something akin to Brownian motion. Given a sufficiently dense Field, its probabilistic impacts upon a single, low-mass atom would cause it to jiggle.

To begin explaining the Theory, let's take the Brownian motion experiment a step further through the use of imagination. Here we'll utilize the Field's cohesive property to explain gravity.

Let's start by creating a new, airlike, gaseous medium with cohesion as an imaginary property. We'll call this new gaseous medium "unobtainium" because it's useful in imagining the concept, but very difficult to obtain. Unobtainium will be identical to air, with one additional property; it will have internal cohesion. In other words, it can be stretched in tension like rubber. It has a "spring rate," so to speak.

Now, we'll imagine a new Brownian motion chamber, a transparent, rectangular box about 3 feet long, 1 inch deep, and 4 inches wide. After filling this new chamber with our unobtainium, let's visualize a thin slice of it, 2 inches wide and 3 feet long, as if it were a very thin sheet of rubber clamped at both ends of the chamber. With an imaginary felt tip pen, let's mark this sheet of "stretchy air" with equally spaced parallel lines one-quarter inch apart across its width for its entire length. These lines are a way of labeling the initial density of our new airlike gas. Equal spacing of these lines indicates that the molecules of our new gas are uniformly distributed. Our unobtainium has a uniform density throughout the chamber. In fact, if we place a particle of smoke anywhere within our thin slice of unobtainium, its motion will be indistinguishable from classic Brownian motion in normal air. It will jostle and jiggle around in random fashion due to the same molecular collisions we've previously discussed.

The stage is now set for us to experiment with the special, imaginary, internal-cohesion property of our unobtainium. Two clamps are placed near the middle of, and across, our sheet of unobtainium. They are parallel to each other, six inches apart, and each clamped down tightly across the sheet. A mechanism between them allows me to pull these clamps together until they are one inch apart. Watch the lines on our sheet of unobtainium as I actuate the mechanism and pull the clamps together.

I've just caused a localized compression of our airlike gas near the center of its length. The grid lines between the clamps are now closer together, indicating the density of our unobtainium is higher between the clamps. Now let's look closely at the grid lines outside the clamped area. We note that they're no longer equally spaced. They are, instead, stretched apart. The greatest amount of stretch is closest to where I've squeezed it together, near the clamps, at the center of the sheet. The stretch asymptotically approaches zero at the ends of the sheet. The initial equal spacing indicated uniform gas density. The increased distance we now see between these lines indicates that the initial density of our airlike gas has been changed along its length. The molecules are no longer uniformly distributed throughout the chamber. The number of gas molecules between the lines has remained unchanged due to the imaginary property of internal cohesion, but outside the clamps they now occupy a greater volume. A physicist would say they are of lower density.

At the ends of the sheet, least stretched, the density of our gas is close to the original, unstretched value. Near the center of the sheet, most stretched, the density is less then the original value. We've introduced a density gradient along the length of the sheet. Anywhere along the sheet the gas density is lower toward the center and higher toward the ends. Any incremental slice, perpendicular to the direction of stretch, will have this density gradient.

Now, using the image we've built of a closed chamber filled with unobtainium, air with a density gradient, we can ask an interesting question, "Using the Brownian motion model, what will happen to a smoke particle that is placed anywhere in the stretched region of unobtainium within our chamber?" Well, we can see that the number of random collisions of gas molecules with the smoke particle will be biased by the density gradients we've induced. The density is greatest nearer the ends of the chamber and lowest near the center. So, there ought to always be a greater number of air molecule impacts against the side of the smoke particle facing greater density, the ends of the chamber, and fewer such collisions on the side facing the localized compression, near the center of the chamber. So, the answer to the question is that a smoke particle placed in the chamber anywhere along the stretched region of the sheet should be accelerated toward the center of the chamber by this imbalance in the number of collisions. In fact, an outside observer not seeing the lines on our invisible, magical gas might say, "Hmmm, the clamps appear to be extending a force like gravity outward, and it's pulling the smoke particle toward it!" But we know what has really happened. We've induced a density gradient in the gas surrounding the smoke particle, and the now-biased numbers of random molecular collisions are propelling it toward the clamps. The clamps aren't extending a pulling, attractive force on the smoke particle. The particle is being pushed toward the clamps by the imbalanced number of collisions with unobtainium particles, because of the density gradient the clamps induce by localized compression of the gas. Gravity is a push, not a pull.

Now, imagine that we replace unobtainium with our extremely dense, cohesive Field of purely randomly acting energy that can be visualized as electromagnetic in nature. Imagine that Field extends throughout the entire physical universe. Substitute a single atom of matter for the smoke particle. All we need is an explanation of localized compression of the Field to explain the force of gravity acting on that single atom of matter.

So, what about the unobtainium between the clamps in our experiment? The lines on that part of the sheet are very close together. What does that mean?

In terms of Ed's Theory, it means the Field is compressed. If it's compressed enough, that area of the Field is Matter! That's what, according to Ed's friends, Matter is. It's localized compression of the extremely dense Field of energy we've been talking about. Matter and Electromagnetic energy are the same thing. Remember Einstein's Electromagnetic Energy = Mass times Speed of Light Squared, $E=mc^2$? That which we call electromagnetic energy and mass are two different forms of the same thing. They are both things that appear to be different from one another, but are really just different manifestations or forms of a single thing, the Field.

More Than Gravity

I hope you've been able to follow my attempt to translate what Ed's friends told me and have been able to make sense of it. His friends continued their discussion to explain various facets of the theory in more detail. They talked about the formation of matter, how the Field is compressed, and what holds mass together at the atomic level. They gave an explanation of why a mass is limited to traveling below the speed of light within the Field they described. They discussed super-conductivity in terms of the Field also.

To continue their discussion here would take more space than I can allot in this book. Suffice it to say that they were very thorough in their explanations, and I was satisfied that it all fit together in a coherent pattern. With what I've included here, I hope I have given a taste of the sort of information accessible through the Afterlife. I'm sure that, if you could find the right person There to talk to, there isn't any question you couldn't find an answer to.

How to Change or Eliminate an Old, Outdated Belief

What I've written in this appendix is intended to provide a means of changing beliefs. People often ask me how to accomplish such a seemingly difficult task. For me such changes were necessary to further my goal of exploring the Afterlife. Whether or not you need to change your beliefs is strictly a matter of your personal choice. I've included this information in the spirit of providing assistance to those who desire to do so.

The method I give here is based on one taught to me by Rebecca. It assumes you have already identified that a belief is currently limiting your ability to perceive and experience. It assumes you desire to change or eliminate such a belief.

The most basic assumption of this method is that some aspect of yourself is holding the belief for you. At some point in the past, you decided, consciously or unconsciously, that the belief was useful to you. You asked some aspect of yourself to hold that belief and cause it to be applied at any time that aspect felt appropriate. It wouldn't necessarily be required to make itself or the belief known consciously, just apply the effect of the belief at appropriate times.

A simple example might be a belief that falling can injure your body. Through experience in the physical world I've come to believe this. I've stored that belief within an aspect of myself. So whenever I think about putting my body in a position where it could fall a great vertical distance, some aspect of me resists. This is a useful belief-based limitation affecting where I'm willing to put my body. Try to get me to stand on a tightrope sixty feet off the ground and I feel resistance to doing so. I might not be aware of the specific beliefs involved, but I will still feel resistance. The aspect of myself holding that belief will do whatever it can to stop me from climbing up onto that tightrope. My arms and legs may suddenly feel too weak to climb. I may become frozen in fear. That aspect I've entrusted to hold that belief will do whatever it can to stop my body from getting on the tightrope. A simple, silly example perhaps, but what follows might help explain the concept of changing a belief.

Changing A Belief

Suppose I wanted to learn to walk that tightrope. I'd have to change those *falling injury* beliefs at least as far as tightrope walking is concerned. To illustrate the method I'm suggesting, I'll use an imaginary conversation with the aspect of myself holding the beliefs about bodily injury due to falling. We'll start with me at the bottom of the ladder I have to climb to get to the tightrope. I'm feeling weak-kneed and paralyzed with fear. This leads me to suspect that I have a limiting belief. To begin the belief changing process, I'd close my eyes, relax, and begin my conversation. Focus 10 or Focus 12 would be good choices to relax into.

"I'd like to speak to the aspect of myself preventing me from climbing this ladder."

"Yeah, what do you want?"

"I want to climb this ladder. Why can't I?"

"Are you kidding! That sucker goes at least sixty feet up in the air! If I let you climb this ladder you might fall and wreck our body!"

"Where did this belief come from?"

"You took on beliefs about that at a very early age, little falls, little injury; big falls, big injury. This could be a really big fall!"

"How are you applying this belief in this case?"

"This belief seems to apply to this situation so I'm sending out signals of fear to paralyze our body so you can't move it up that ladder."

"But I really want to learn how to walk a tightrope!"

"Not if it's going to wreck our body, no way!"

"I appreciate that you are holding these beliefs for me and acting to limit my activity in accordance with them, but in this instance the belief doesn't apply."

"Why not?"

"Because I desire to learn about tightrope walking!"

"So?"

"So I'm going to take responsibility for the safety of our body. I'm going to move very slowly up the ladder and be very careful to hang on and not fall off."

"But, preventing that very thing is my function! That's why I hold and apply this belief for you!"

"You can continue to act as I've come to believe about falling and injuring our body in every other case except this ladder climbing right now. In this case we're going to change those beliefs. I take responsibility for this change."

"But, but . . ."

"It's what I desire."

"Okay. I'm still going to signal a little fear just so you don't forget to be careful, but not enough to paralyze our body."

"Thank you, you've understood my desire to change this belief."

At this point I've met the aspect of myself responsible and expressed my desire to change my beliefs to learn something I want to learn, tightrope walking. That aspect has relinquished control to the point I can climb the ladder. Let's move to halfway up the ladder.

"Are you sure you desire to do this? We're up pretty far. If you slip and fall our body is going to get messed up bad."

"Look! I desire it! Signals from that old belief interfere with concentration needed to safely climb. If you don't change it, your meddling thoughts may be responsible for me losing concentration. If I slip and fall, you'll be responsible! We both want to complete this climb without injury to our body, so be quiet unless you have something constructive to say."

"Okay. Watch out for the third rung up. It's a little slipperier then the rest. Otherwise everything's okay."

"You're right. I can feel it's a little slick. I'll take special care on that rung. Thank you for your input."

So I keep climbing up the ladder toward the platform. I get to the platform and I'm about to take my first steps onto the tightrope. My knees start to feel weak and wobbly, and I can't let go of the platform railing.

"Hey, I told you I desire to learn about tightrope walking. Why can't I move?"

"The ladder was one thing, that rope is different. It's pretty easy to fall off that skinny little rope."

"You're right. I might fall off the rope."

"We might fall? From way up here?"

"Yes we might, but if you'll look below us you'll see there's a safety net. We can fall without injury to our body."

"But . . . but . . . I'll have to experience falling? Everything about the belief I hold for us is based on never letting our body fall. Never, never, never!"

"Well, in this case it's safe to fall. In this case, on a tightrope with a net, change that belief to *falling is okay*. I've taken responsibility and prepared for that possibility. We can safely fall into the net."

"But, but . . ."

I force myself to take two steps out on the tightrope. I'm maintaining my concentration and balance just fine when...

"But what if you lose your balance and we fall and get hurt! I can't let you do this! I'm going to freeze up every muscle in our body with fear to stop you . . . Whoops!"

The aspect's method of controlling the body that's always worked before just caused me to lose my balance, and we're falling toward the net. After landing in it safely and bouncing a few times . . .

"That was absolutely terrifying! Body doesn't seem to be injured anywhere. Lucky for us the net was there."

"It wasn't lucky. I took responsibility and arranged for the net to be there. That's why you can change the belief in this specific case. We were doing fine until you tried to take over control. Freezing up with fear caused the fall!"

"Yeah, guess the usual paralyze-with-fear method isn't going to be effective to protect our body in this situation. Maybe I should try something else? Wait a minute, you're climbing up the ladder again? Didn't you get enough the first time?"

"No I didn't. I desire to learn more about tightrope walking!"

"Really?"

"Yes, and I suggest this time you put your efforts to control the body into something instead of paralyzing fear."

"Like what for instance?"

"Like maintaining my body weight balance once we get on the tightrope."

"Oh, okay. I'll put all my efforts into balancing body weight directly over the tightrope."

"Great! That's how tightrope walking is done. It's all about learning to subconsciously control balance on the tightrope. That's the change I want you to make to my belief in this case. *Balance prevents falling and injury!*"

A silly example perhaps, but it contains all the elements of the process to change an outdated belief. They are:

1. Recognize you're being limited. You can't do what you desire to do.
2. Ask to communicate with the aspect of yourself responsible for the limiting belief.
3. Engage that aspect of yourself in conversation; dialogue with it.
4. Understand what the belief is and how it operates to limit you.
5. Express the desire to change the belief *in the situation you desire to learn about.*
6. Attempt to do what you desire to do again.
7. Continue to dialogue with that aspect of yourself as more facets of the limitation of the belief come up.
8. Repeat this process until you can walk the tightrope without even thinking of maintaining your balance. Then you know that aspect has incorporated the desired change in your belief.

Eliminating a Belief

Sometimes a limiting belief needs to be eliminated rather then changed. My belief that physical-world-like senses of sight and hearing were necessary to explore the nonphysical world completely blocked my perception of that realm. It's an example of a belief that had to be eliminated, not just changed.

Those of you who recall reading about experience during my first Lifeline program in *Voyages Into the Unknown* may remember my perception was blocked. I expected, believed, I would get to Focus 27 and see and hear There just like I do Here. Instead I found myself in a complete void. I couldn't see, hear, smell, touch, taste or sense anything. As far as I could tell there was absolutely *nothing and no one* in Focus 27. Until my belief in using analogous physical world senses was eliminated, my nonphysical world perception remained completely blocked. The process for eliminating an old, outdated belief is similar to changing one. I'll use the same dialogue method as above to illustrate the process.

I was extremely frustrated by my lack of perception in the nonphysical world. I was convinced the Lifeline program was a scam and Focus 27 was like the story of the emperor's new clothes. Nobody in the program wanted to admit they couldn't see or hear anything There, so they claimed they did. Rebecca suggested that what I was trying to sense were very subtle energies, perhaps requiring a different form of sensing. After I'd relaxed into a Focus 10 state, my conversation with the aspect of myself responsible for the limiting beliefs could have gone something like this.

"I want to communicate with that aspect of myself which is blocking my perception of the nonphysical world."

"What do you want?"

"I want to perceive clearly in the nonphysical world."

"So, what do you want me to do about it?"

"First, tell me why you're blocking my perception?"

"I hold and apply the belief that *if I can't see it or hear it, it can't be there.*"

"And that's why I can't perceive nonphysically?"

"Yep! It's nonphysical! Can't see it with my eyes, can't hear it with my ears, it can't be there."

"How does that belief block my perception?"

"It's like an equation in math, if your eyes can't see it or your ears can't hear it, then I make it not there."

"You make it not there?"

"Of course, that's my function! I make sure whatever is there can't be perceived, to fulfill the belief I hold for you. It's just as real as two plus two equals four. Eyes can't see it, ears can't hear it, equals block its perception."

"Simple as that?"

"Yep, just as simple as that!"

"I want to change that belief."

"Can't just change it. It's hardwired in."

"What do you mean by hardwired in?"

"This a very old, core belief. It's been around so long it's connected to too many other beliefs in the system to change it without affecting a very large number of other beliefs. All other beliefs based on or connected to core beliefs will have to be changed also. It could take eons to find all those connections and gently, gradually undo them."

"But I want to change this belief now; what do I do?"

"Eliminate the core belief which feeds and holds all the connected beliefs in the system together. Cut the stem of a plant off at the root and all the leaves die too. Understand?

"Yes I do, so let's go ahead and eliminate the core belief right now."

"This could have unpredictable, far reaching effects. This one's a deep core belief supporting lots of branches and leaves. This is your identity we're talking about here, and if we cut this belief off at the root so many others will die that the whole system may crash."

"I want to eliminate it."

"You don't want that belief anymore? Are you sure you understand the implications of this decision? This could feel a lot like dying, you know!"

"It can't be that big a deal! I want to eliminate it!"

"You don't need me to hold and apply that belief for you anymore?"

"That's correct. Before this point in my life I thought I needed that belief to be operative. I'd like to express my gratitude to you for fulfilling your function so well all these years. You've been performing a valuable service. Thank you for doing that for me. Your function is no longer necessary. I release you from your duty to fulfill that function starting right now."

"Okay. Glad to have been of service."

"Now I'd like to institute a completely new function."

"Okay. What would you like?"

"From now on a new function will be operating. That function is: Whenever I desire to be aware of nonphysical energies they are to be brought into my awareness by whatever ability there is to sense them."

"Can I have an example so I'm sure I know what you mean?"

"If I intend to be aware of the presence of a Guide in the nonphysical world, you are to bring that Guide clearly into my awareness. If I intend to communicate with anyone or anything in the nonphysical world, you are to bring it clearly into my awareness."

"So if you intend to be aware of anything in the nonphysical world, my function is to bring it into your awareness as clearly as possible by whatever ability available?"

"Yes, and if a new perceptual ability is possible to improve my perception further, you are to assist me in development of that ability; that's also part of your new function."

"Very well, I'll hold the belief that is possible, and perform that function."

"Thank you. I'd like to express my gratitude to you for agreeing to perform that function."

In the very next Lifeline tape exercise I became aware of the presence of a Guide in Focus 27. As this function continues to operate, my ability to perceive in the nonphysical world grows. Each time I encounter a limit to that perception ability, the process above can be used to eliminate it. That process made the new function progressively stronger. Sometimes, as in the chapter titled *Last Voyage with Doubt*, the belief I eliminated erased more connected beliefs than I realized it would. The disorientation, grief, and depression that followed was a fairly long stretch of bumpy road.

To outline this process for eliminating an old, outdated belief and removing its blocking effect:

1. Recognize you're being blocked. Realize you're blocked from doing what you intend to do.
2. Ask to communicate with the aspect of yourself responsible for holding the belief causing the block.
3. Engage that aspect of yourself in conversation; dialogue with it.
4. Understand what the belief is and how it operates to block you.
5. Express gratitude to the aspect of yourself that has carried out the blocking function up to this point.
6. Release that aspect of yourself from continuing to hold that belief and carry out the blocking function.
7. Carefully frame the wording and intent of the new function if you desire to replace the old one. Sometimes a new function is not necessary. If it is, it might be necessary to give the intent of the new function considerable thought. Think through the implications of your choices.

Use *positive wording* for the new function. *I desire clear perception* is an example of positive wording. *I don't want my perception blocked* is not a positive wording of the same desire.

Use *present tense wording* for the new function. *Whenever I want to perceive, it is brought into my awareness* is present tense wording. *My perception is going to get better* is future tense wording. A function with such future tense wording may act to keep better perception in the future and not allow it in the present! Wording can be tricky.

8. In a meditative state, Focus 10 for example, express your new, carefully worded function and your desire that it take affect.
9. Express your gratitude for this new function being carried out.
10. You only need to do this once, then expect your desire to be fulfilled.

From experience I know both of these processes work to change or eliminate beliefs and their effects. It might feel a little strange to talk to yourself as I'm suggesting, and maybe that's another limiting belief to investigate.

If you use these processes, you should be aware that beliefs can be part of our identity and that elimination of beliefs can cause a pattern of uncomfortable feelings. I experienced these feelings in several ways: as a loss of identity, as a feeling like I might die soon, as grief, and as depression. If after experiencing something that challenges your beliefs you begin to experience any of these feelings, please remember what is said here. This is *very* important! *As you integrate your new experience into your new identity, these feelings will dissipate.* Be gentle with yourself; allow yourself time to integrate and get to know the new you.

As you identify and remove beliefs which block your perception, examples of progress and growth in your experience will happen. That's my belief and it works for me.

Guidelines for the Novice Ghost Buster

Several times a year I get a call from someone concerned about a presence, usually in their home. Some callers, like Helaina, are frantic, worried the ghost might do them harm. Others, like Mai, are more concerned for the welfare of a ghost, like her friend, Chelik. There are some simple things anyone can do to assist in moving a ghost to a better place. Before getting to them, let's cover some basics and, hopefully, clear up a few misconceptions.

First, the most important thing to know is that ghosts are just human beings not living in physical bodies. These are people just like you and me. Like people everywhere, ghosts can be friendly, scary, smart, stupid, and everything in between, but they're just people.

Second, at its most basic, the reason you can be aware of a ghost is because its attention is focused at the level of physical-world reality. There can be many reasons why a ghost would do this. They may be unaware that they're dead and are staying close to familiar surroundings or people. Sylvia was an example of such a ghost. They may be aware of their death, but confused about what they're supposed to do. Chelik was such a ghost. A ghost such as Joe, Sylvia's husband, may have a message that they want to give someone still living in the physical world. Helaina's Jack-the-Ripper type ghost was here to feed on fear. There are many reasons why a ghost's attention may be focused at the level of physical-world reality, but that focus of attention is what brings them to your awareness and keeps them here.

Third, you have nothing to fear from a ghost. Despite what Hollywood horror films would have us believe, such a person is not a threat to you. While projecting one's own fears onto a ghost can certainly appear to give evidence to the contrary, Helaina's story illustrates the basic truth. By the time the ghost she most feared sat down next to her on the sofa, she was able to permanently send him away by merely expressing her desire that he leave. The only assistance she needed from me was to remind her to do so. By the end of our phone conversation, she knew, through her own direct experience, that she had nothing to fear from any ghost. Helaina knew all the supposed poltergeist activity in her apartment was nothing more than manifestation of her own fear. Too many people I work with have bought into Hollywood's fear-inducing images and are scared out of their wits, thus adding to their problem.

Fourth, there are Helpers living in the nonphysical world who will gladly assist you in your attempt to move a ghost along. All you have to do is ask. Oftentimes the Helper is someone like Ribby, already actively trying to assist Chelik, but unable to reach him. Or like Maggie who came to assist Marla's grandmother the instant an opportunity presented itself. Sometimes they're like Sylvia, waiting to assist her dying husband, Joe. The Afterlife abounds with Helpers willing to volunteer their assistance whenever such an opportunity presents itself.

Fifth, as I explained in my first book, *Voyages Into the Unknown*, since you still live in a physical body, you have a special advantage over Helpers. Since the ghost's attention is focused at the level of physical-world reality, it's aware of you. For the same reason, the ghost is most likely not aware of the Helper's presence, but the ghost can see you. It can hear your thoughts. That means you can communicate with the ghost even when a Helper can't. That's your special advantage. If, through your communication, you can bring the Helper's presence into the awareness of the ghost, the Helper will take over from there. For the novice ghost buster, that's the most important power you have, the ability to communicate with the ghost. If you succeed in connecting the ghost and the Helper, that Helper will move the ghost for you. It's not necessary that you be fully aware of communication coming to you from either the ghost or the Helper. While it might be fun and interesting to have that awareness, it's not necessary to accomplish the task of helping a ghost move on.

So, all that's left for me to do is help you learn a simple method of facilitating a connection between a ghost and a Helper. It's simpler than most people think, and you've probably heard it before. When Helaina saw the ghost standing by her front door, she used this method. She said, "Look for a Light. When you see a Light go to it." Many of us have heard people say "send them to the Light." Most of us have only a vague notion of what it means or why it might work. Before outlining the entire procedure for a novice ghost buster, I'd like to share my understanding.

During my first Lifeline program, when I was completely unable to communicate with anyone in the nonphysical world, Rebecca's advice was the key to making my connection. She advised that I open my awareness to the possibility that the subtle energies I was trying to sense required a new way of sensing. The very next time I attempted nonphysical communication in Focus 27, I was asking for the assistance of a Guide. Guides, it turns out, were nothing more than Helpers. When I asked for the assistance of a Guide, my first clue that one had come was that I felt a presence. The next clue was that I saw a light. At first, it was a dim, ill-defined, fuzzy ball of light, but with each successive contact, it became clearer and brighter. That's generally how anyone not skilled in nonphysical-world perception first becomes aware of a nonphysical person. If you're reading these guidelines because you are experiencing the presence of a ghost for the first time, chances are good that this is the way you first encountered it. You've at least experienced the feeling of a presence, and perhaps you've seen a "light."

That's also how Helpers first appear to anyone not skilled in nonphysical-world perception, including ghosts. The ghost will first feel a presence, and then see a light. That light is the Helper. That Helper is the light! They are one and the same. The light is another human being who has come to offer assistance. That's why so many people who experience a near death talk about seeing a light. They're seeing the person who has come, as Sylvia did for Joe, to meet and assist them at their death. Some of these Helpers are incredibly powerful, loving Beings called 'Graduates.' Being radiated with a Graduate's light provides a powerful feeling of peace and pure, unconditional loving acceptance. In my fourth book, you'll be reading more about these Graduates. All that is necessary to assist a ghost is to facilitate their awareness of the light, the Helper.

How do you do that? The same way that I became aware of the Guide and that you became aware of the ghost. Direct their focus of attention to seeing a light. The procedure below is the one I suggest to people who call me asking how to move a ghost. From their feedback I know it works. Eddy's experience is an example.

As it happens, I had finished writing everything else for this book except these guidelines. I'd opened the word processor file once to write these guidelines, but just couldn't seem to get started. Two days later a man named Eddy called asking for my help with ghosts in his house. My conversation with him crystallized my thoughts into the guidelines you're reading. As I said, Helpers abound in the nonphysical world to offer assistance at any opportunity. You'll find the guidelines outlined below, after I recount my conversation with Eddy. I've added a little here to that conversation to illustrate the complete procedure.

"Before you begin working directly with the ghost, it's often helpful to ask for the assistance of a Helper. You can use whatever image of a Helper fits with your beliefs."

"Image of a Helper? What do you mean?" asked Eddy.

"If you believe there are Angels, you can ask for the help of an Angel. If you believe in Spirit Guides, you can ask for one of them."

"And if I don't have any particular name I'd use?"

"Than you can just ask for a Helper."

"How do I do that?"

"First sit or lie down and relax. A meditative or prayerful state of mind is helpful, but just a relaxed state of mind, fairly free of distracting thoughts, will do fine. Then you might say something like, 'I'm trying to move a ghost out of my house, and would like the assistance of a Helper', with the thoughts in your mind. Use whatever word for helper you prefer, Angel, Spirit Guide, God, Jesus, or Whatever."

"What if I don't know how to meditate or get into the relaxed, distraction-free state of mind you describe?"

"There are many places to learn to do this. Sometimes local schools or metaphysical bookstores can help you find a class in mediation. Or, I can give you the 800 phone number for The Monroe Institute. They have Hemi-Sync tapes available which can very quickly teach you to reach a suitable state. The state they call 'Focus 10' would work very well.

"Do I have to be aware of the Helper's presence, or of an answer to my request for assistance?"

"No. If all you do is get into a relaxed state of mind and ask for assistance, that's all that's necessary."

"Do I start trying to move the ghost right after I ask for help?"

"You can, if you're feeling an awareness of the ghost's presence. Once you've asked for a Helper's assistance, it will come at any time in the future when you're trying to help the ghost move on."

"I don't have to ask for help again after that?"

"No. Asking for a Helper to come kind of puts them on alert that you'll be trying to move the ghost. One will be waiting to assist whenever you do that. Once you feel the presence of the ghost, it wouldn't hurt to ask the Helper to be ready just before you start, but it's not necessary. Helpers are always willing to cooperate to assist a ghost out of being stuck."

"Then, how do I actually move the ghost out?"

"The next time you sense the presence of the ghost, look in the direction where you feel it to be. Pretend you're starting a conversation with the ghost. You can speak out loud or speak with your thoughts."

"Pretend. What do you mean when you say I should pretend my conversation?"

"Pretending is a way of opening the power of imagination. Imagination is a tool of communication. It carries your message to the ghost. Everyone knows how to have a conversation with your voice in your head. That's what I mean; intend to have a conversation with the ghost using your voice in your head."

"Does it have to be a two-sided conversation? Do I have to pretend the ghost's side too?"

"No, as long as you intend to have a conversation with the ghost, and say in your mind what you want to say, the ghost will hear you."

"Is there anything special I should be feeling as I'm doing this?"

"No particular feeling is necessary; the ghost will 'hear' your words or thoughts as long as you pretend your conversation toward it."

"Is there anything I could be feeling that would make my intent to move the ghost more powerful?"

"Yes, the best is to be feeling love."

"How can I make myself feel love?"

"Remember an event in which you felt loved or loving. Maybe it was the first time you held your baby, or the last time you petted your cat. Just remember what that felt like. The most powerful thing you can do to help move the ghost is to be feeling love and speak from your heart."

"Speak from my heart?"

"This can be as simple as pretending your words or thoughts are coming from the center of your chest. Speaking from the heart, at its most powerful, means to send your love to the ghost with your message."

"Okay, so I sense the ghost's presence. If I know how, I feel my love and send it with the message of thoughts using the voice in my head. What do I say?"

"Feel for the presence of a light." Wait for a moment and then say; "Look for a light." Wait for a moment again and then say, "When you see a light, go to it."

"It's that easy?"

"It's that easy. If you could see the ghost you intend to help after you say that, you'd see it looking all around. You'd know it saw a light when you saw the ghost disappear."

"What if the ghost doesn't see a light? Maybe the Helper didn't come or the ghost just couldn't see the Helper?"

"The Helper will always come, but it's possible that the

ghost may not see the light the first time you direct its focus of attention toward it. In my experience, the ghost almost always does, but it's possible it might not see the light the first time you try. If not, you just tell it again."

"How will I know when the ghost is gone?"

"That depends on how you are aware of the ghost now, when it's around. If you just feel the ghost's presence, you'll feel that presence suddenly leave. If you see the ghost as some kind of light, that light will disappear. If you see the ghost in more human form, you'll see it looking around in the air. If its looks like the ghost sees something, looks at it and then disappears, that's how you'll know it's gone."

"How many times should I use this method if the ghost doesn't seem to leave?"

"You can use it every time you sense the presence of a ghost. Each time you'll be giving it an opportunity to see the light and make a connection to a Helper."

"What if it feels like the ghost leaves and then comes back again?"

"That almost never happens. It's far more common to find multiple ghosts in a house. If you have a little more than average sensitivity to a ghost's presence, you may be able to sense differences between them. I've personally never seen a ghost return once a Helper has moved them on. If you feel the same ghost leave and return, your first contact in all likelihood scared it. Remember that ghosts are just people. The first time a total stranger walks up to you and starts a conversation out of the blue, wanting to get away is not an uncommon reaction. In a ghost's nonphysical world, just wanting to get away is a force sufficient to propel them away from you."

"What should I do in that case?"

"Do what you would do with anyone who was frightened away by your first attempt to talk to them. Invite them back to talk. Assure them you intend no harm. When they come back, try again. Eventually they'll get used to your contact and stick around to hear what you have to say."

Eddy and his wife were aware of six different ghosts in their house. They'd seen one on several occasions, a young woman they called Annie. Another, a man they called Henry, was a heavy breather, and they'd hear him in the house and pacing the floor of a smokehouse on the property. There were two older women they could sometimes hear talking in the house. The other two were children they'd hear laughing and playing outside in the yard. There were others Eddy didn't know about.

There were so many of them to start with that I moved those first six out myself the following day. When I called to let Eddy know they were gone, he told me about one he'd encountered the night of our first phone conversation. He'd just walked upstairs and into the bedroom. As he entered the room, something at the window caught his eye. He saw a man's face looking in the second-story bedroom window. Eddy said that he knew it had to be a ghost because he had to be standing in the air more than ten feet off the ground to see in that window.

"Quick as I could, I spoke from my heart and told him to look for a light and when he saw the light he should go to it," Eddy told me. "I saw a little movement of his head and then he disappeared."

Eddy's request for help was a gift to me. It pulled all my thoughts together into the guidelines below.

1. In a quiet place, where you won't be disturbed by ringing phones or other loud unexpected noises, sit or lie down and relax into a meditative state. If you don't feel confident about doing this, you can try the rest of the procedure without this step. That often works. If you'd like to quickly learn to relax in this way, contact The Monroe Institute at Route 1, Box 175, Faber, Virginia, 22938-9749. I'm not employed by The Monroe Institute, and suggest this because this is where I learned. While still in this relaxed state, proceed to the next step.
2. Ask for the assistance of a Helper, using whatever label fits your beliefs. A simple sentence spoken in the thoughts of your mind such as "I intend to move a ghost out of my house and request the assistance of a Helper" is all that's necessary for this step.

3. The next time you are aware of the presence of the ghost, feel for where it is. Stand facing that direction as though there is a real person there. There is a real person there, of course, just not one in a physical body. It may help to close your eyes when you feel for the ghost's location.

4. Feel the love in your heart. Intend to speak your message from the heart. This step isn't absolutely necessary, but it is a powerful boost to the intent of your message.

5. Pretend you are addressing the ghost as you would any other person you intend to start a conversation with.

6. You can do this next step either out loud or with your voice in your mind. Say to the ghost; "Feel for the presence of a light."

7. Wait for a moment and then say; "Look for a light."

8. Wait for a moment again, and then say, "When you see a light, go to it."

9. Express your gratitude for the assistance of the Helper. A simple "thanks" will do.

That's the entire procedure. When you use it, you may be aware of the Helper's arrival or you may not. You may be aware of the ghost's leaving or not. If you have been aware of the ghost's presence in the past, you will most likely feel its absence. In any event, none of this matters. This method works. I've never known it to fail. If you feel the presence of this or another ghost in the future, repeat steps three through nine.

If you or anyone you know is aware of the presence of a ghost, I encourage you to use the above guidelines. It's the greatest kindness you can do for such a person. Annie and Henry, two of the ghosts in Eddy's house, had been stuck there since the turn of the century. They and the others are now free to continue on their paths in any way of their choosing, with the help of other people in Focus 27. There are many more choices for them now than they had when they were stuck in that house.

APPENDIX D

Glossary

For those who haven't yet read *Exploring the Afterlife, Voyages Into the Unknown*, I've included this glossary. A fuller understanding of these terms will be gained by reading the first book in the series.

Chakra: One of the seven energy centers of the spiritual body according to Yoga philosophy.

CHEC Unit: Controlled Holistic Environmental Chamber. A Pullman-berth-like space that participants use as sleeping quarters and a place to listen to Hemi-Sync tapes during six-day programs such as Gateway Voyage. Each CHEC unit has a mattress, pillow, and blankets and provides a level of isolation from outside sound and light. Each is equipped with stereo headphones connected to the control room, lighting, and its own fresh air supply.

DEC: Dolphin Energy Club. During each six-day program, TMI teaches a method of self and remote healing supported by Hemi-Sync. The image of a dolphin is used in this method, hence the name. Participants who wish to continue practicing the remote healing aspects of this training can join a group of other individuals to do so. TMI takes requests for remote healing, disseminates them to DEC members, and provides feedback to members on results.

Exploration 27 Program: A TMI program for graduates of the Lifeline program. In Exploration 27, participants explore the infrastructure of Focus 27 and learn more about the various "places" There. Introduction to the Planning Center, Education Center, and Health and Rejuvenation Center are included as well as more detailed exploration of the Reception Center. Participants also explore Focus 34/35, an area Bob Monroe referred to as *The Gathering* in his second book, *Far Journeys*. Here participants have the opportunity to communicate with intelligences from other areas of our universe.

Focus Levels: Each focus level is a specific *state* or *level* of consciousness or awareness. Each has specific *properties* or *activities*, which program participants learn to access and utilize using Hemi-Sync sound patterns.

Focus C1: The level of ordinary, physical world consciousness. The level of physical world reality in which we **normally live.**

Focus 10: (Mind Awake/Body Asleep): The state of consciousness in which the physical body is asleep, but the mind is awake and alert. In this state, one can develop conceptual tools for use in reducing anxiety and tension, for healing, remote viewing, and other information-gathering methods. In Focus 10, much like an awake dream state, one learns to think in images rather than words.

Focus 12: (Expanded Awareness): This is a state where conscious awareness is expanded beyond the limits of the physical body. Focus 12 has many different facets, including exploring nonphysical realities, decision making, problem solving and enhanced creative expression.

Focus 15: (No Time): The state of "No Time" is a level of consciousness which opens avenues of the mind that offer vast opportunities for self-exploration beyond the constraints of time and space.

Focus 21: (Other Energy Systems): This level offers the opportunity to explore other realities and energy systems beyond what we call time-space-physical-matter.

Focus 22: The state of human consciousness where humans are still in physical existence and have only partial consciousness. In this state would be those suffering from delirium, from chemical dependency or alcoholism, or from dementia. It would also include patients who were anesthetized or comatose. Experiences here might be remembered as dreams or hallucinations. My personal experience of this area is that many here appear deranged, lost, or confused. This can make them very difficult to reach and communicate with.

Focus 23: A level inhabited by those who have recently left physical existence, but who either have not been able to recognize and accept this or are unable to free themselves from ties of the Earth Life System. It includes those from all periods of "time." Those who live here are almost always isolated and alone. Often the circumstances of their death have left them confused about where they are; many times they don't realize they've died. Many maintain some form of contact with the physical world, and thereby limit their ability to perceive those who come from the Afterlife to assist them.

Focus 24, 25 & 26: This covers the Belief System Territories, occupied by nonphysical humans from all periods and areas who have accepted and subscribed to various premises and concepts. These would include religious and philosophical beliefs that postulate some form of post-physical existence.

Focus 27: Here is the site of the Reception Center or the Park, which is the hub of it. This is an artificial synthesis created by human minds; a way station designed to ease the trauma and shock of the transition out of physical reality. It takes on the form of various earth environments in order to be acceptable to the enormously wide variety of newcomers.

Focus 34/35: A level of consciousness beyond human consciousness, also known as *The Gathering*. Here intelligences from other areas of the universe are gathered to observe the earth changes. Here contact, communication, and interaction with these intelligences is possible.

Free Flow Focus Tapes: A Hemi-Sync tape with minimal verbal instruction and maximum free time in the focus level.

Grainy 3-D Blackness: A specific level of consciousness characterized by its coarse grained, holographic imagery. An *eyes-closed* blackness with depth as well as width and height. Also described by many as a *blackness with texture.* This level seems to be a connection point with all other levels.

Hemi-Sync: The following explanation is taken from a Monroe Institute pamphlet with the institute's permission:

"The Monroe Institute is internationally known for its work in the effects of sound wave forms on human behavior. In its early research, the Institute discovered that nonverbal audio patterns had dramatic effects on stages of consciousness.

"Certain sound patterns create a *Frequency Following Response* (FFR) in the electrical activity of the brain. These blended and sequenced sound patterns can gently lead the brain into various states, such as deep relaxation or sleep. A generic patent in this field was issued to Robert Monroe in 1975. Drawing upon this discovery and the work of others, Mr. Monroe employed a system of 'binaural beats' by feeding a separate signal into each ear. By sending separate sound pulses to each ear with stereo headphones, the two hemispheres of the brain act *in unison* to 'hear' a third signal, the difference between the two sound pulses. This third signal is not an actual sound, but an electrical signal that can only be *created by both brain hemispheres acting and working together simultaneously.*

"The unique coherent brain state that results is known as hemispheric synchronization, or 'Hemi-Sync.' The audio stimulus that creates this state is not overpowering. It is noninvasive and can easily be disregarded either objectively or subjectively.

'While hemispheric synchronization occurs naturally in day-to-day life, it typically exists only for random, brief periods of time. The Hemi-Sync audio technologies developed by The Monroe Institute assist individuals in achieving and sustaining this highly productive, coherent brain state."

Hemi-Sync—My Explanation: If you're a technical type, maybe my own explanation of hemispheric synchronization will be easier to follow.

Using stereo headphones to acoustically isolate each ear, two different-frequency audio tones are supplied, one to the left ear and the other to the right. For example, a 400-cycle-per-second tone might be supplied to one ear and a 402-cycle-per-second tone to the other. If you watched a real-time brain wave frequency pattern analysis of the result, you would see the brain wave frequency spectrum of both hemispheres begin to synchronize to two cycles per second. The brain wave pattern of both hemispheres synchronizes to the difference between the two input frequencies (402 - 400 = 2). If this brain wave frequency pattern were the same as, say, REM sleep, which it's not, then the person listening would begin moving into REM sleep. Another pair of audio tones could be simultaneously introduced which match an alert, wide-awake brain wave state. Then the state the individual would move into would be Mind Awake/Body Asleep or Focus 10 in Monroe Institute jargon.

The most important point seems to be that both hemispheres of the brain come to a balanced, cooperative, information-sharing state which is facilitated by their synthesizing the third tone. In this balanced state, both hemispheres of the brain, with their well-documented differences in perception and analysis abilities, cooperate constructively. In that balance comes Knowing.

Helpers: Nonphysical human beings who have lived in the Afterlife long enough to *know the ropes*. Helpers often volunteer to assist physically alive people exploring the nonphysical realities. They also provide volunteer assistance to other nonphysical humans, usually upon entry into the Afterlife, or at any time the assistance is requested or would be helpful.

Interpreter: An aspect of me that searches my memory for anything associated or related to what is presently within my awareness. My Interpreter also brings such associated or related things into my awareness as a means of building memory of new information.

Gateway Voyage Program: The first of the series of six-day residence programs TMI offers and a prerequisite for all other TMI programs. Gateway Voyage introduces participants to Focus 10, 12, 15 and 21 in a structured program of learning. It teaches one how to access each focus level, and various conceptual tools for their use.

Guidelines II Program: A six-day residential program at TMI that teaches participants to access Guidance.

Lifeline Program: A six-day residential program at TMI that introduces participants to Focus 22, 23, 24, 25, 26 and 27. This is the area of the Afterlife in which participants learn to contact and communicate with those who inhabit these levels, including Helpers and other nonphysical humans. Lifeline uses the vehicle of retrieval to teach participants how to access and explore these focus levels.

The Park: An area of Focus 27 also known as The Reception Center. (See Reception Center)

Perceiver: An aspect of myself that brings into my awareness perceptions of the nonphysical world. This aspect is capable of perception only. It is incapable of building memory of what it brings to my awareness.

The Reception Center: An area of Focus 27 in which the newly departed are assisted in their adjustment to leaving the physical world and entering the Afterlife.

Retrieval: The act of locating, contacting, and communicating with a nonphysical human stuck in an area of consciousness from Focus 23 through Focus 26, and moving that person to Focus 27. Retrievals are the vehicle of training used in the Lifeline program to learn to explore the Afterlife.

Stuck (as in a focus level): A nonphysical person who is completely without contact with other nonphysical humans in the Afterlife is said to be *stuck*. This usually results from beliefs held by that individual at or prior to death. The circumstances of such a person's death may also lead to being stuck.

Hampton Roads Publishing Company

. . . for the evolving human spirit

Hampton Roads Publishing Company
publishes books on a variety of subjects including
metaphysics, health, complementary medicine,
visionary fiction, and other related topics.

For a copy of our latest catalog,
call toll-free, 800-766-8009,
or send your name and address to:

Hampton Roads Publishing Company
134 Burgess Lane
Charlottesville, VA 22902
e-mail: hrpc@hrpub.com
www.hrpub.com